Petrolhead

Petrolhead

The Life and Times of a Classic Car Buff

Roger Austin Learmonth

PARAPRESS
LIMITED

Also published by Parapress:
Sound the Trumpets, Beat the Drums,
Military Music Through the 20th Century,
ed. by Gordon Turner and Colin Dean
England's One Test Wonders by Roderick Easdale
Your First Great Dane by Angela Mitchell

This book was first published in the UK by
PARAPRESS LTD
9 Frant Road
Tunbridge Wells
Kent TN2 5SD
www.parapress.co.uk

ISBN 1-898594-78-3

A catalogue record for this book is available from the British Library.

Design and typesetting by Mousemat Design Limited.
www.mousematdesign.com

Printed in Great Britain by Biddles Ltd, Guildford and King's Lynn.

Contents

The author with Tom Coldicott and XK150 on the 1998 Claret & Classics

This book is dedicated to my dear wife Kathleen, without whose support and indulgence I would merely be looking at other people's classic cars. Also to my good friend Tom Coldicott, who harangued and encouraged me until I finally put pen to paper.

Acknowledgements

My grateful thanks go to the many people and organisations who have helped with the production of this book.

Special thanks are due to Nick Baldwin, who raided his archives for me and provided many of the pictures I lacked.

Thanks also to all the following for providing additional photographs:
CK Bowers (various), Peter Rodgers Classic Cars (the delightful Bradfords), Vivienne Learmonth (TR4A), Russell Lucas (Ford V8), Dennis Harris (prize-winning Rover), Shirley Learmonth (Alfetta), Hardy Kruppa (MGB), Stan Williams (superb XKs), Mrs Ena Stringer (Talbot), Alan Passmore (Ford Squire), Peter Scott (his lovely SS Jaguar saloon), Richard Green (his excellent Rover 14) and Juliet Rashbrook (XK150), Brian Sherer at Vauxhall Motors Heritage Cenrtre (Velox, Wyvern and Cresta).

Also to Alec Fry and to Derek Skinner who undertook some early reviews and made many invaluable comments.

Finally, my grateful thanks to Peter Simpson, who undertook the mammoth task of technical editing and to Elizabeth Imlay for her editing and project management.

Introduction

I was born on 26th September 1945 in the JJ hospital in Bombay, India. My family brought me to the UK when I was three months old. But enough of that. This isn't my life story but it is the story of the cars in my life. I've been crazy about motor cars for as long as I can remember and over the years I've been involved with quite a few.

I wish I could claim that they were all exotics, but I can't. It would have been equally wonderful to write about the Bugattis and Astons that Father drove, but sadly it was not the case. Our family transport was more mundane: Morrises, Vauxhalls and the occasional Jaguar take a disproportionate share of the limelight. When I started into motorcar ownership, I was always struggling to make it above the parapet of extreme mediocrity.

I imagine that much of my early life with cars will ring bells with those who have experienced the frustration of not having sufficient cash to indulge their taste. I was always a Lagonda and Ferrari man at heart but, when I could afford anything at all, I tended to own Triumphs and the occasional battered Jaguar. I have also been a life-long fan of the domestic product. The passing of the once dominant British car industry has been a bitter and tragic pill to swallow. Inappropriately, for someone not involved in the trade, I seem to have taken it personally. I feel the demise of the old makes as keenly as though I had lost dear and valued friends. If you want to see a grown man choke with emotion, then mention names like: Alvis, Armstrong-Siddeley,

Austin, Daimler, Hillman, Humber, Jowett, Lanchester, Morris, Riley, Singer, Standard, Sunbeam, Triumph and Wolseley. (And what of Rover?) Then of course there are those marques that are still around but are no longer in the hands of their former owners. But please don't get the wrong impression: this is not a tirade against the unfortunate tide of economic affairs, or a denigration of foreign cars.

It is essentially a very personal tale of someone who started, as a lad in south-east London, spending far too much of his time fooling around with automotive tin and never losing the habit. I was always going after something a bit different. While my contemporaries made do with Hillman Minxes and Austin 1100s I was out chasing Triumph Roadsters and XK Jaguars. But I've also had more than my fair share of cooking machinery. As the years passed I have, to a limited extent, been lucky enough to indulge my passion and gather around me a small set of "presentable" old metal.

It was my good friend and rally co-driver, Tom Coldicott, who suggested that I might like to write about the cars that have filled my life in good times as well as bad. I suspect his ulterior motive was to stop me boring him to distraction with my endless anecdotes by getting it out of my system. It has been made possible by the rather uncharacteristic way in which I have kept a record of all the cars that have passed through my hands. How I wish I had also kept a comprehensive photographic record but, alas, my early pictures are few and for the most part execrable. A small compensation is my cache of original receipts.

These days I idle away my time playing with my "old motors" rather like a small boy playing with toy trains. My very indulgent wife lets me out, perhaps too often, to frolic in foreign climes on classic car rallies and even turns a blind eye to my pathetic attempts at historic motor sport.

I hope there is something of interest in these unworthy pages.

CHAPTER I

Early Days

I was christened Austin after the make of taxi that Father was driving at the time. Not of course quite as up-market as my brother, Bentley. My parents always claimed he was called Bentley because he was conceived in the back of a very smart 8-litre that Dad drove when he worked for Lord Mulrooney. It has always been a cause of great sadness that in my case they couldn't have held off until Father got his new job with Lord Withers. His Lordship had a decidedly sporty taste in cars and, all things being equal, I could well have been called Alfie Romeo. It's an old joke, but I've got to start somewhere.

My earliest automotive memory was riding in my Uncle Jim's Ford lorry. Alas, Uncle Jim is no longer with us and I know only that he ran a timber business and operated an ex WD (that's War Department to the youngsters) truck that he acquired in the late 1940s. There's a picture showing me at the wheel. My mother tells me I spent all my time playing in the cab whenever uncle came around. I was about two at the time, so my memory is a little hazy. All I remember is that it was a straight six, side-valve unit with three on the floor and a tendency to pull to the left under heavy braking. No, not really, I'm only kidding, the brakes were fine.

Our family went though a lot of upheaval in the late '40s and early '50s, and by the time we got our act together the family car was a 1937 Morris. I think it was an "Eighteen" but I can't be sure, it was certainly a big saloon. By then I was five and a complete car

This was the sort of Morris that we had as our family car.

nut (I think the modern term is 'petrolhead') and could recognise most of the makes on the road. I drove my parents crazy by doing just that whenever I was taken out in an automobile, usually in a loud, piercing and incessant voice (so what has changed?) In those days cars were hard to come by and for people like us, new ones were unobtainable. We lived in Keston in Kent, which was quite a smart neighbourhood, and I remember one of my father's colleagues visiting us in his brand new Ford Consul. It would have been about 1950. Virtually the entire road turned out to have a look at what a modern car was like. Our next-door neighbours were an elderly doctor and his wife who had an immaculate 1934 Austin 10. On our street (which was a private one with poles at each end so it must have been a bit posh), everyone who had a car, had pre-war iron. Dr Goss and his Austin were very much the norm.

Nearly every week, summer and winter, rain or shine, we

automotive front were easing up and there were a few more vehicles around as people re-commissioned old cars laid up for the war.

The Ford was replaced with a magnificent 1937, two and a half litre SS Jaguar saloon. It's hard to believe that this was any less expensive to run than the V8 but my dad adored it so much that I suspect he would rather have got rid of me than his pride and joy. But as luck would have it, I stayed and the car went. I think it had something to do with the gearbox, which broke into lots of pieces on the Bromley road. It was, it seemed, not to be replaced for less than a king's ransom and the lovely old girl was forced to join another household.

We had a succession of oddballs starting with a BSA Scout. I must have been six or seven but even I knew a truly horrible car when I rode in one. For good or ill it was a front-wheel drive four-wheeler, not one of the quaint three-wheeled jobbies that might

SS Jaguar 2 ½ litre

went to the pictures. We'd pile into the Morris and go off to Catford in south-east London. There were four cinemas to choose from so, although I was only five, there would always be something suitable for the family. Parking was never a problem. The Plaza even had its own car park and there was always plenty of room. You could get in up to a dozen cars but it was never full. I remember coming out of the show on freezing winter evenings wrapped up in my winter coat. I'd sit in the back while Mum, usually under protest, worked the throttle and Dad stuck the handle through the grille and turned for all he was worth. More often than not they'd end up in an argument but I can't ever recall not getting home under our own steam. When it was foggy (it was the time of the "pea soupers"), we'd open the windscreen and crawl along at a snail's pace. There wasn't a heater but we had a real chamois leather for wiping the windows.

The old Morris met its end one Sunday afternoon in March. My brother, his pregnant wife and I were in the back, with Mum and Dad up front. Funnily enough we were off to the cinema to see a cowboy film. We must have been in a jolly mood because we were all singing our hearts out. As a special treat I'd been given a bag of chocolate caramels and I was cramming them down as fast as I could when someone turned out the lights. All I can recall is searching through the grass for my sweets and clutching the empty bag. Another unfortunate had run into us side-on at a crossroads. Both cars were pretty mangled. Mum cracked some ribs and my sister-in-law broke her collarbone. All the men, me included, were fine although I never did find the missing caramels. The poor Morris was a write-off.

Luckily, my nephew was born without problems a few months later and mum's ribs healed nicely and, oh yes, we got a rather splendid Ford V8 car to replace the crashed car. I don't remember much about it except it was grey. It was a British-built 22-horsepower job with a torquey side valve that used a lot of petrol. I think father liked it a great deal but, as it was a definite drain on resources, it had to go. By that time things on the

This is really a photo of my brother; the V8 Ford is purely background.

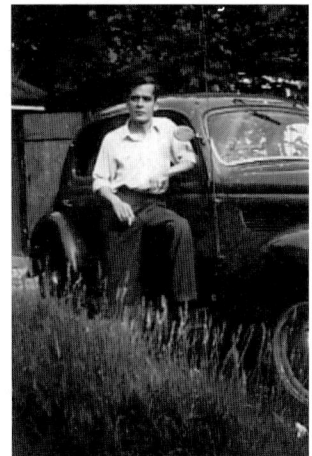

actually have been fun. It had seen much, much better days and I suspect when it finally left us it was ready to turn in its permit as a road-going vehicle. I can't remember whom we passed it on to but if it wasn't a breaker's yard it should have been. I have a fleeting memory of a few days spent with a little Triumph saloon with just one headlamp and no brakes. This car was so unutterably awful that my mother threatened hysterics unless Father took it away at once. He was a strong man but not that tough, and the Triumph was history within hours.

BSA Scout

Father's Triumph was seriously horrible.

I imagine these rather ignoble little heaps were the result of a serious shortage of cash and I don't know of any windfalls at the time but Father appeared one day with Alfie. Alfie (I have no idea why he called it that) was a stately, green Talbot three-litre saloon of early '30s vintage, the complete antithesis of the BSA and Triumph. She was, I think, a pre-selector model with a magnificent long-stroke engine that looked like a work of art. I remember being shown the dynostart. This clever device was a starter cum dynamo fixed directly to the crankshaft, so obviating the need for a ring gear. The car would start completely silently without the usual whirring and clatter of a starter dog engaging. It was a seriously smart motor and we loved it, Mother included. That was until I fell out of the back. Well, I didn't actually fall out but the back door came open while cornering at speed and I almost fell out. Father fixed the lock and Mother was placated. Then I nearly fell out again and this time Mother couldn't be placated, so Alfie had to go. It was a shame really because she wasn't replaced for more than five years, as our lives took a dog-leg turn and we ended up in the Far East in somewhat reduced circumstances.

This blurry old photo, that I acquired quite recently, shows my grandfather with Alfie, Dad's green Talbot.

We didn't own a car while we were in India (although Grandmother had a rather splendid, chauffeur-driven 1937 Lincoln Zephyr) but that's a story for another time. We got back home in more or less good form apart from recurring bouts of malaria that reduced all of us to quivering jellies at random intervals for many years afterwards. Within days of our return Father started looking for a job. I was just twelve and, as none of

Our Talbot looked something like this. If the rear door catch hadn't given way at awkward moments, we might have had it still.

Grandmother's Lincoln was cream and, for the period, quite flamboyant. Nichols the chauffeur spent a lot of time polishing the old girl (the Lincoln, I mean).

my enthusiasm had been extinguished, I was delighted when it was announced that we were off on an expedition to Sheffield where Dad had secured several interviews. Exhaustive evaluation revealed that the cheapest form of transport was a venerable Morris Fourteen that Dad had been offered by a dealer. The plan was to motor up to Harrogate, where Mother would stopover with a friend while Father and I journeyed on to Sheffield to spend a few days while he met prospective employers.

I was in a fever of excitement waiting for the new car to arrive. We knew it had a reconditioned engine and was in fair-to-middling condition. A 1938 model, it came without a boot but access to storage space was possible by removing the back of the rear seat. This arrangement had the unexpected benefit of converting the rear into a passable double (often used by the family as a triple) bed. My father paid £10 for it, so it wasn't the smartest car on the block. Starved of automotive involvement for so long, I was a somewhat uncritical audience when it finally arrived; it looked all right to me.

It's not uncommon for fathers and sons to share secrets and the one that Dad shared with me was that the car's only major fault was a broken chassis. Not a bent chassis or a cracked chassis or one with a little tear, but a chassis where on both sides the metal had completely parted company. Just behind the engine one could clearly discern a front bit and a totally separate back

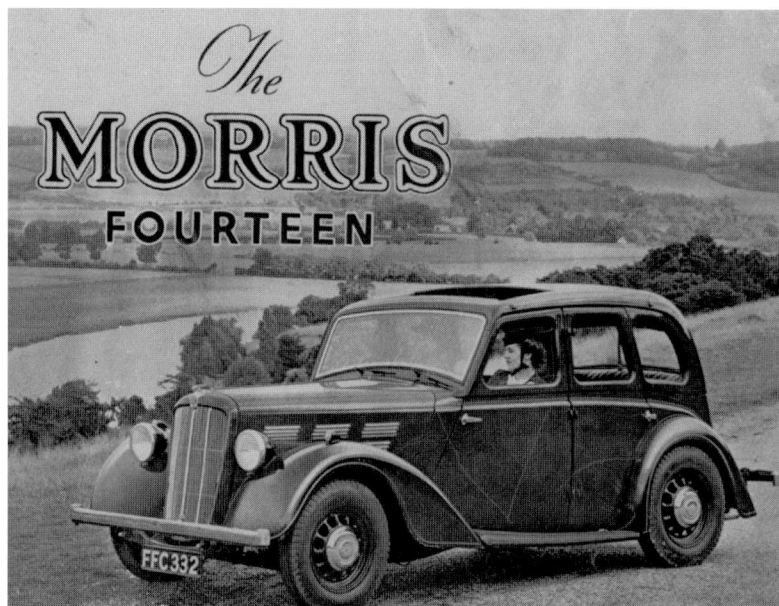

bit. One mustn't get the impression that nothing had been done to rectify the situation; some thoughtful soul had actually attempted a repair. There was evidence that welding had been tried but the rot had set in too decidedly for it to be a serious proposition. The repair consisted of angle iron laid across each break and then bound tightly with cable. Actually, I think it was piano wire. Once you'd been told that the chassis had a problem, the discernible sag in the middle of the car was a definite give-away. Closing the bonnet was a knack only Father acquired. There was no MOT test in those days, so you had to be really unlucky to be collared for driving an unroadworthy vehicle.

Don't push it too hard, the dealer had advised. Under cross-examination, Father revealed that "too hard" meant anything over 40 miles an hour. For all our reservations (Father's and mine, that is; Mother was blissfully unaware of potential trouble), the old girl ran there and back without a problem. Apart from a blow-out on the A1, for which I completely blame my dad as he had irresponsibly let the speed creep up to 45, the journey was a joy – in sort of slow motion.

We stayed up there for a couple of days. I'd sit in the car reading while Dad was being interviewed, sometimes for three or four hours at a stretch. In the evenings we'd drive out into the country, find a lay-by and sleep in the back. Morning ablutions were courtesy of a "wash and brush-up" at a public convenience. It sounds awful, but in the '50s, for six pence (2½p) or maybe a shilling, a cheerful attendant would provide a basin of hot water and a clean towel. If you were away for more than a week you could avail yourself of the slipper baths provided in most towns.

Father wasn't offered a job in Sheffield, for which I occasionally still sink to my knees in grateful thanks (sorry, Sheffield) but he got one in Kent. He became area rep for a firm that sold furnace linings. His official title was "fuel efficiency technologist". I didn't know what it meant either but I do know that he got paid to sell things, more if he sold a lot and nothing if

Ours was a beauty. It was a '38 14-horsepower, the one in the photo is a '39. We had the four light sportsman saloon with wire wheels.

The Rover dash

he didn't sell any, so I suppose he was a salesman. Apart from furnace do-dahs, his employers offered big and heavy welding machines, so Dad was expected to carry one around with him. The Morris's lack of a boot became a serious drawback. Lifting out the back seat and shovelling out a couple of hundredweight of appliance several times a day took its toll. He borrowed £100 from Granddad and bought a Rover.

I remember this car with nothing but the greatest affection. It wasn't so much a car as a member of the family. It was a 1938 Fourteen. The manufacturers referred to it as a 'sportsman saloon', which meant it had four and not six side windows, a sunroof and a quick-release window on the driver's side. Someone once told me that the quick release was to allow an owner hastily to let down the window, get out a gun and take shots at passing game that had been foolish enough to show itself. It sounds daft enough to be true. I'll have to find out for sure before I write about it. Another feature was a freewheel option that effectively disengaged the engine from the transmission when not under load. I suppose it was a petrol-saving device, and blooming dangerous, at least it would be in modern traffic conditions.

We bought it from a dealer called Cooper in Greenwich who gave us back the £10 for the Morris. That was in 1958, and of course my memory could be faulty (it probably is) but if someone had told you our Rover was only a couple of years old, apart from the archaic styling, you would have believed them. After twenty years she had her original black paint complete with gold coach line and green grill. She was a tribute to the quality and excellence of British engineering. The wonderful brown leather interior was in excellent order and superbly comfortable. The well instrumented, triangular dash always put me in mind of what I imagined a fighter plane would look like. My father soon mastered the crash gearbox and he was forever showing off his clutchless changes.

That car heralded a settled period in my family's life. We had come back to England with little more than the clothes we stood up in and we started the long haul back to solvency with our trusty Rover in support

The Bradford Van (not the Utility) complete with its single windscreen wiper. It has a certain ungainly charm.

It was during this time, as Father got back on his feet, that he began to think of ways of supplementing his income. As chance would have it Mr Cooley, who lived at number 47, became the proud possessor of a smart Bradford van. No, I'm wrong, not a van but a utility; there was a difference. The van version was an unashamed utilitarian commercial load carrier. The utility was an altogether more up-market proposition. While it was possible to turn it to the carriage of goods, it was also possible to use it as a perfectly acceptable passenger vehicle. It had seats in the back, side windows and a chromium-plated front bumper. The *pièce de résistance* was its chromium-plated grill assembly. This latter item I think, moved it even further up the ladder into the deluxe category.

Somehow we leant that Cooley had given a princely £85 for his treasure. All this in itself was unremarkable and of no significance until my dad came across a Bradford van in a dealer's yard: a van and not a utility, mind. He took me down to

The Bradford Utility with chrome bumper and grill. The rear had sliding windows and two upholstered seats. I have discovered that the mushroomish colour was officially known as "Catalina Tan" which has been likened to butterscotch flavoured Instant Whip. This model also sports twin windscreen wipers.

see it in great excitement. The plan he outlined was elegant in its simplicity: buy it, do it up, flog it. Hopefully for 85 quid or thereabouts. He had the vision of the Cooley equipage firmly in mind. When I saw it I was less enthusiastic. To my poor schoolboy mind if, on some arcane scale, Cooley's motor rated a ten then the van, at a push, was a generous one and a quarter. There was no way this particular sow's van could be converted into the silk utility of Father's imagination but he was determined to give it a go. He paid £10, which included delivery.

The project played havoc with our relationship. It came at the wrong time when, as a spotty adolescent, I was more interested in girls (actually the prospect of seeing as much of their unclad bodies as possible) than motors, and certainly bored to distraction with a grubby little Bradford van. Father worked like a Trojan (pardon the pun) and at the same time became more and more exasperated with my lack of enthusiasm and what he saw as idleness (he was, of course, absolutely right). About this time we moved from the flat we had rented from my grandfather in Forest Hill to our own maisonette in Sydenham, which we bought from my Aunt Ruth and Uncle Will. ("Maisonette", what a twee little word.) The logistics of towing the van and its associated clutter from behind Grandfather's house to its new lodgings were somehow overcome. Dad hired a lock-up garage in a derelict yard not far from where we lived and spent most of his spare time slaving over the contraption. The yard was owned by a charming fellow who had run a business there for many years. We had got to know him because he had an even better old Rover than ours (a '37 twelve-horsepower). When he retired he shut the place down and let off bits to eccentric people playing with ancient and decrepit motors. We fitted in rather well.

I'd get dragged along to spend weekends in futile attempts at undoing rusted bolts and freeing off seized fasteners of one kind or another. Dad and I got scratchier with each other by the week. The deal was that I would be let off around 5 o'clock on Saturdays so I could get home to watch the Lone Ranger on TV. On the occasions that I had been particularly dilatory and useless he was inclined not to let me go. This caused all kinds of family friction and Mother usually took my side, so I suppose he felt isolated and fed-up.

At this point it might be worth saying a few words about Bradford vans. Jowett Cars of Bradford were a well known and respected firm of automobile builders with their roots in the light car business as far back as 1906. Perhaps their most famous product was the highly acclaimed Javelin saloon designed by Gerald Palmer. The earliest Jowetts had utilised a horizontally opposed twin of simple design and proven longevity. In 1946 this engine was re-commissioned in 1005cc form for the Bradford van.

Everybody knows about "austerity" Britain and the economic climate after the Second World War. It was a place where manufactures of basic, cheap vehicles found a ready market and producers like Reliant with their girder fork vans and Sharp Commercials with the Bond Mini car went into serious production. Jowett, with the development of the Bradford, got into this low cost market very successfully. The Bradford was essentially a product of its time: "minimalist" sums it up quite nicely. It had most of the bits required to make it go and stop but only just enough of each for it to happen.

Father battled manfully to convert the derelict commercial into something desirable. He unseized the engine, repaired the gearbox and fettled the ancillaries, cleaning and scrubbing and generally getting things going again. When it came to putting in rear windows, he ran up against Customs and Excise who demanded £9 duty for the change of use. He paid up like a lamb. After several months of solid effort his handiwork was ready for painting. Mr Cooley, who was indirectly responsible for the whole thing, no longer lived up the road so we couldn't just go and have a look. Anyway we didn't need to; we could both recall his utility well enough. I remembered that it had been painted a sort of vibrant beige, if that's not a contradiction in terms. The precise colour was Mushroom, we were told. In any event Father's and

The Bradford light truck (I think Jowett sold it as a lorry). Shown for no other reason than, having discussed the Van and the Utility, I thought the reader might like to see more of the range.

my memory of the exact shade must have been at variance, because when he returned from the paint shop he'd brought back what I described as light pink. We had a small argument but it was his van, and so on went two quarts of pink Valspar Lacquer. When I mentioned that I thought hand painting might let down the finished product, I was assured that Rolls Royces had been painted that way for years. Actually, all things considered, he made a jolly good job of it. We finished up with a pink (or mushroom depending on how you see colours) body and black wings. Mechanically it got to the point where it would cold start on the handle after a little coaxing. Sometimes, but rarely, if had been thoroughly warmed, it would go on the starter, which most of the time refused to turn at all.

And so to the first advertisement in the *Exchange & Mart*; I think Father put it in at £80. There were no responses. Re-advertised, we had a few desultory calls at £70 and someone came to look at it for £60 but didn't buy. It wasn't put in again for a few weeks, while Father reviewed his options. It must have been purgatory for him, with Mum and me insisting that we'd told him so (Mother had now joined me in the sceptic's camp).

It finally went back into the magazine, this time for a trifling

£50. Again, not a sausage. Then several weeks after we'd given up hope, a man rang to ask if my dad would care to swap it for a telly. Now the subject of TVs was a sore point in our household. My father wasn't a fan and only grudgingly allowed the 9-inch set we'd got for nothing from Granddad. Of course even in those days it was an antique, a curtains-pulled, watch-in-the-dark set that only picked up the BBC. So there was no 'Popeye', 'Wagon Train' or 'Sunday Night at the London Palladium': I was seriously culturally deprived. I suppose we hounded a reluctant Father into the deal, which included delivering the vehicle to the chap's flat in Plaistow in East London. He didn't have transport, he told us and couldn't come to see it. Looking back it seems a rather bizarre set of circumstances but that's how it happened.

We must have set off with the intention of doing the deal, but we made no arrangements for getting back with a television set. We dragged the Bradford from its den on the appointed Sunday morning and managed to get it started. Two of the tyres were flat but it was hardly the time to start investigations so we took it in turns with the foot pump until they were up enough to get it to a garage forecourt. We had our hearts in our mouths the entire journey. It was probably the first time the thing had run under its own steam in ten years or more. Going up Sydenham Hill, Father double de-clutched into first and we made it by the skin our teeth. Most alarming was the oil pressure, which sank to zero as we neared the crest with the engine churning furiously. Mercifully, the roads were clear and we had a fairly uninterrupted run. I think I said a quiet prayer as we chugged through the Blackwall tunnel but we finally made it and thankfully pulled up outside the address we had been given. Father switched off the engine, which wheezed and clanked and gave us the definite impression it had no intention of ever going again. We got out cautiously and headed for the garden gate. On impulse we both turned and gazed at the Bradford sitting in the gutter. Notwithstanding Dad's months of work, it looked a total heap. We quickly turned away and went in. The man with the TV came down and walked round the vehicle a few times. The thing I relished least in the world was the prospect of trying to make it back home in that damned van.

He didn't even ask to hear it go. "It got here so it must be OK," was his only comment. We went up to see the television. It was lovely. A 14-inch Sobel that looked as modern as you'd like, certainly a lot prettier than the van. We were cannier than our friend and gave the set a thorough road test; it worked fine. And so to the exchange. The man seemed very relaxed about the whole thing. Dad and I manhandled the TV down the stairs and left it in the hall while we went off to sort out the logistics of the journey home. It was only then that he told me we'd probably have to get back to Sydenham on the bus. We had walked half way around the block when we came on a chap washing his Morris Traveller in the road.

"Interested in earning ten shillings?" father asked him.

"What have you got in mind?" he replied, and the transaction was arranged. We popped back for the telly and by the time we reached the corner with it, we noticed that the tyres on the van had gone down again. What the two of us must have looked like, shuffling along a residential street on a Sunday morning with a telly between us, goodness only knows. We were almost back to the Traveller when we heard rapid footsteps behind us. Our hearts sank into our boots. It was the van's new owner.

"Here," he shouted after us. I was tempted to drop the telly and run. "You ain't left no keys." Dad explained that the economy-minded Jowett Company had not provided an ignition lock on this austerity model, just a switch on the steering column. He went off happily enough. We almost ran the rest of the way and were driven home in what seemed like sumptuous luxury.

That's not quite the end of the tale for, although we never heard from the man with the van again, the television conked out on its second evening. Dad played around with it for a bit and discovered that overheating seemed to be the problem. He affected a temporary repair by propping a fan heater behind it, naturally without the heater bit on. Provided you didn't mind a bit of whirring with your viewing it worked perfectly satisfactorily. Dad said he'd get it fixed properly but it was five years later, when the set finally gave up the ghost, that we were able rescue the heater for its rightful purpose.

And that was the end of the Bradford episode, which over time passed into our family's folklore.

I suppose I really am a chip off the old block because, while I was between the ages of about thirteen and sixteen, Dad was always hoping to acquire something upmarket and smart, a tendency to champagne taste and beer pocket that I very definitely inherited. Mother on the other hand was always the voice of good sense and refused to allow some of the more bizarre notions to which Father would otherwise have succumbed.

The first flight of fantasy I can recall was a 4½-litre WO Bentley that he was offered by an acquaintance. The car had been recently restored and the Rexene-covered body had been done in blue instead of the traditional racing green. She looked absolutely wonderful and I pleaded with him to acquire the jewel. Little did I know at the time that it was no more than a pipedream. Firstly, the asking price of £600 was way above our limits, and in any event my mother was never about to countenance such a ludicrously unsuitable vehicle as regular family transport.

The next exotic I can remember was a very early '30s Rolls Royce 20-horsepower. The car was in a scrap metal yard in Charlton. When Dad took me to see it, it was sitting up on blocks *sans* wheels but still looking quite the part. It was painted a dull battleshipish grey, and we were assured that it had driven in under its own steam and was raring to go. Father and I were as keen as mustard and for a time we plotted to wed Mother to the idea of ownership, but she would have none of it. People like us didn't have Rolls Royces, we were informed. With a car like that we would be laughing stocks, she told us, and she was probably right. It was particularly galling as the asking price was only £100, which was just about manageable. Like the Bentley, the body was of the tourer style with a very approximate hood and ill fitting front and rear side screens (I don't know if these latter items were part of the deal) so of course, completely unsuitable for the intended purpose. It's arrival would have caused more than a little domestic discord had it ever been brought home.

For a while Dad flirted with the acquisition of a mid-'30s vintage, 3-litre Lagonda saloon that sat a little forlornly in a yard on the A20. This was an altogether more viable prospect, as it had all the features required of a family car such as a watertight top and wind-up windows. I can recall lifting the bonnet and being shown what seemed like a very impressive engine. I don't remember why we never bought that car but we didn't and, as with the others, her memory soon faded.

During my last few years at school Dad moved from being a wage slave into the property development business, and his first acquisition was a mechanics' workshop on Kirkdale Road in Sydenham. When he finally got possession, the premises were filled with an assortment of old machinery. There was a war-time Humber staff car complete with massive wheels and bulbous tyres, a couple of old vans, an Armstrong Siddley Whittley saloon and a very respectable 3½-litre Derby Bentley sports coupé, a Park Ward model, I think. Dad told me that the Bentley belonged to a

This is very like the first modern car we owned. Ours was a 1956 Velox not quite as adorned as this 1957, top-of-the-range Cresta.

customer of the former proprietor and was awaiting collection. I learned later that he had acquired all the vehicles as part of the deal, since the workshop had been bought as a going concern. He had no interest in the business, however, and was bent on splitting up the site and selling it off in more lucrative bits. He subsequently told me that he had pretended the Bentley wasn't his so that I wouldn't pester him to keep it and get it back on the road. He eventually sold it for a princely £75.

All through this period we had our faithful Rover. Having been extensively used for commercial travelling, she was beginning to look a little shabby. Then she developed the habit of squirting oil out of the radiator cap, usually onto the windscreen, which could be embarrassing if you needed to look through it.

Dad had several goes at fixing her. He took the head off and replaced the gasket a few times, but it didn't cure the problem. Meanwhile fashions were changing. It was 1961 and Britain was getting more prosperous. My parents were beginning to find their pre-war jalopy an embarrassment. The boys at school had fathers with smart new Zodiacs and Crestas and there was I being ferried around in a banger. And so the fateful day came when the Rover was traded in for a metallic green, 1956 Vauxhall Velox. We were allowed £45 for the part exchange. A new era had arrived: we had our first post-war car.

A few months after the deal, Dad got a letter from the licensing authority telling him that our Rover had been abandoned on a by-pass somewhere. They still had him down as the registered keeper. We couldn't bear the thought of such an ignominious end for our old friend and resolved to go down and retrieve her. Even Mum was convinced it was the right thing to do. The reconnaissance for the retrieval was set for a Sunday morning and I went to bed the night before in a state of high excitement. But Mum and Dad had chatted in the night and on Sunday morning the operation was called off. We never heard of the Rover again.

During the Velox years, I started getting involved with my own transport and became less concerned with Dad's cars. I know

Taken from a period Vauxhall brochure, this is the kind of thing my parents lusted after. We had in turn both the Velox and the up market Cresta.

my parents were great admirers of Vauxhall's PA Cresta and they spent ages trying to negotiate a deal for a pink and white example at Shead Motors in Tulse Hill, but it came to nothing. Dad finally acquired a black PA Velox that I remember was cheap but not quite right. The steering column was bent and the wheel wobbled when it turned. It must have been about 1962 when he traded it in for a 1960 PA Cresta. He had that car for quite a while, eventually swapping it for a Jaguar XK 150, but that's a story for another chapter.

CHAPTER 2

A Car of My Own

From my description of events in the previous chapter, particularly the affair with the Bradford, it could be that one might see Father as something of a fool. Nothing could be further from the truth. He was without doubt one of the most able men I have known. There was nothing he couldn't turn his hand to. Not only was he a gifted automotive engineer who could make parts at the drop of a hat (he would never buy anything if he could make it), but he would often solve complex mathematical problems in order to do so. If he had a fault it was his stubborn bullheadedness, which often resulted in his pursuing projects long after he and everyone else knew they were futile. But he taught me a great deal, not least the value of persistence and hard work. My only regret is that I leaned the lessons so late.

All through my early life the myth that went with my love of motorcars was that I would acquire one on my seventeenth birthday. As it turned out I didn't pass my driving test for more than two years after that date so I didn't get on the road until I was almost twenty, but that didn't stop me acquiring my first car before the appointed day. In truth, not so much acquired one as had one thrust upon me.

It was my father, kind and very supportive of my passion for motors, who arranged my first vehicle. "I've found you a car," he announced one day.

I was taken aback. Visions of the delightful MG TC that I so coveted flooded into my mind, but only for a second. I knew the

Father – a gifted engineer

The car in Wally's yard was very like this one but in horrible condition. The illustration is taken from the pre-war Morris Ten sales brochure. The post- and pre-war cars were almost identical.

old man too well to believe he'd spring for anything like that.

It turned out to be a 1946 Morris Ten, a non-runner needing lots of work. It was propped up in a scrap yard in Charlton that was as disreputable as the car itself. Father took me to see it and my heart sank. The term "pile of junk" is the one that comes to mind. It was a scruffy little saloon with a scabby body in regulation black. The engine had seized solid and the interior smelled of vomit. We hated each other on sight. The owner of the yard, an irascible Scot called Wally, guided me over the trophy.

"Just needs a bit of work, Jimmy," he volunteered. When I questioned him about the duff engine, he insisted that it had come in perfectly well under its own steam. "A bit of elbow grease, laddie," was his parting shot as he wandered off to his caravan-cum-office.

I nurtured the hope of getting out of the deal by claiming it was too costly, but neither Wally nor my father were prepared to discuss money. In truth they were in cahoots and planned on giving me the car for nothing. Unfortunately, that was about what it was worth. I suppose I sound ungrateful, but really! As a callow sixteen-year-old with very little mechanical knowledge, I was hardly likely to unseize an engine and get the heap back on the road. Nevertheless, for several weeks I spent each Saturday at Wally's yard pouring penetrating oil down the bores and dusting down flaking bodywork with a wire brush.

I laboured pretty half-heartedly and spent a lot of time observing Wally at work. I remember a phalanx of pre-adolescents coming into the yard one day. They had an old but, we were assured, perfectly serviceable refrigerator perched on a pram. "What's it worth, mister?" they asked him.

Wally said nothing; he wheeled the contraption to the nearest plug point and, after some stripping, stuck bare wires into the electrical outlet. The old appliance at once began to hum as the compressor came to life. Wally ripped the wires out of the wall. "It's nay gud," he told the kids, "it doesne' work, bugger off and take your crap wi' ya."

They tried to argue, but the threat of physical violence soon saw them off and forlornly they wheeled the pram and its cargo away. When I cautiously mentioned that I had heard the compressor kick-in he made a sour face. It was clear he didn't want to discuss it. I went back to treating various parts of the Morris with engine oil.

A few hours later I stepped out to get a cheese roll and there, halfway up the road, was the fridge, dumped on its side. Of the pram or the children there was no sign. When I got back I mentioned what I had seen to Wally and he gave me a crafty smile. A few minutes later the fridge was on a handcart and back in the yard.

It was by chance that I witnessed the end of the episode. At half term, much against my will, Father hounded me down to the yard, ignoring the sanctity of my precious holiday. He insisted on driving me over himself so there was no chance of escape. We arrived in time to witness Wally standing by the refrigerator chatting to a very down-market car dealer. "There's absolutely nowt wrong wi' it," he was saying. "It'll keep your beer cold in the

I had to include this drawing also taken from the same Morris brochure. It shows an artist's impression of the model presumably, speeding down a country lane. Why does the term 'artistic licence' come to mind?

summer. I've had it mysel' fer 'ears, belonged to me mam." He sold it for 30 shillings.

Nice one, Wally, I thought.

It must have been obvious to everyone that I was getting nowhere with the Morris and even clearer that my heart wasn't in it. Having poured a gallon of oil down the bores, I still couldn't turn the engine. At this point I should make it clear that turning the engine was a strictly manual operation consisting of a starting handle and lots of physical effort. I had managed to acquire a battery, but not one capable of turning over a lawn mower let alone four reluctant cylinders.

"You can borrow whatever ye want from the pile," Wally had offered, pointing to a mound of scrap accumulators. "I'll charge ya five bob if you can find a gud un," he added. I did eventually find something that gave a feeble spark but, I'm happy to say, never parted with the five shillings.

Father came down one Saturday to vet progress. I'd had a belly full. "I've poured enough penetrating oil down the bores to sink a battleship." I told him. "It'll never free up. It's had it," I added in exasperation. To add weight to my words I leant heavily on the starting handle, then jumped up and put all my weight on it. Nothing: it didn't budge. I hovered there balancing precariously like a sick parrot on a perch.

My father looked sceptical. "Let me have a go," he said and taking over the handle gave it a sharp tug. His efforts were no more successful than mine. He put all his strength into it and started to go red in the face. It looked as though my goal was finally in sight. If he couldn't move it then nobody could and the purgatory of my weekly visits to Wally's would soon be over. Suddenly his determination overcame years of corrosion as the pistons once again moved in the bores. Worst of all was the look of triumph that came over his face. If it had been to hand I would have happily hit him over the head with that fridge.

Freeing up an engine and getting it started are two different things. I spent several days swinging that damned handle.

Working on my own, it wasn't easy to check for fuel and sparks and turn the engine at the same time. In theory all that was necessary for internal combustion was there, but the blighter wouldn't catch. Once more my father came to see how I was getting on and I was in terror of him again succeeding where I had failed. He wore himself out before giving up. But my smugness was soon dispelled.

"Come on," he said, "we'll get the battery out of the car." I can't quite remember how it all hooked up but, with my dad on the job, hook up it did. We spent an age churning the thing over, but luckily for me it was to no avail, the old banger resolutely refused to go. Mindful that we would need the dregs of our battery to get us home we called a halt before it was completely drained. That, it seemed, was finally that.

We returned the borrowed part from whence it came and went back to pick up tools. I knew this wasn't the time to start raising the topic of abandoning the project. Father was unusually silent; I knew he didn't like being beaten. I gently closed the bonnet. He had insisted we put everything back, including Wally's worn-out battery. I suspected I'd not heard the last of that dreaded automobile but it was getting late and growing colder as the sun began to set. We'd soon be home, I figured.

"You've left it switched on," Father admonished, noticing the feeble glow of the ignition telltale through a side window.

Who the hell cares? I thought. "I was planning to have one last swing at her," I lied. Grasping the handle, I gave it a feeble turn. The engine burst into life, throwing out plumes of acrid smoke.

"That's just the penetrating oil burning off," Father said enthusiastically. "She'll be fine when she's warmed up." I wasn't sure whether to laugh or cry. We stayed on until well after dark, at least until the petrol ran out. At one point Dad suggested siphoning some from his car but, by some happy miracle, he abandoned the idea and we set off for home.

He was in high spirits and chatted away merrily about the finer points of further restoration. In his enthusiasm I suppose he

SOME USEFUL FEATURES

More illustrations from the brochure. Note the cup and saucer and the rather curly sandwich on the parcel shelf under the dash. Whether these were intended to be left in situ whilst driving along is unclear.

failed to notice the dejection of his offspring slumped in the passenger seat.

And so to yet more miserable weekends wasted on that beastly car. The end came unexpectedly. It was Dad's normal practice to chivvy me out of the house on Saturday mornings and give me a lift down to the yard on his way to work. One morning we arrived to find the place shut up and no sign of Wally. My father passed by several times after that but never found the place open. It was a while before we learned that Wally was dead. He'd just keeled over one day while going about his business. I never found out (or cared) what happened to my Morris. Years later when I passed by they were building a block of flats on the site. I hope his family benefited from the transaction. I never again considered owning a Morris Ten or any other kind for that matter. Sorry, all you Morris fans out there.

CHAPTER 3

The Wilderness Years

During my sixth-form years (I went to school in Forest Hill) the boys were divided into two groups, motorbikers and sissies. There were one or two car owners but too few to form a recognisable classification. As I had no hope of swelling the latter's numbers and I didn't fancy being a sissy, the only option was to get a bike. My parents were violently opposed to this, and not without cause. Nearly everyone who had one, came off his bike at one time or another: some were less fortunate than others. I don't have the statistics, but a depressing number of young men either died, became permanently disabled or endured long periods of hospitalisation. What probably saved me from serious harm was a change in the law that came about at the time. Perhaps because of the youthful carnage, the government decided to restrict learner riders to machines of 250ccs or under. This had the dual effect of letting in the Japanese (who systematically destroyed the domestic motorcycle industry) and of keeping lots of young men alive and intact.

My dream machines, and those of my contemporaries, were things like Triumph Bonnevilles and Trophies, BSA Gold Stars and Rockets as well as Vincent Black Shadows and Norton Dominators, all pretty standard fantasy fare of the period. Of course, given my schoolboy finances there was no hope of acquiring one of these lusted-after machines but old, serviceable, big bikes could be had for under £50. A 350 or 500cc BSA,

Matchless/AJS or even a Triumph would have been easy to find. Blue jeans astride a "big-banger" was my self-image, such as it was. Then the legislators stuck in their oar. Suddenly my options were down to two-stroke pop-pops, Triumph Tiger Cubs and 'Noddy' Velocettes. I wasn't quite so keen to play and more inclined to listen to what Father had to say so the idea of a Bond Minicar, oft mooted by my dad, was revisited.

As I mentioned in the opening chapter, post-war Britain spawned a rash of budget cars and commercials. Lawrie Bond, a sometime racer and committed evangelist for the microcar, came up with an attractive design for a low cost and practical three-wheeler. The idea would have died had it not been for the firm of Sharp Commercials of Preston whose managing director conceived the project as being financially viable. From 1949 to 1966 some 26,000 three-wheeler Bond Minis rolled off the production lines. They developed from the very basic, early mark "A" through to the only slightly less basic mark "H".

At sixteen, I liked the idea of owning such a vehicle for a number of reasons. First, it looked a bit like real car, three wheels notwithstanding. Second, in heavily used but still usable condition they could be bought very cheaply. Third, you could drive one on a motorcycle licence and fourth, you could drive one on a provisional licence unaccompanied, although there was some confusion about whether it was possible to carry an unqualified passenger (i.e. someone who hadn't passed a driving test).

Father liked them on my behalf because they were under 200ccs, with a power-to-weight ratio that made them significantly less lethal than motorcycles in whatever form.

There were some ancillary reasons for my interest in these rather masochistic little contraptions. I was playing in a band at the time and the Minicar, unlike a motorbike, offered useful accommodation for my instrument and its associated electrical gubbins. I was also courting, and having my own transport had its appeal, hence the investigation into the finer points of who could or could not be carried. Another "minor" attraction was that my parents, in their desire to keep me away from motorcycles, were prepared to contribute significantly to the cost of purchase.

Once this last point had been established and confirmed, in other words my father formally agreeing to cough, I was in a muck sweat to get my hands on one. We must have travelled to every corner of south-east London in our quest to secure a Bond in working order, for £30 or less that is. Each Thursday I'd queue at the newsagent at the crack of dawn in order to get an early copy of the *Exchange & Mart* (its full and proper title in those days was *The Bazaar, Exchange & Mart* or the "Totter's Bible" as Mum called it) and scan it for likely candidates. In any event we must have seen more than a dozen of these little monstrosities.

The first was in Camberwell. It was a mark C or D and seemed in acceptable condition. It had been fitted with a modification intended to overcome the lack of a reverse gear. If the driver turned off the engine, threw a switch and then re-started, (which was achieved by pulling a cord rather like that on a lawn mower), the engine would run backwards and *voilà*, reverse. Of course, the whole operation had to be repeated in order to go forward again. When we got there the owner wasn't in, but was due back at any moment, his wife assured us. We had a good look at the car and my dad even gave it a road test. He came back a little shaken; he'd never been in one before. He was decidedly less enthusiastic than he had been, while I on the other hand was as keen as mustard. The chap didn't show, although we hung around for quite a while. We left our number but he never called. I must have tried to get him on more than twenty occasions over the next week but he was never in. His wife was always as nice as pie and assured me that the vehicle was still for sale and her husband was about to get in touch. He never did. When I tried to phone him the following week I got no reply. The week after that the number came up unobtainable. I shall never know what happened.

This is pretty much the sort of think I went to look at. This particular example is a Mark C, so I would most probably have ended up with one of these. The D models had a self-starter and rather better windscreen wipers. Earlier cars had a manual handle for reversing. All were very basic.

We saw a few others that weren't as nice as that first one and were rejected out of hand.

We found a very nice example in Herne Hill but the owner wouldn't let it go for what we offered. I made big, sad eyes but Father didn't want to know. We finally did a deal with a man in Catford and I had high hopes. He promised to have the vehicle MOT'd (the ten-year test had been introduced). Dad was minded to offer a bit less and take the car as it stood but the owner was adamant.

"If it's for the lad, I'd be happier if I knew it was right," he told us sanctimoniously. We shrugged our shoulders, we didn't have anything to lose, or so we thought. He wouldn't take a deposit. "It's down to you," he assured us. Three days later he'd sold it to someone else. "I wasn't sure you were that interested," he said when I called him, "anyway you didn't leave a deposit."

Father got tired of trailing around and I had no transport so the search went cold for a while. I did find a car not far from home in Forest Hill but when dad came to look at it he said it was a pile of junk.

Then I got distracted by my pal Steve, who had decided to buy a motorcycle combination. Believing in my extensive knowledge of things automotive, he prevailed upon me to go with him and look at an "outfit" he was considering. (Isn't it funny how there is an established nomenclature for these things?) My main contribution was doing the deal; I negotiated an outstanding price. Steve got it for £10 which, given the initial asking price of £35, was good going. What I failed to spot was that it was totally clapped out, mainly of course because I knew very little about such things. It was a BSA of late '50s origin, an A10, Gold Flash I think. It had a big Watsonian, double adult sidecar that was in reasonable shape. It went, but only just. I rode it home from Bell Green and Steve walked because we weren't sure whether learners were allowed to carry unqualified passengers.

Basically, the thing needed a new engine, but we were too ignorant and inexperienced to know. It had no pick-up, no performance and no redeeming qualities of any kind, except that without any serious compression it was very easy to start. Steve pottered about unhappily for a week or so. One day, while wandering around in Myers, the local bike breakers, we met Clive, a nineteen-year-old man of the world and an established motorcycle guru. He said he'd be happy to give the Beezer a "once-over" but when we got it down to him he pronounced it a terminal case. He did, however, offer to swap it for a very decrepit Matchless outfit, a 500 single with a box. No, that's not an "in" term for a fancy type of sidecar. It just means that instead of a sidecar it had a crudely made, oblong, wooden box bolted to the chassis. Its saving grace was that in comparison with the BSA it went like the clappers. It was working transport and Steve was happy, so we had a deal. Three days later the clutch went. Steve phoned Clive in high dudgeon. He came over, took a look and confirmed the diagnosis. Off we went to Myers to see if they had a second-hand replacement. The man in-charge pointed at a pile of parts.

"Have a look in there, mate," he told Clive, "I think you'll find a clutch in that lot somewhere," and wandered off. Clive found what we wanted and instead of taking it to the front as I expected he opened up his leather jacket and stuffed it inside. He must have seen the look of shock on my face. "Shut your mouth," he warned me. My cheeks must have been burning scarlet and I certainly had trouble with my breathing as Clive sauntered out of the shop with me trailing miserably behind.

"Wasn't one there mate," he told the man at the counter. I was in shock and it was not until we were back at Steve's that I remonstrated with him, but he was a big lad and quickly put me in my place. He had the job done in an hour and the old Matchless gave Steve good service for quite a while.

My friend's success with his motorcycle combination turned me off the Bond Minicar idea. Once I had experienced the electrifying performance of a big bike, even with sidecar attached, there was no prospect of my ever accepting life with an asthmatic, two stroke three-wheeler.

I soon found a combination of my own, a 650cc Triumph

Thunderbird with a skimpy but attractive sidecar that had seen better days. (I made it roadworthy with some two-by-fours and a bag of galvanised nails.) The T-bird was a '53 or '54 with telescopic front forks, and rear suspension courtesy of a sprung hub. It was probably the fastest vehicle from 0 to 60 that I have ever owned. I don't know what the numbers were but golly it was quick! I remember sitting at the lights with the driver of a 3.8 Jaguar Mark 2 giving me the eye. It was done up like a dog's dinner, louvred bonnet and all. He obviously fancied his chances against my old combo but it was no contest: I was in the next county before he got the clutch up.

With iffy brakes, no lighting (I remember on one occasion riding through the West End after dark with hand torches strapped to the front and back), no MOT or road tax but, of course, with devastating performance, it was the ideal vehicle for an impetuous seventeen-year-old.

Luckily, I survived without mishap the main lesson of riding motorcycle combinations. The design of these vehicles is peculiar, with the wheel of the sidecar in line with the rear wheel of the bike. This results in an asymmetric three-wheeler that has some rather odd handling characteristics. (In the UK, because we drive on the left, the sidecar is fixed on the left of the bike so the rider is always on the outside.) This geometry means that right-hand bends can be taken at amazing speeds; in some cases it seems almost impossible to discover the limit. Contrary to what one might expect, left-handers on the other hand must be negotiated with great care: it doesn't take much for the sidecar wheel to lift alarmingly and tip the outfit over. For the unwary, this, as the cigarette ads suggest, can be seriously damaging to your health, sometimes terminally.

When I was seventeen, I started learning to drive. Still anxious to keep me away from motorcycles, even ones with miniature mobile homes strapped to them, Father put my share of the promised Bond money into a Bedford CA van. Its dual purpose was to haul building materials (he'd moved into buying old properties and doing them up), and to act as my tuition vehicle. He had the wrong disposition for teaching me to drive and I had the wrong one for learning with him. Most of the time he was having hysterics and I was in a panic. I hated going out with him and he hated taking me but each of us kept screwing up our courage and giving it one more go.

The end came in Church Road, Upper Norwood (by then we'd moved to Crystal Palace). He'd coaxed me out on a Saturday morning and we were heading in a southerly direction down the busy high street when - my version first - Father panicked, for no reason becoming agitated about my speed and the proximity of a group of pedestrians on a zebra crossing. His version was that I was going too fast, hadn't seen the old woman and child and was about to run them down.

We both agreed about what happened next. He screamed in a somewhat unnerving way and snatched the wheel from my grudging hands. I of course, snatched it right back but not before the van had veered across the road and mounted the opposite pavement. We proceeded to scatter shoppers in all direction before bumping once more on to the road and getting back to the proper side. It all happened so fast, one moment we were careering out of control along the pavement on the wrong side (is there a right side of the pavement?) the next, we were cruising serenely along as though nothing had happened. Frankly, I was unnerved although my father pretended not to be. Actually we

These Bedford CA utilities appeared in many guises, vans, campers, mini-buses and even tippers.

were both shaken witless. I was in shock for several days. Anyway, that put paid to driving lessons with Dad.

I gave up the idea of ever owning a motorcar and concentrated on being reckless with my combination. I had lots of scrapes and near misses and nearly got mangled several times. On one occasion, going up Highgate Hill, I went for a gap between two lorries but at the last minute a coach overtook the oncoming truck so I aimed for what had become a significantly smaller gap and sailed through with my eyes shut.

My new girl friend lived in Archway, which is a long way from Norwood, and the Triumph was pressed into regular service across London. One evening on the way home I got a flat tyre in Villiers Street just outside the Coliseum. I had neither tools nor any way of dealing with the situation. The bike wasn't even taxed or tested. I sat there for an hour then telephoned home. Dad asked where I was and told me he'd be over. He arrived 40 minutes later with a set of tools, and proceeded to get the wheel off. There was no way we could get a puncture fixed at midnight on a Sunday so we drove around looking for a new inner tube. It was an education, and I discovered there were some very odd places in London and even odder people around in the wee hours. While we were in the midst of our adventure, someone cut a blooming great hole in the window of the jewellery store opposite and made off with a haul. At one point we were engulfed by police. I hadn't noticed anything; I guess I was a busy with other matters. We eventually found what we were looking for and Dad got me back on the road. I got home a good bit before him; boy, that Triumph was quick! It certainly beat the pants off Dad's Velox. Actually we got in about four in the morning and I expected my parents to blast me to hell but they were as nice as anything. It wasn't the first or the last time that my dear old Dad got me out of a jam.

My luck seemed to have run out one afternoon on Annerley Hill. Steve and I were horsing around and, as we came out of a chip shop, I suddenly jumped on his Matchless and roared up the hill; he followed on my Triumph. What we didn't notice was the

Traffic Division officer behind us on his big, white Tiger 110. He cautioned us and then started to test our respective vehicles; needless to say he found them wanting. He threw the book at us.

But worst of all, he threatened to collar Steve on what seemed like a serious charge. It was duly noted that we met no statutory requirements regarding such things as road fund licences and test certificates, although we both had insurance for our own bikes. By good fortune, because I had helped Steve with his acquisition, I was also insured to ride his machine. The problem was that he wasn't insured on mine. The officer gave me a choice. Either I admitted to

My thunderbird was a lot like this one except with a sidecar.

aiding and abetting Steve riding my bike without the obligatory RTA cover or, I could claim that he had taken it without my permission. The latter meant that on the aiding and abetting charge at least I was off the hook but Steve would be charged with "taking and riding away" for which he would be ferried to the local nick and accommodated in a cell. Steve not surprisingly was in funk. For the sake of our friendship, I put my hand up to the accessory bit.

The officer must have been with us for an hour or more. When he started showing us his bike and demonstrating its virtues we should have taken heart. As we talked, he gradually relented and let us off the long list of charges one by one. We were finally left with the insurance issue. "That's a very serious matter," he told us, "I can't let you go on that one." He asked us to show him our respective insurance documents and I gave him my certificate, which I always kept screwed up in my back pocket. Steve went off to his outfit to get his.

"Well, at least you have both done the right thing by getting insurance on your own bikes," he said. "I won't penalise you for a silly mistake this time. Don't let it happen again." With that he got on his bike and rode away. When Steve came back with his piece of paper it took me ten minutes to convince him we had been let off.

Nevertheless the incident unnerved me and, as I had little

prospect of getting my machine through any kind of test, I began to use it less and less. This meant that I was forced to stay over at my girlfriend's more often, which of course had its advantages.

Ownership of the Triumph coincided with a number of important changes in my life. For one, I left full-time education. I also reached my eighteenth birthday and I got my first job. I hadn't received my exam results at the time so I suppose it was always intended as an interim measure. I applied to an advertisement in the *Evening Standard* for an assistant production manager, went to interview and got the job. The Arcy Manufacturing Company was in Kentish Town on the opposite side of London from where we lived in Crystal Palace. The hours were 8 till 6. I'd catch the first bus, the 6.40, from Palace Parade and get home at about 8 in the evening. I rarely used the combination. The place was owned by a Jewish gentleman called Strauss. He had come out of Austria in 1938 by the skin of his teeth and landed in England with his wife, two daughters and £5. He'd built up a prosperous little business making anoraks for stores like C&A, Marshall and Snelgrove and Selfridges. He was a kind and generous man and ran an Auntie Rover 100. He was in the process of reducing his involvement and I worked directly for his son-in-law Martin, who was progressively taking over the business. Most of the other managers were from Berlin or Vienna and told terrifying stories of pre-war Nazis in Germany and Austria.

The title "assistant production manager" was a euphemism for production manager's assistant; I wasn't much more than a glorified gofer. I got on well enough though, partly because I was comfortable with numbers and was able to memorise all the style codes and also because I was good on the 'phone with suppliers, something with which the rest had difficulty. I was soon given the job of ordering braids and buttons. The great thing about that job was the pay. I got £12 and 10 shillings a week, in cash on Fridays. My first priority was to save up for a ring for my girlfriend and the next, to pass my driving test, junk the Triumph and get some serious wheels. I'd spent too much time in the automotive wilderness.

CHAPTER 4

Getting Started

With cash in my pocket for the first time, I opted for a series of driving lessons with a professional. Dad didn't feel in the least put out and in fact was so pleased that he replaced the Bedford with an ageing Ford Squire in which I still had a half share. Ford produced two estate versions of the popular (excuse the pun) 100E saloon, the Escort and the Squire. Both models had the van body, but with side windows and rear seats. The interiors were properly trimmed and the back was equipped with the latest split tailgate. The Squire was the countryman version, with a small amount of wood fixed to the outside. Not as "Tudor" as a Morris Traveller but woody nonetheless. Ours was in Dagenham beige, a colour much favoured by Ford at the time.

I'm going to offend a lot of people, but I've never been a fan of Ford side valves. They guzzled far too much petrol for their size and that awful three-speed box with its massive gap between second and third made them painful to drive. You were either in second with the mill churning fit to burst or in top and about to stall the thing.

The Squire had the dubious benefit of being the first car on which I carried out major maintenance. Almost as soon as it arrived the gearbox fell apart. Father and I

The Squire was the countryman version of the Prefect. It had the nasty 1172cc side valve and a hopeless three-speed gearbox. Ours was a nondescript beige colour. After the CA Bedford van, it was at least compact. If you mounted the kerb and aimed at pedestrians, you were likely to mow down fewer than with the Bedford.

YKJ 565

removed the offending item and managed to pick up another from a breaker's yard easily enough. I got home early one Friday afternoon when Dad wasn't around and decided to install it on my own.

Working in the drive, I rigged up a crossbar from which to suspend a pulley, block and tackle and was lowering in the engine and box when the ramshackle contraption gave way. I saw it coming down out of the corner of my eye and got most of my head out of the way in time. But not quite far enough, because the bar caught me a glancing blow on the temple and laid me out cold. The motor and transmission were upended in the engine bay, and the fuel pipe, which I had tied out of the way, came adrift and the stuff poured out of the tank. My mother found me lying in the drive soaked in an ever-widening pool of petrol. At first she thought I was fooling around and then realised my predicament was for real. Luckily, I recovered in time to stop anything more serious occurring and was able to staunch the flow before staggering inside for some TLC. After a short rest I returned and finished the job. I had the car on the road that evening. I suppose it's possible that the blow on the head did some lasting damage; there are a lot of people who will swear that it did.

I was still using the Thunderbird combination. When my girlfriend's shared flat broke up she decided it would make sense to move south of the river. My dear mother, against her better judgement, agreed to let her move into our spare room. "Only until she finds a flat and for absolutely no longer than two weeks." Mum was adamant. We used the bike and sidecar to move her stuff to Crystal Palace. The first few days were a whirl of activity, talking to agents, scanning lists and looking at property. Gradually the tempo dropped and then the search stopped altogether. She finally moved out three years later when we left to get married.

The time had come to turn in my handlebars and I sold the Triumph to a young man who planned on getting her through the MOT test. I hope he succeeded; she had given good service and I was sorry to see her go.

With a regular income and the best of intentions, I signed up for a set of driving lessons with a professional school. My instructor was a brave man and gave me the option of taking lessons in the Squire or using his dual control Volkswagen Beetle. As his car was virtually brand new, it was the one I chose. Apart from the trials and tribulations of learning to drive on busy suburban roads, I enjoyed the VW a lot. If I'd had the cash, I would have been happy to own one. The instructor's boast was that he had never taught a pupil who hadn't passed first time. The proviso was that all tests had to be taken at the Carshalton centre where he knew all the testers: mainly because he had been one of them for the previous ten years.

I presented myself on the appointed day and, I am glad to say, kept my instructor's record intact. I rushed home, arranged insurance and threw away the L-plates. I took the Squire out for a cruise and kangaroo hopped my way around the block. That evening my girlfriend and I went to the West End to celebrate; naturally we went in the 100E. I was told later that parts of the ride were a little hair-raising, but I remember it as going rather well.

Dad and I both agreed that a shared vehicle harboured too much potential for trouble so we stuck it in the good old *E&M* and it was sold in no time at all.

I found a Vauxhall Wyvern in a dealer's yard near Peckham Rye. It was a 1956 model "E" that, apart from some scabby paint on a front wing, seemed in good shape. The price tag said £60. Dad started it up and it was obvious that it had "run an end". When we pointed this out, the dealer was as surprised as could be and immediately dropped the ante by £30. I was all for accepting the deal, but my shrewder father held out and we got it for 20 quid. Apart from the serious engine problem, she was the perfect vehicle for a young man setting out on the road to car ownership. The Wyvern was a big roomy saloon with a column change, so it could accommodate three passengers on

My Wyvern was black with a rather nice red interior. It provided comfortable seating for six.

the front bench seat. It was the smaller engined, four-cylinder sibling of the more powerful Velox and, in theory, more economical. (From experience, I have become sceptical of the claim that small-engined versions of big cars give better gas-mileage.) I was thrilled to bits. I was a little less ecstatic, however, when we whipped off the sump and discovered a case of terminal big-enditis. Most of the journals were already 60 thou oversize and on their last legs. The one that was knocking like a jackhammer seemed to have been fitted with a made-up custom shell of indeterminate size. The journal itself was positively egg-shaped.

Undaunted, we set off once again for the local breaker. He had exactly what we wanted: nestling in a corner was a battered Wyvern. "That one drove in," the man assured us. "The engine's a good 'un." But he wanted £7, a bit pricey we thought. Then I spotted a very decrepit Bedford van under several layers of bric-a-brac.

"How much to buy the engine out of that?" I asked.

"That one was pulled in; I've never heard it run," the breaker replied. "But if you want to take a chance it's 50 shillings." I accepted with alacrity, fully expecting to have to lift it out ourselves. "But I can't get to it this week," he added. "Come back on Tuesday and I'll have it ready to collect."

He was as good as his word. When we got it home and cleaned off the grime we found a re-conditioner's plate riveted to the side. The legend informed us that the engine had been rebuilt 18 months earlier. It ran beautifully.

The old Wyvern provided reliable transport for quite some time. The three-abreast seating in the front meant that my girlfriend, my pal Steve and I could meander through the countryside in a decidedly convivial manner. It let us down once in Tunbridge Wells on the way back from Hastings, when it refused to run on more than two cylinders and only just made it into Caffyn's garage. I had a look but could find no obvious reason for the failure. The works mechanic was called out and assured us that the carburettor had given up the ghost. I was sceptical but he was the expert. They let us leave the car on the forecourt but none of us had enough cash to get back home, so the pump attendant kindly lent me £5. I did, however, have to leave him my rather valuable guitar as surety.

As usual, it was my long-suffering father who came to the rescue. He drove me back to the garage the next day and soon identified the problem. A stud holding the rocker shaft had sheared, resulting in malfunctioning valves. He managed to get out the broken fragment but we couldn't find a replacement stud. We did, however, find a coach bolt that, with a few packing washers, did the job. "As soon as you get home, fit the proper stud," my father warned. When I sold the car six months later his temporary repair was still doing service. I repaid the fiver and got my guitar back.

It was at about this time that I came to the end of the road, musically speaking that is. My electric band had been abandoned for some time and Steve and I had formed an acoustic duo, but this too was running out of steam. "Steve Silver" and "Roger Gold", it seemed, had had their day. Steve was a real musician and went on to become one of the country's leading baroque flautists. I, apart from having very little talent, was increasingly inclined to liquidate the capital tied up in my musical equipment and squander it on a motorcar.

My exam results duly arrived and, although I'd managed three "A" levels, I decided against university. A regular, weekly pay packet once experienced was not easily relinquished. I enrolled instead in evening classes at the Regent Street Polytechnic. The avowed aim was a BSc in Economics. The course consisted of five years of intensive study; just who I thought I was kidding I've no idea. I suppose the only one I fooled was myself but even that wasn't for very long. I'd also thrown in the towel at Arcy Manufacturing and taken whiter collar employment in the accounts department of the London branch of BUPA. The pay was only £520 a year, a sizeable reduction, but the hours were a lot shorter. As a career move it was one of the shrewdest I ever made, but not for any reason I could have guessed at the time.

The Wyvern began to play up, refusing to start each evening when I retrieved it from the station car park. I tried a replacement battery and a new coil but to no avail, and cold starting became an increasing problem. To make matters worse, the back axle started making crunching noises when cornered hard. At least the coachwork still seemed sound.

I got a puncture one day and lifted the car using the proper jack – a wind-up device that fitted into a hole in the middle of the sill. I changed the wheel without difficulty and was just about to let it down when there was a loud cracking sound and the two halves of the car came down on their own. The jack stayed in position still holding up the centre. I lowered it gently, then opened the doors and jumped up and down on the sill until the body was once again more or less in line. So much for sound coachwork.

It was time to say good-bye, and an ad in the ever-faithful *E&M* resulted in an eager buyer at £55.

With money to spend, I set off on the trail of something

sporty. I was in the happy situation of having the cash and no definite idea of what I would get with it. As with most young men, my tastes ran ahead of my pocket. The strategy was to find a vehicle that would normally cost about twice what I had available and then, by hard bargaining and accepting something in less than ideal condition, secure it for a smaller sum. I developed a thick hide, which was sorely needed when offering vendors only a fraction of their asking price. There were occasions when I escaped serious physical harm only by the skin of my teeth, but I did buy a lot of cars very cheaply.

The normal tactic was to get hold of the *Exchange & Mart*, that came out on Thursdays, as early as possible. By then I had discovered a source that would let me have the magazine on a Wednesday evening, thus enabling me to steal a march on other would-be bargain hunters. (These days I wear spectacles and I maintain that this is a result not of old age but of those early years when I spent so many hours scanning the small ads in the *E&M*.) On this occasion, because I didn't have a specific make or model in mind, it meant an exhaustive search from A to W (Yugos weren't imported at the time). What I found was a Ford Consul convertible being offered from an address in Bermondsey. These were always desirable cars, with the drop tops following the normal practice of holding their value better than the saloons. At the time a '57 convertible in good order would have fetched about £150, so an ad quoting £75 for one requiring a little attention was seriously interesting.

The main disadvantage of selling before buying was the problem of getting to see the goods. I recall it was a filthy night and, as Father couldn't be persuaded to play ball, I went out alone by public transport. It wasn't an easy trip from the Palace, but where there's a will there's a way. The man selling the car turned out to be a dealer with a yard full of junk. The look of the place should have persuaded me to turn around and go home, but the prospect of picking up the two-tone convertible at the right price was too appealing. It was the worst possible night to evaluate a prospective purchase: in the open with the rain sheeting down and the wind blowing a gale. What can I say? – blinded by wind and rain, I mistakenly thought that the car looked all right.

I persuaded the dealer to take me for a run. To say the

Consul Convertible

An illustration from a contemporary sales brochure. Ford's second attempt at the Consul (1956-62) was another handsome design. With the top down, the convertible was a stylish motor. The 1703cc engine was more than adequate and performance was acceptable for the time.

demonstration was a disaster is an understatement. The route around the back streets of Bermondsey was strewn with parked cars, which under normal circumstances would have limited our progress to crawling speed. On the evening in question, in the dark with only a single, out-of-line headlamp for illumination, we didn't even do that well. We were not helped by the windscreen wipers which, as in most Fords of the time, were operated by a ludicrous system that worked on engine vacuum. This meant that the speed of the wipers varied with engine load: hard acceleration often meant they virtually stopped altogether. On this particular, clapped-out example of Dagenham's handiwork they mostly didn't go at all. For some reason the passenger side worked marginally better than the driver's. It was not an inspiring drive, but worse was yet to come.

We went bowling along in the near blackness, as the dealer attempted to prove that the car, contrary to indications, was really a spunky little sportster. I saw the cyclist plodding slowly along the line of vehicles at the kerb and assumed that the driver had as well. It was not until the bike was almost under our wheels that I realised he had not. I screamed out a warning and we managed to stop with the cyclist pinned between the Consul and a parked van. Fortunately, he was shaken but unharmed. It was a close call and we crawled back to the yard badly unnerved. Again, this would have been an ideal opportunity to catch the bus home and forget all about the old wreck. But, let's face it, with the dealer having come so close to facing a manslaughter charge, surely it was an ideal time to extract a real bargain? I bought the Consul for £52.10 shillings, which included delivery. When I got home from work next day the car was sitting in the gutter; the keys and the paperwork had been pushed through the letterbox.

Of course, in the daylight and without the rain it was even worse than expected. Everything was either worn out or had rusted away. The engine smoked and threw out great globs of oil, the back axle whined, the electrics were a joke and the wipers I've already discussed. The seat frames were broken, the interior was a tip, the hood was slashed and the boot full of water. The floors were rusted through, barely covered by sodden carpets and most of the body edges had been remade with plastic filler. All in all it was extremely nasty, and it was mine. The first car I had bought without my father's explicit approval had turned out to be a pig in a poke. My best hope was to await a hurricane and then try selling it to a deaf, dumb and blind mental defective. Needless to say, I was fairly dejected. I left the car in the kerb and considered my options.

In order to appreciate what happened next, one should know something of where we lived in Crystal Palace. My parents' house was on what was thought to be the steepest road in London. At one point the gradient was as much as 1 in 3. We were used to parking with a wheel firmly turned into the kerb. I even got into the habit of carrying around a couple of house bricks to chock the offside wheels.

About a week after my acquisition, I was alerted by the sound of high revving and furious wheel spinning in the road. I went out to find a big, flat-bed truck attempting to reverse up the hill. Without a load on the back, burning rubber off the rear wheels was all the driver could manage. The nose of the truck was resting against a tree planted at the edge of the kerb, so the vehicle was also unable to move forward. It was, in a word, stuck. Father and I tried standing on the bed over the driving wheels but our combined weight just wasn't enough. We even attempted pushing while the driver gunned the engine, but that too proved futile. Then I came up with an idea. We used a bottle jack under the beam axle to lift the front. We then pushed the cab sideways so that the jack toppled over and the truck moved a few inches to one side. Although it took three of us to achieve the desired effect, it was quickly evident that the strategy was working and we repeated the process several times.

Unfortunately, as soon as the lorry was free of the tree (the driver being out of his cab and helping to push), it took off down the hill like a bat out of hell. The man made a valiant attempt at scrambling back but was thrown clear as the vehicle gathered speed. The truck careered off out of control. There were homes on all sides. If the runaway had got to the bottom and gone through the front of a house the potential for tragedy was unimaginable. But, at just the right moment my dear old Consul came to the rescue. Fortunately, it had been strategically parked between the truck and disaster. The lorry, now travelling at speed, ploughed into the back of the car and then mounted it as though attempting some form of automotive coitus. Locked together, with sparks flying, they skidded a few feet further and then came to rest. Serious disaster had been narrowly averted; except of course that the Consul was a write-off.

A few days later the insurance assessor came and had a look. He licked his pencil, sucked his teeth and said rude things about my poor, mangled car but he did at least authorise removing the remains. The breaker then arrived to scrape up the salvage. He too was unkind, but gave me £10 and carted it away.

There followed numerous phone calls to the trucker's

The Standard 8 Drop Head was quite rare and had coachwork by Mulliner.

insurers. I was sent forms to complete that were lost in the post and the process had to be repeated. After several weeks, I gave up hope and started looking for another car. With the £10 from the salvage and another tenner I'd saved, the options weren't exciting, but I'd managed the Wyvern for £20 so maybe I could do it again. This time perhaps I could even find a car with a serviceable engine.

I found the very thing in the form of a 1948, Standard 8 Drop Head coupé. I got her from a Polish gentleman in South

Performance wasn't spectacular but the package was a delight nonetheless, although somewhat reminiscent of Noddy and Big Ears.

Norwood. He was asking £20 and we settled on £15. He had lavished an enormous amount of care and attention on her. He had re-trimmed the interior, sadly not in the original leather but had used an acceptable vinyl substitute. Surprisingly, he had made a good job of it. He had also renewed the hood. The body was as sound as a bell, without a trace of rust or filler. The only two drawbacks were, first, the colour, which was a rather anaemic air-force blue, and second, that it had been applied by hand. Even this the owner had done tolerably well.

I thoroughly enjoyed driving her around and she never let me down, except when I forgot to fill her with anti-freeze. In the cold English winter she froze up solid and warped the head. The little side valve was easy to work on. I whipped off the head and had it skimmed but had difficulty finding a replacement gasket. Somebody put me on to a firm called "Clare's" in Gypsy Hill. This was in 1966, and when I went in it was like stepping through a time warp. It was as if I had been whisked back to the '30s. More like a grocer's shop than a car parts supplier, the shelves were neatly stacked with tins and boxes of new "old stock". Everything was clearly labelled with legends like "Morris 8 crown wheels" and "Austin 12 water pumps". The man behind the counter, wearing a brown dustcoat, was at once attentive and helpful. The conversation went something like:

"Good morning Sir, how can I help you?"

"Er, I'm looking for a head gasket for a 1948 Flying Standard 8 Drop Head."

"Yes Sir, I think we have some of those right here."

He turned to face the shelves and just there, up and to his right, dangling from a nail, were half-a-dozen of the things.

I visited Clare's several times after that and usually found what I was after. That strange, anachronistic little business lasted several years more before finally making way for a modern filling station. I'm sure old car buffs everywhere mourned its passing.

It's strange, but of all the motors I have owned that little Standard is the one I regret selling the most. She was in every way a delightful car. If I owned her now I'd re-trim in leather, re-spray her a nice colour and convert to 12-volt electrics. She'd be just the thing for sunny, Sunday rallies. I saw one in immaculate condition the other day and it brought a lump to my throat. What a silly old fool I am!

It must have been about four months after the destruction of the Consul that I received a letter from the trucker's insurance company. I opened it up half expecting another excuse for prevarication but instead found a cheque for £125. My joy knew no bounds.

The temptation was to blow the lot on something fast and fancy, but wiser counsel prevailed. I was on the verge of matrimony and was persuaded to invest £100 in a savings plan that I was assured would grow over time into a useful nest egg. I nonetheless quickly disposed of the Standard and went seeking better things.

A particularly incompetent picture of BCF 176

Down in darkest Dulwich, I came across the car that made my heart beat faster. I had answered the ad for a 1948 Triumph Roadster 1800 with circumspection. Reading between the lines the description did not inspire confidence. But when I saw it, it was love at first sight. My whole life had been building towards this. The man was asking £75. Apart from some cracking on the front apron, the paintwork looked wonderful. It also ran tolerably well (at least, as well as this particular model could). The major drawbacks were a hideously tatty interior and an almost unusable gear change.

These cars were originally made with a very unusual right-handed column change. The car in question had been modified to a floor shift by fitting what I later discovered was a Standard Fourteen gearbox top. This mechanism operated directly on

Another dreadful shot of BCF. Its saving grace may be that it shows the hill and for that matter the actual tree where the fateful lorry got stuck before writing-off the Consul.

the selectors, which meant that, without an extension to bring the stick reasonably within the driver's reach, changing gear was peculiarly difficult. Cog swapping was preceded by furious rummaging beneath the instrument panel and then by a howl of pain as the driver bashed his knuckles against things sharp and knobbly under the dash. All in all, a most unhappy state of affairs.

Of course, it didn't put me off in the least. At worst it was an inconvenience requiring a change of driving style, but at best it was a huge and effective bargaining point. I got BCF 176 for £50 and drove her home that evening.

That Triumph Roadster was the first car on which I voluntarily lavished attention. She was definitely different and, while my contemporaries were driving around in Minis and Anglias, I was the man apart, the intrepid adventurer in my British racing-green goddess.

Unlike many immediate post-war models, the Roadster had not been in production before 1940. The Triumph Company had been bought by Standard in 1945, with the intention of moving it into the territory occupied by companies like Rover and Jaguar. In fact, the '40s Triumph

The boot was also a passenger compartment with the pop-up screen windows on top.

Renown saloon was not unlike a razor-edged version of the contemporary Rover 14. On the sports car front, although Jaguar had warmed up their pre-war saloons for the post-war market, they had not re-introduced the SS 100. Nuffield offered the MG TC sports car, but it was no more than a lightly modified version of the pre-war TA. Sir John Black, the managing director of Standard, saw an opportunity in the market and came up with an all-new car (although I suspect much of the work had already been done at Triumph before the take-over). The first models came off the production line as early as 1945. Steel was in short supply, so the body tub was aluminium over a coachbuilt, ash frame. A pair of bulbous, steel wings with big, separate headlamps dominated the design. A tubular chassis of mammoth proportions was supported by cart springs at the back and a single, transverse leaf spring in front. The car had hydraulically operated drum brakes all round.

Here is a proper picture of a Triumph Roadster 1800. The car had lots of quirky features. When the dipswitch was depressed, for instance, the left beam was lowered by a solenoid-operated, tilting reflector and the right light went out. You could just about make out a London bus at ten paces in the dark.

I think it fair to claim that the Triumph Roadster was a unique motorcar. Although a familial resemblance to the pre-war Dolomite tourer is evident, it was really one of a kind. The column gear change allowed space for a bench seat that accommodated three passengers. There were additional facilities for two more, provided by a pair of fold-down dickey seats in the boot, the lid of which flapped back and was held in position by stays. A unique feature was the provision of a separate, pop-up windscreen for rear passengers. People who see Roadsters for the first time are often puzzled by what appears to be windows in the rear tonneau panel.

You either love or hate the styling. At the time I loved it, now I'm not so sure: it's definitely quirky. I suppose the package was let down by being hopelessly underpowered. Standard, for whatever reason, dropped in the overhead valve version of their pre-war 14-horsepower engine. I suppose it was partly because a car-starved Britain wasn't too fussy about what was under the bonnet, and possibly because the package just wasn't up to handling more horsepower. It's not that this engine was a bad one; in fact Jaguar used it to power their 1 ½-litre cars. When the 2008cc, wet liner Vanguard engine came on stream, Standard fitted it instead of the 1800. Unfortunately, they also deleted the four-speed Standard 14 box in favour of the Vanguard's three-speeds, although they left the gear change on the column.

I spent a lot of time working on my car, hoping to improve it. In the process I desecrated the interior, but my excuses are firstly that I didn't have the cash to do a proper job and secondly, whatever travesties I created could all have been undone by a more sympathetic owner at a later date. It must also be borne in mind that BCF 176 was my everyday transport and there was no prospect of keeping her off the road for lengthy restoration. (With so many excuses, it must have been bad.)

The bench seat was falling apart but it was nothing that a competent trimmer couldn't have handled; unfortunately, that wasn't the route I took. Instead I slung it away and fitted a pair of awful, plastic Triumph Herald bucket seats. I found a stall in the local market that sold cheap vinyl by the roll, so I re-trimmed the interior in padded, check-patterned plastic. I supplemented my handiwork with garish, mottled living-room carpet. I think it was foam backed. At the time I reckoned it looked OK: today the thought of it makes me cringe. At least I didn't recondition the polished wooden dash by painting it purple. I do own up, however, to fitting big, plastic traffic indicators by screwing them to the wings.

The gear change was hard to live with and somebody told me that the 1½-litre Jaguar used the same box but with a different top that incorporated a rather snazzy remote shift. The quest was to find the appropriate part, but I had no luck. Then one day, driving back into London on the A20, I went past the two huge breaker's yards that used to sit side by side on the Sidcup bypass. I think one was called "ZB" and the other "Frank Barwick". One of them used to advertise by having an old car (a Wolsley Hornet?) on a pole outside the premises. The second one of the two produced the goods. When I asked the chap in charge for the part I wanted, he paused for a while, then nodded.

"I've seen a Jaguar gearbox top around here somewhere," he said, "but I can't think where. Just give me a moment."

Then it came to him. He strode over to a huge pile of scrap awaiting collection. After warning me not to follow, he bounded up the veritable mountain of old car parts that tottered 20 feet into the air. He stuck his hand into the heap and brought out a Jaguar 1½ litre gearbox top, complete with stick. It cost me 30 bob and was worth every penny.

I drove that Triumph like a lunatic, four-wheel drifting through suburban roundabouts and screaming off the lights leaving Ford Populars and Morris vans gasping in my wake. The quoted maximum speed was about 75 mph but I often had 85 up on the clock and that was just in the 30-mile-an-hour zones.

I joined the Triumph Roadster Club, but became increasingly unpopular as my philistine and hooligan tendencies manifested themselves. I behaved like a Wally, but for the most part got away with it.

It wasn't long, however, before I began to realise the old girl's limitations and started to hanker for something with a bit more sparkle. Cash was still tight, but things were looking up as my firm moved me from accounts clerk to trainee computer programmer in their new data-processing department. The prospect of better things loomed.

CHAPTER 5

Early XKs

I sold the Triumph in order to acquire my first XK, and so began a long love affair with Jaguars in general and XKs in particular. Between the ages of nineteen and twenty-one I owned half-a-dozen XK sports cars; they ranged from rather good to absolutely appalling. The Triumph Roadster had been my first car with sporting pretensions and, to me at any rate, it felt like a quick motorcar. When one considers that the 0 to 60 time was nearly 30 seconds, one begins to appreciate just how electrifying the XK120 seemed when it first came on the scene.

I've lumped the stories of my early XKs together because their near serial acquisition nicely demonstrates my quest for bargain-basement performance. Frankly, it would never have occurred to me to think of owning a Jaguar had my father not come by a rather handsome '150. As I remember, he got it in a straight swap for a Vauxhall Cresta that was past its best and proving difficult to sell. The Jaguar was in excellent order except for a slightly smoky engine. I remember riding home with him as he put his new toy through its paces. Neither of us had ever experienced anything like the power and exhilaration of that Jaguar sports car. From that moment, the thing I wanted more than any other was an XK. Father loved his '150 but it was totally impractical for him and so, still keen to retain the Jaguar feel and performance, he bought himself a Mark 9 that better suited his needs.

I apologise for these two really horrible pictures of OLF. Unfortunately they are the only ones I have. If only I'd had the foresight first, to buy a decent camera, second, learn how to use it and third, photograph every car I owned.

Apart from some body rot in the corner of the boot, she was in fair shape. I never fitted bumpers at the front although I found some rear overriders in the boot after I bought her. I acquired new carpets and fitted wire guards on the headlamps.

As soon as the '150 arrived, I stuck an ad for the Triumph in the *E&M* (what else) and sold it to a very nice couple who were going to treat it as a classic car, so perhaps it got the proper interior it deserved. In any event I accepted £95 on the £105 asking price and they drove away happy. I was without transport for several weeks, which demonstrates my interest in Dad's '150, but it was not to be. He was asking £250 and he needed the cash almost as badly as I wanted the car. I had no hope of saving enough in time, although I did try for a while, at least until the lucky new owner drove the prize away.

I moped for a few days, and then a local garage owner put me on to an acquaintance who was trying to sell an XK. It turned out to be a '120 fixed-head coupé. Not as up-market or quite as shiny as my beloved XK150 but nonetheless desirable. OLF 473 was in a garage in Greenwich. The fellow who owned it had managed to put a rod through the block and had given it to a "spit and chewing gum" repair shop in order to keep the bill down. The mechanic had obtained a Mark One engine and had, so to speak, made one up out of two. Whatever he had done, the result sounded absolutely marvellous and went, at least to my inexperienced right foot, like the clappers. Unfortunately for the owner, the garage proprietor was not going to let it out of his sight until his bill was paid.

The owner was horror-struck when he was presented with a bill for £110. In the days when you could rebuild a Ford side valve engine for a tenner, the poor chap was shattered. The garage's policy of "no pay – no car" did, however, concentrate his mind on finding a buyer. We finally struck a deal at £115, but at the last minute I checked the logbook and found the car he had presented as a 1954 model was, in fact, first registered in December 1953. I made a huge fuss and got a fiver off for my trouble. Very worthwhile, as the saving represented a few tanks full of petrol.

So I got my first Jaguar for £110, and thus began many happy motoring days. I learned a lot with that car, but not nearly enough to keep me out of trouble. My first mistake started with an oil change. Like a good fellow, I decided that regular new oil was what kept an engine healthy. I dutifully looked up the capacity on a garage wall chart and dropped in the recommended 22 pints; I never thought to check the dipstick. Of course, my Mark One sump needed a good deal less, so I had a case of significant over-fill. I cannot remember exactly what alerted me to the error but I don't recall any serious problems in using the car for a day or so. When I discovered the mistake I drained out some oil and everything was as right as rain. What a marvellous old engine that was.

A few weeks later, however, the oil pressure all but disappeared and my mechanic friends were convinced that some serious damage had been done. The first thing I did was to check the relief valve, but with little hope of finding good news. Imagine my delight on discovering a piece of grit caught under the seat. Cleaned out and back together, she once more showed a healthy 50 pounds and I never experienced any trouble with her in that department again.

A recurring problem was a tendency to overheat in traffic. Several times I flushed out the radiator with various proprietary products, but to no avail. During an MOT test the mechanic suggested a simple cure. "The fan's not man enough to cope," he said, "just bend the blades around a bit more and it'll probably be all right." I did, and it was.

I suppose I love the memory of that old car more than I loved the car at the time. I had very little cash to spare and I was forever being told what a fool I was for harbouring such potential for ruinously expensive repairs. Lady luck seemed to be on my side however, and each apparent disaster always yielded to a cheap and simple solution. I even got away with buying a pair of hideous, used remoulded tyres from a scrap-yard for £5. (Even in those days 16-inch tyres were hard to find.) The tread pattern

This is my friend Stan Williams' beautiful XK 120 fixed head. In recent years people have began to appreciate them for the automotive art they are.

was what used to be called "Town and Country". I remember fitting them and blasting up the M1 at over 100 miles an hour in the pouring rain. There is, it seems, a good fairy to protect the young and foolish.

Wiser, certainly more cynical, I was still mesmerised by the mighty XK150. It is hard to believe but, in the early '60s, for the brave and impecunious, XKs represented the chance of acquiring 100-miles-an-hour motoring for less than £100. The cars were probably at their lowest ebb. Good examples were available for little over £250, while road-going but near basket cases could be had for their scrap value. It seemed that Jaguar's build quality worsened with each succeeding model. XK120s were often in sounder condition than XK150s a good many years their junior. I remember being offered a '150 as a straight swap for my '120. The glossy, black '150 looked fantastic and I very nearly accepted the deal, that is until I examined the car closely. The metal where the

mudguards joined the roof and body was virtually non-existent. One could shake the whole structure by firmly grasping a mudguard and giving it a hefty tug. That was in 1966, and the '150 would have been a 1958 model, so in just eight years the body had rusted beyond economical repair.

Again, not one of mine, but Stan Williams' lovely '140 drop-head coupé.

On the mechanical front, poor or no maintenance played havoc with what, in those days, were very sophisticated XK components. Again '150s, with their servo discs and other bits and pieces, suffered most. Everyone was terrified of the twin-cam engines and very few "do-it-yourself" mechanics would attempt to lift out such a huge and daunting lump, let alone mess with those twin overhead camshafts and timing chains. Originality was rarely an issue and one did what one could to keep the old girls on the road as inexpensively as possible. I often marvel at the fact that any cars at all survived the period. I remember once visiting a scrap-yard to get an XK120 idler. The yard was crammed full of dozens of XKs, all gently rusting away in the open. I also remember being outraged at having to pay an exorbitant £5 for the part.

My next XK was a quite excellent XK140 drop-head coupé bought for a now incredible £55. The mechanic owner had almost completely rebuilt her and she was in fine shape. Unfortunately much of the bodywork was still in primer. Although a re-spray and re-trim would have resulted in a very nice motorcar, I had neither the resources nor the inclination to do the work and passed her on to a lucky new owner.

Marriage meant that vacuum cleaners and three-piece suites came before motorcars and the cash I got for the '140 was used for domestic purchases, so that the XK was not immediately replaced by another.

Norma in the XK 120 drop head in a car park at Margate. We had a wonderful summer with KKW.

I accepted humbler transport for a while, until one sunny day my eye lighted on a much used but still proud '120 drop-head at the back of a dealer's yard in Croydon. We haggled for a while and eventually settled on £72.10 shillings. KKW 393 was an excellent buy. My previous XK120 had sported quite a roarty exhaust, but this car was in another league. It was probably the noisiest car I have owned. This had been achieved by dispensing with any form of silencer. The system might literally be described as "straight through". As I remember, two big-bore copper pipes ran uninterrupted from the manifolds to the back of the car. A somewhat lumpy re-spray notwithstanding, she was in moderately fine fettle. Aside from a sticky fuel pump which had the habit of stopping at potentially tricky moments, the old dear never missed a beat. My wife Norma and I spent an idyllic summer chasing around the countryside at high speed in our golden bomb. The car was shod with a set of virtually new Avon Turbo Speed tyres. "Listen, pal, the boots are worth more than I'm asking for the whole car": the salesman's words come back to me still. It was the first time I enjoyed the feeling of security engendered by riding on suitable rubberware and it was to be many years before I repeated the experience.

I seemed to be caught in the fashion for changing one's wheels on a regular basis, and I soon passed the car on to a charming American who wanted it to tour Europe. That dear XK was good but I suspect not quite good enough for the task. I wished him well and off he went leaving me with a substantial profit. I wonder how he and his rather beautiful girlfriend got on?

And very foolish I was to part with my trusty '120! Not satisfied with what I had, and still coveting the more up-market XK150, when I sold KKW 393 I squandered the loot on a fixed-head '150. That car was as horrid as its predecessor had been good. Nothing worked as it should. There was virtually no oil pressure, certainly no brakes and decidedly "iffy" steering. The cheap re-paint job looked superficially attractive but barely disguised the comprehensive application of body filler. The car had the habit of sticking in first gear, which was particularly embarrassing when one parked nose first against a wall.

Following in the tracks of the Consul, here was the second non-human entity to leave a lasting scar on my psyche. It was another occasion when I experienced that awful sinking feeling of discovering that I had parted with hard cash for a complete lemon. The XK150 I wanted so much and that had looked so bright and appealing was, in reality, a pile of junk. Perhaps it was the times, or maybe just my youth that allowed me, so amorally, to pass on my bad judgement and ill fortune to another unsuspecting soul. (Actually, I'd already had practice with the sale of the Wyvern.)

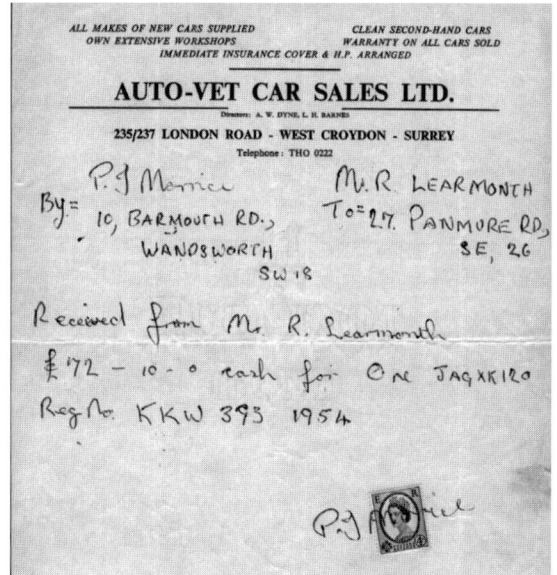

Just to prove it cost £72.10, here's the receipt for my gold XK120 drop-head bought from a dealer. I remember he also had a K2 Allard that I could have had for the same price.

The whole episode was made even more unsavoury by a bizarre turn of events. I had sold the gold '120 with a view to picking up some other car that had caught my eye, and was certainly not expecting to get my hands on another XK. I was very surprised a few days after the sale, however, to find a tiny line advertisement in the London *Evening Standard* for the afore mentioned '150 fixed-head. At the time my parents were on vacation and Norma and I were back at Crystal Palace, house-sitting until they returned. Being without transport, I managed to persuade the owner to drive the car over and the deal was that I would pay for his petrol. I added a sweetener by suggesting that I would provide the taxi fare home if I decided to buy the car then and there.

This was the scrappy bit of paper that, as it turned out, was some sort of evidence that I had come by PDM 817 honestly. The signature of the seller looks suspiciously indecipherable. The original piece of paper, which I still have in my possession, is jagged at the edges as though torn out of a paper bag. It was a curious episode, which I have no wish to repeat.

The chap duly arrived, and the sight of what I had coveted for so long blinded me to the dreadful shortcomings of the offering. A deal was struck at £125; he had been asking £150. I borrowed a tenner from Norma and, with the proceeds of the '120 sale still hot in my sticky hands, I parted with the cash. Of course with an extra ten shillings for the cab ride.

I had PDM 817 (is she still out there? I doubt it) less than a week before I realised my mistake. I was fortunate, because at the time the advertisement for the gold XK120 was still running in the *E&M*. As prospective buyers were still calling on the car, I was able to convert one of them to the '150 for a few pounds more. At the time I was delighted to see the back of it.

It was about nine months later that a solicitor's letter arrived. Over the next few weeks the story unfolded. PDM had been stolen from a lock-up garage one night. The owner had foolishly left the relevant papers in the glove box so it wasn't too difficult for the thieves to dispose of their spoil to the dealer from whom I'd bought it. I hadn't registered the car, and neither had the man to whom I sold it. No doubt discovering his error, he too had quickly passed it on. The new keeper had

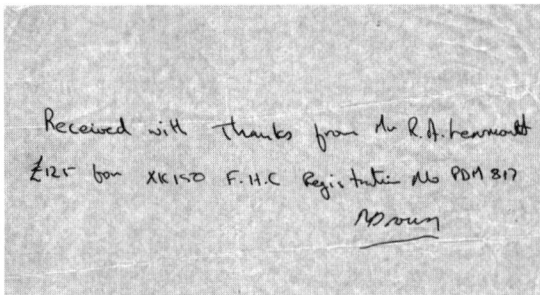

Received with Thanks from Mr R.A.Henniott
£125 for XK150 F.H.C. Registration No PDM 817

This isn't a picture of the worst XK150 in the world. In fact it's a nice example of an FHC with wires and a sunroof, which I am not sure is original, but a good feature nonetheless.

undertaken an extensive refurbishment and the car had been off the road for the duration. As soon as he applied for registration, however, the police pounced and had taken him in for questioning, and the vehicle away for return to its rightful owner.

The unfortunate buyer had traced the trail back to me and I was visited by the police. As it was clear I wasn't the thief, they soon lost interest. I suspect the fellow at the end of the trail never saw a penny of his money, but it seems that the lucky original owner got his car back in much better shape than it had been when stolen.

I was interviewed by the police officer who had been on the original case. According to him, the theft had been reported soon after it happened and they had fairly quickly turned up the dealer who had sold me the vehicle. They had thrown him into the back of a police car and for several hours had toured my neighbourhood while he tried to recall exactly where the XK had been delivered. Naturally they were hoping to see the car still parked at the kerb outside my parents' home. Unnervingly, this had happened while the vehicle was still in my possession. I remember that I had moved the XK into the side yard, fully intending to remove it before Dad got home. Unfortunately, or not, depending on your point of view, the blooming thing got stuck in first gear and I had to leave it where it was for a few days. Dad, as cross as anything, was forced to park up behind me, thus obscuring any view of the XK from the road.

It took me a while to work up, through a series of cooking saloons, to a nice, blue MGA. The MG was in every way an ideal car for a young man seeking the joys of open-topped motoring on a limited budget. Youth, however, is often unwise and wants what it should not have. Someone smarter offered me a good price for my faithful and trusty MGA and, one dark and rain-sodden evening in the depths of Manchester, I squandered the lot on the world's most evil XK150. "Not another '150!" I hear you cry, "Will this man never learn?" Alas, it seemed not, for this fixed-head was determined to be the nastiest car I had ever owned.

Again, I was seduced by a shiny exterior that barely covered a rusting hulk liberally laced with plastic filler. In the few months I owned the vehicle, I do not believe it ever started without massive coaxing and cajoling. I still have memories of stuffing petrol-soaked rags into carburettors in order to restart at traffic lights and roundabouts where the monster had decided to give up the ghost. The batteries were on their last legs, not helped by the constant drain of interminable attempts at starting. I was forever jacking up the front and removing wheels in order to get at the wretched things for recharging. 678 EBB broke my spirit, and with it went my desire to own an XK150. I became fatalistic about my bad luck with them. If the good Lord had intended that I should own one he would not have let me suffer so. When the chance came to trade it for an XK140 fixed-head and a little cash, I jumped at it with alacrity.

The joy of once again owning a car that started more or less on request was dimmed only slightly when I discovered the few non-standard features of my new possession. In order to overcome a slight corrosion problem, a previous owner had dispensed with the piping between the rear mudguards and the body and filled the joints with great splodges of paste. It had been smoothed over nicely and given a fresh coat of crisp, white paint.

A somewhat fuzzy image of the handsome XK140 fixed-head coupe. Unlike the earlier '120 equivalent, it had two tiny seats in the back.

I swear I only noticed the travesty after several days of ownership. Nevertheless, that '140 was a reasonably good car and, I believe, restorable for a relatively small outlay. I used it for while but, when the clutch began to slip, I gave up and traded it in for an old Rover 90; but that's for another chapter.

I suppose XKs have got to me like no other motorcar. I still have a bad habit of buying the occasional example that needs remedial attention and then failing to dispose of it, so their numbers have rather built up. There were five at the last count. The trouble is that I feel terribly sentimental about the old girls and just can't bear to part with them. Actually, it would have been six but for a piece of heroic self control.

A short time ago I was flicking through a car magazine, when my eye lit on an advertisement for another publication. They were highlighting a story about a chap who had bought a succession of old Jaguars in his youth. One of the cars in the picture was none other than OLF 473, my first '120. It was like being reacquainted with an old love. Well not quite, more like once again meeting someone who despite her devotion had received rather shabby treatment. I recalled that, several years after disposing of the car I had, by the merest chance, run across the chap who had bought her from me. Excited by the prospect of picking up on how she had fared, "How is OLF?" I asked in eager anticipation.

It took him a while to identify the vehicle I meant. "Oh, that old thing," he finally replied, "I drove her into the ground and then crashed her. Sold her to a chap who seemed to have a yard full of breakers." I could have slugged him. "Mind you," he added, "she always went like a bomb."

That had been the last I had heard of my first, and in retrospect most cherished XK, but here she was again, albeit in a 30-year-old photograph. Following a letter to the editor and several phone calls, I traced the history of OLF virtually to the present day. She had survived after all. For a long while I contemplated my next move. I knew where she was and it was possible therefore that I would be able to buy her back. We'll never know. Enough is enough, she has survived and that's worth knowing. I hope her new owner looks after her as well as I should have done.

CHAPTER 6

Dog Days

Between 1966 and 1969 I owned fifteen cars, six of which were the XKs of the previous chapter. Although owning Jaguar sports cars sounds exotic, they were all absolutely bargain basement examples: the most expensive cost me £145. In between the XKs I made do with a pretty uninspiring catalogue of automotive tin. Perhaps "Bangers and Trash" would have made a more accurate chapter title. The one exception was an MGA, but more of that anon.

I left BUPA and joined Colgate Palmolive in February 1967. I was now a fully-fledged computer programmer, earning roughly twice what I had the year before, although it was a long time before the extra cash trickled down to motoring expenditure. Norma and I got married in April of the same year and we finally moved from my parents' home in Crystal Palace. We went to live in Sydenham, in fact only two doors from where I'd been during the Rover/Bradford years with Mum and Dad. The aunt and uncle who had sold my parents their maisonette now rented another to Norma and me. Having our own home was wonderful, but from a car-owning standpoint it had the disadvantage of not providing off-road standing, and certainly no shed full of Father's tools.

After the sale of the drop-head XK140, for a good profit may I say, domestic requirements took care of the proceeds and I made do with bangers while I tried to consolidate my funds. The horrors were, in sequence, a 1955 Singer 1500 SM, a 1960 Citroen ID19 and a 1958 Ford Zephyr automatic.

The 1500 SM, bought for £15, was bodily very sound. Unfortunately it was also irredeemably boring, its only saving grace being that it would go from A to B without fuss and drama. The bearings in the engine were on their last legs, but by then I had learned how to drive without invoking the dreaded big-end

The 1500 was the last gasp of the independent Singer Company before it was gobbled up by Rootes. Its only noteworthy feature was a nifty overhead camshaft engine.

knock. I used her until I had saved up enough to get my hands on something better. I think she was the only car that failed to sell through the *Exchange & Mart*. I finally ended up selling her to a pal for £9. He needed to get to Glasgow in a hurry. It was a long way and, in view of the creaking bottom end, I helped him on his way by filling up the engine with EP 90 gear oil. It certainly helped the sale and kept things quiet down below for a few hundred miles. The fellow made it up there without mishap but wasn't quite so lucky on the homeward leg. But, for goodness sake, what did he expect for under a tenner?

My next purchase was a very distinctive French Citroën, which had the dubious prestige of being the newest car I had owned to date. A 1960 model, it was basically sound if a little worn. I collected some cash and paid a couple of wide boy dealers

Very French and very idiosyncratic, the ID and DS series were like no other car. Wildly ahead of their time in 1955 when they first appeared, they replaced the ageing "Maigret" design.

£70 for it. Apart from also being a little "endy", the Citroën was in good shape. It had all the little stylistic touches that made the cars so avant-garde. The one-spoke steering wheel was unusual, as were the roof-level rear indicators. Unlike the DS model, mine was the cheaper ID with a column change and a four-speed, manual box. Top was a real overdrive gear and with only 1900ccs she was still a fast and very economical cruiser.

At the time one would have expected to pay at least twice as much as I gave for this particular model so, given the spivvy types I'd got her from, I was always on tenterhooks awaiting some catastrophic failure that never occurred. Even the hydraulic suspension worked, although it was a little slow getting going. Once parked, the car would quickly settle into the kerb as the body collapsed down on to the wheels. It was necessary to allow a few minutes after starting, to enable the old girl to pump herself back up to her full, commanding height.

I used this car for a number of months and almost started to enjoy her. One rainy morning on the way into town through the Elephant and Castle, I got into a race with a Cortina. It was made all the more interesting because the traffic was heavy and necessitated a good deal of dodging and weaving. (My only excuse is that I was twenty-two years old and must have been producing testosterone by the gallon.) As we came roaring up to take the right-hand sweep around to London Road, I out-braked my rival and catapulted into the lead. Unfortunately, the Citroën refused to make the turn as I requested and went sailing on. I suppose I wasn't used to front-wheel drive, because my steering wheel twiddling was to no avail. I hit the foot-high kerb with enough force to wreck the suspension and bend the front wheel into a weird shape. By some miracle the tyre stayed up and I drove back home at ten miles an hour. I parked in the gutter and I never saw her go under her own steam again. I spent a few desultory weeks attempting an inexpensive fix, but the downside of owning a foreign exotic was the price of maintenance. The stricken hulk stood around long enough for the neighbours to start getting shirty and in the end she went to the breaker, who carted her away for £15. For the first time in many years I made do without a car for a while but, when a work colleague offered me his cast-off Zephyr, I was back on the road.

The MK2 Fords were quite the thing in their day. This is the sleek low-line model that began in 1959. The picture, another taken from a period Ford brochure, shows the flagship Zodiac model in the foreground and the slightly less luxurious Zephyr at the back.

Linton Moss, who worked with me at Colgate, had a very different strategy from mine. Each time he bought and sold, usually at a profit, he put the proceeds into his next acquisition. Over time he progressed to some very desirable machinery. The Zephyr was no more than a stopgap to cover the period while his Lotus Elan was being repaired following a crash. Linton was one of life's great characters, with a fabulous sense of fun. Always desperately keen on flying, in later years he bought an aeroplane and became something of an ace. Sadly, before his fortieth birthday he was killed while stunting at an air show.

The Zephyr, an automatic, was another "nothing" sort of car, its only interesting feature being that it had a serious fault. Normally it ran beautifully and would climb hills without effort; the weakness, however, was in reversing. Provided it was on the level, the auto box would handle things without a problem but, if asked to tackle any sort of gradient while going backwards, the car would behave extremely unsportingly. The symptoms were a strong smell of burning followed by a complete refusal to move, no matter how hard one worked the throttle. Too much of this treatment resulted in a boil-up and an engine bay full of scalding water.

It was easy to sell because in those days cheap automatics were in short supply and I had a dozen responses to my ad. To my dubious credit, I screened out the disabled before passing it on to a healthy young chap from Camberwell. I hope he had no requirement to motor uphill backwards.

A curious thing about the '50s and '60s was the way motor manufacturers thought that buyers would be attracted by advertising the non-standard features of their cars, usually in chrome script on the boot. The Zephyr, for instance, had the word "Automatic" prominently displayed. "Overdrive" and "Deluxe" were other popular boasts often screwed to the bodywork.

During my days at BUPA a colleague made me quite envious by acquiring a Triumph TR2. I never actually saw the car, but heard a great deal about its scintillating performance and its potential for serious fun. One day he phoned me in great distress. During a burn-up with an MG on the Chiswick flyover he had managed to put a rod through the block. A new engine was needed but, without the wherewithal to acquire one, he was in near despair. Sworn to secrecy lest his mother should find out, firstly that he'd been stupid enough to play boy-racer and secondly that he had wrecked his car as a result, I tried to help as best I could.

In truth my knowledge of the subject was at best sketchy but I was, as always, ready to offer advice. Having failed to obtain a TR engine for anything like the funds he had available, I persuaded him that the Standard Vanguard had essentially the same mill. I was also able to procure a used example on his behalf for a fiver. He was duly grateful. I later found out that, although the engines were of the same family, there were a number of very significant differences.

In the event he was never faced with attempting the transplant. I heard from him again almost a year later when he was desperate to sell. The package came with the Vanguard engine still in the boot. Actually, the story is rather a sad one. Unfortunately, the poor chap lost his job but just couldn't face telling his mother the news and for several weeks went each day with his sandwiches to the park. He quickly ran through his savings and started disposing of his possessions. I suppose at the time the TR was one of the least useful. Unsurprisingly, he found a severely limited market for a Triumph with a terminally busted engine. I really didn't want the project, but I couldn't resist a bargain at £20. There can't be many people who bought a TR for a score.

The TR2 was the first in a long line of Triumph sports cars.

I took on the work determined to make a job of it: not for me a simple engine swap. I was aware that the TR mill developed almost twice the horsepower of the Vanguard version, so I wasn't about to sacrifice grunt for an easy life. In effect, I made one up out of two. I kept the Vanguard block, rods and pistons but had the TR crank, which had been only slightly damaged, metal-sprayed and reground. It was important to retain the TR item because, although the cranks were nominally similar, the TR journals were cross-drilled for improved oil flow. I also used the TR camshaft and head. I hit problems with head studs, which were much thicker on the TR than the Vanguard, but got round the problem by retaining the saloon's set-up and fitting collars into the TR's larger-diameter holes. I also recall a lot of fiddling around with push-rods, as neither set seemed to fit; the TR rods were shorter and hollow. I must have solved the problem somehow because I got it running, and it seemed to go well enough.

What I loved about the TR was its no-nonsense, functional cockpit. The stubby gear lever was a joy to use. Overdrive was available on TR3s onward.

By the time I had the car operational, I had disposed of the Zephyr, so I was keen to get the TR on the road. Having confirmed that the "made-up" engine worked, I fitted everything else under the bonnet, only to discover that the radiator was beyond redemption. I searched the *E&M* and found two candidates. Without wheels, getting to them was courtesy of London Transport. One was in Ilford the other on a council estate in Golders Green. First thing one Saturday morning I went to Ilford, mainly because it was the easier journey. The man who had described the rad as perfect was a liar, so I turned around and went back home. On Sunday I went to Golders Green and bought a better one.

The following weekend I started work at the crack of dawn. In theory, getting a radiator out of a TR is straightforward: that is, if the front apron can be removed; but if your 20-quid example has had the front glued on with filler paste and glass mat then that isn't an option. Getting out a radiator with the apron in place can be done, but it isn't easy and involves the removal and refitting of most of the stuff under the bonnet. I worked through the whole weekend, barely stopping for sustenance. At 10 o'clock on Sunday evening I filled the new rad with water and was gratified to discover that it stayed put.

I was cock-a-hoop: after months of effort I was able to fire her up and experience the thrill of having brought back an automobile from the dead. Gingerly at first I took her on our maiden voyage together. Gaining in confidence, I gunned the motor and felt a surge of power push me back into my seat. Suddenly there was an almighty bang, followed by an unholy clatter and I was engulfed in smoke, or steam, I wasn't sure.

I limped home making a fearful din. Under a street lamp I discovered the problem. In reassembling the area around the new radiator I had neglected properly to screw down one of the windtone covers. Under fierce acceleration it had fallen off, struck the fan and bent the blades forward. They had neatly cored out the centre of the new radiator. It was steam and not smoke. I let down the bonnet, went to bed and, I am ashamed to say, shed a tiny tear for my wasted weekend's endeavour.

On the following Saturday I made the return journey to Ilford (I knew the way) and acquired a less than perfect replacement. On Sunday I was back on the road: this time with the horn tops firmly bolted down.

The battered old TR was my first big project tackled without my father's assistance. I suppose all in all, apart from some crass mistakes, I was fairly lucky. Of course I had no garaging or off-road facility of any kind, so the entire project, including the engine rebuild, was done in the open, either in the front garden or out in the road. Ah, those were the days!

The actual TR2 replete with Vanguard block.

I used the car without problems for a while and then got a bee in my bonnet about wanting an MG TC, so I advertised in the exchanges section of a well-known magazine. I got no response from MG owners looking for a trade but I was unexpectedly contacted by a very upper-class young chap who turned up at my door the same evening. On the proviso that I was prepared to deliver, he paid me £80 and went on his way.

As I recall, the moment I had the cash, the washing machine turned up its toes, so a chunk of the dosh was purloined for domestic requirements. A year later I was driving past a dealer's yard in the Old Kent Road when I spotted my TR on the front. I stopped and went to look at her; she was up for sale at £95. I started the engine and it seemed healthy enough, so it had lasted at least twelve months.

There followed a very smart Standard 10, a 1957 model with four doors and a proper boot. I remember that Norma and I, on the way back from a day in Brighton, gave a lift to a couple who were hitchhiking back to London. We were soon sorry we had. They smelled so bad that we were almost gagging by the time we let them out in Croydon. I tried for ages to get the stench out of the car and eventually had to sell it in order to rid us of the unpleasant odour.

I bought a scruffy little Farina A40 from a dealer in Catford

The Standard 10, a good, solid but unexciting British car of the'50s

and drove it into the ground. My father acquired a mini about the same time, which must have belonged to a boy racer because he found that the track had been widened by the application of after-market wheel spacers. He took them off, and I put them on. I recall four-wheel drifting the car around in ludicrously inappropriate circumstances when the steering suddenly went funny. After nursing her back home I found that two of the studs on each front wheel had sheared. I suppose the spacers were a bad idea.

One evening I went out for a drink with some work pals and we met up with a bottom-of-the-market car dealer in a pub in Golders Green. We started chatting about motors and he showed me an MGA he had just acquired and asked if I wanted to buy it. I had a look at the car, took it for a run and was very impressed by how well it went. He was willing to take my A40 in part exchange but wanted another £55. I didn't have the cash and told him so but one of my friends stepped in and offered to lend me

I can't quite make up my mind whether this picture is intended to show an A40 or the VC10 aeroplane undergoing tests. Anyway, the car, which came out in 1959, ushered in Pininfarina's more angular styling which was to run through the entire BMC range.

the money. I accepted and drove home in the MG. It turned out to be a little cracker.

A blue 1956 MGA 1500, it was another of my cars that I remember with affection. When I got her, although she was mechanically sound, the bodywork was decidedly tatty. The outer sills under the door had completely rotted away, so I made up replacements from aluminium sheet. I found a spray can of BMC paint that proved an acceptable match. I rubbed down and touched-in the tin-scab where it had broken through and significantly improved her appearance. I gradually invested in overdue replacements like a new hood and, one happy day, I was

The delightful MGA 1500. It was an excellent package based around a sturdy chassis and BMC's "B" series engine. I remember lusting after one of these racy-looking cars as a schoolboy

My MGA on holiday in Devon. Norma was learning to drive.

even able to afford a pair of side screens. (Life without side windows had been rugged and not a little damp.) When I finally secured a set of bumpers for £10, my restoration was complete. Two days later, driving through the city in greasy conditions, I managed to stop but the fellow behind didn't. It wasn't a bad crash but it did mangle my shiny, new overriders. All was well however, when he gave me £25 on the spot for my pain and suffering.

Colgate had a soap factory in the North-west and, when I was asked to work on a project there, the MG saw significant service between London and Salford. Although the hood was new, I had fitted it to the original wooden bow. On that particular model the hood was fixed to the top of the screen with two screws that clamped it to the screen rail. I suppose the old bow may have been a little warped, but there was certainly also a design flaw because on later versions of the car a third, centre catch, was added. In the wet, at normal speeds, a little water always found its way through, but at high speed, on the motorway, the trickle became a flood.

Once underway, the water soon overcame any attempts to staunch the flow with rags and dusters and came pouring into the cockpit. I soon developed a clever modification, however. On rainy Friday evenings I could be observed in the Colgate car park preparing for the journey home by donning my two-piece, specially prepared rain suit. This consisted of two plastic bin liners, one with holes for my feet and the other with similar apertures for head and arms. Thus attired in my customised outfit, I would drive the 200 miles home as quickly as I could.

Norma and I went down to Devon for our summer break in the "A". The weather was wonderful and we had a marvellous time. Apart from a failed battery, I never had a moment's trouble with that car; she always started on command, used very little oil and maintained excellent oil pressure. I wonder if she survived? The registration number was 344 AWL; does anyone have her still?

The hours I spent in Salford gradually increased, so the firm organised a flat near Sale in Cheshire and Norma left her job and moved up with me. While scanning the small advertisements in a local paper my eye fell on an ad for an XK150, but that's a tale I've told already.

The monstrous '150 was followed by the not-so-bad '140 which quickly developed a slipping clutch. When all the available adjustment was gone, I swapped it for a 1955 Rover 90. The Auntie Rover was in many ways a lovely old car and supremely comfortable, with an odd centre gear change that looked peculiar

Auntie Rover, a testament to stolid British engineering. Actually a fine, quality car with legendary longevity.

but fell nicely to hand. Norma was now pregnant and this led to her needing frequent medical consultations, so she went back to London and the Rover was pressed into regular motorway service. It performed this duty adequately, cruising at 80 and burning up the miles fairly serenely. There were only two problems. The first was that she used a gallon of oil for the 200-mile run. I would set out from Salford, get on to the motorway and then stop about half way, at the Watford Gap Services on the M1, and drop in the first half-gallon. I would then top up with the other half when I got home. The procedure would be reversed on the way back. One of the nice things about the Rover was a button on the dash that allowed the driver to convert the petrol gauge into one that measured the oil in the sump. On my car, if you held it down, you could actually observe the level falling as you went along.

The second problem was that the kingpins were progressively seizing up. I tried everything to free them off, but years of neglect had resulted in the mixture of rust and grease inside them freezing solid. It was impossible to introduce any lubrication, so I modified my driving technique instead. Because there was very little movement in the steering, I discovered that the best practice was to drive in the centre lane. (Anyway, if one drives quickly, excessive steering movement isn't needed.) I got used to the limitation and became quite accomplished at managing with only a couple of inches' movement at the steering wheel. The biggest downside was the tendency for the car to change lanes on its own when it hit a bump violent enough to shock the swivel joints into action. Hence the trick was to leave lots of space around you.

When things got really bad, I took the car to my father to get his advice about possible remedial action. He went out in it for a trial run and came back ashen-faced. "It's a death trap," he declared, still shaking.

For the first time, desperately short of cash as usual, I bought a car on hire purchase. It came from a dealer in Romford and was hardly better than the Rover except that the steering was more or less OK. It was a 1959 Sunbeam Series One Alpine with steel

wheels and a hard top. The price tag was £275 and the dealer allowed me £60 on the Rover, so there was a hefty HP loan. He must have been on a big margin, because he didn't even road-test the Rover (which was just as well). I remember going to collect the car after the paperwork was done. The dealer drove the Alpine off the front and I left the Rover in the kerb. I still have memories of sitting at traffic lights with the forecourt in view, watching in the rear-view mirror as the poor chap tried to reverse the Rover into the gap vacated by the Alpine. Some hope!

The Alpine wasn't such a bad old bus, but the tin-worm had already taken hold and it needed a lot of attention if the dreaded rot was to be eradicated. It never got any. It was at once put into service on the northern run and, because it had overdrive, it would cruise at an indicated 85.

It was driving the Alpine that resulted in my developing a bad habit which has proved difficult to eradicate. The Rootes

This is a series 111 Alpine (mine was a series 1). The hardtop on the earlier car was beautifully rounded at the rear but provided limited headroom if you were foolish enough to attempt cramming in a passenger behind the front seats.

gearbox operated in overdrive when in top and third gears, an inhibitor switch in the cover dropping it out when not in those ratios. The switch was faulty and the car had the disconcerting habit of coming out of overdrive even when the gear lever was in the right position. At high speed, on the motorway, this would cause the engine to rev alarmingly near its "blow-to-bits" point. I discovered, however, that by constantly holding the lever in a "down and to the right" position, I could stop the problem occurring. Thus I developed my "right hand on the wheel and left on the gear stick" style that I have not been able to shake to this day.

It was another of my cars in which the oil pressure left a lot to be desired. When well and truly hot she would run at an indicated 20psi. She always idled at or near zero, but she never rattled or let go.

It was at this time that the great tragedy of my life happened.

One day I got a phone call at work: Norma had been taken into hospital and was in a serious condition. I drove down to London at breakneck speed, covering the 212 miles in just over two hours. When I got to Lewisham hospital, Norma was dead.

CHAPTER 7

Deals on Wheels

In this chapter, I'll take a break from the sad times that I left at the end of the previous one, and look at something less tragic.

Constantly buying and selling my cars brought me into contact with quite a few dealers, most of whom were in the back-street cowboy category. Nearly all my early cars were bottom-of-the-barrel buys, so I was well acquainted with that end of the market and it was hardly surprising that I got involved in a bit of casual auto trading.

My first speculative venture was an early Vauxhall Victor F-Type. Up till then General Motors' UK arm had had a reasonable reputation for middle-of-the-road family transport. The F-Type all but ruined it. Typical of late '50s transatlantic styling, this model featured a deep wrap-round windscreen and the most rust-prone bodywork imaginable. I wouldn't be surprised if they had started falling apart while they were still in dealer showrooms. The reputation of Vauxhall was not helped by the fact that the startlingly modern styling and contemporary good looks resulted in high initial sales. The corollary was that there were soon lots of disgruntled first and second time owners cursing the name of Vauxhall.

I bought my Victor from a dealer in West Dulwich. It was one of those cars that would never see the forecourt, but linger around the back until traded out, usually as one of a batch, to a "sell from the kerb" dealer. The Victor's only saving grace was its

The dreaded, rust-prone FA Victor

superficially bright exterior, which masked rather a lot of faults, most of them serious; but I figured it was worth a punt at £20.

I've already mentioned that Father had started in the real estate business, and by that time he was operating a thriving portfolio of rental properties. One of these was a large Victorian house in the Crystal Palace Park area. A distant relative and his family rented one of the flats in the building, and as part of the road test I thought that I would pop round for a visit. The basement was occupied by a rather odd fellow who had decided unilaterally to use the front garden as a forecourt for his embryonic car sales business. He had collected a bunch of decrepit old wrecks, written prices on the windscreens and was attempting to inveigle passers-by to invest in his wares. Now it happened that he was in the yard when I arrived in my latest acquisition and, having a professional interest, I naturally inspected his stock at some length. It soon occurred to me that my Vauxhall was the perfect addition to his assembly of tinware. I guess I was just plain lucky in having exactly the right offering in the right place at the appropriate time. He was clearly in the throes of building up his stock and we did a deal on the spot. I went home on the bus with £30 jingling in my pocket.

My father was enraged when he discovered, a week later, that one of his tenants was using the front garden as business premises. The council, incidentally, was also in an uncooperative mood. Needless to say, the poor fellow was persuaded in short order to terminate his enterprise. I recall that I neglected to mention the transaction to my dad. I didn't go round there for a while, although I was tempted back when we were told that the wife of the fledgling dealer was minded to dance naked in the back yard during the times of full moon. They were certainly a family that put the gardens to intensive use.

One of the characters I met during this period was a flamboyant fellow called Marty Bowden. Over the years I bought a number of cars from Marty, as well as selling him a few. Marty was a marvellous person to know because he would never refuse anything. If you took a car around he'd always make you an offer, often a very tiny one, but an offer none the less. In effect, Marty was my back door if all else failed: he would take whatever it was off my hands; usually at a loss, but it did mean that I was shot of it. This worked in all cases except, of course, when Marty himself had sold me the goods in the first place. In other words, you couldn't always rely on Marty taking back what he had unloaded onto you. That's how I got stuck with the Skoda.

I found this very blurry picture of a model 445, 1200cc Skoda on the Internet. I have never seen another like it before or since owning mine, which was a very rare right-hand drive version.

The Skoda was a 1956, 1200cc model the like of which I have never seen before or since. Marty let me have it for £20 and delivered it to a lock-up garage that I rented near my home. I cannot say how many of this model had been imported into the UK, but this particular example was a right-hand drive version. It had a wonderfully roarty exhaust note and went like the clappers for its modest sized engine. It had two

shortcomings. The first was a rather tatty interior where the light grey cloth had failed to withstand the test of fair wear and tear. The second was the brakes. There weren't any. None at all. There was a nice hard pedal but no actual friction at the wheels. Unfortunately, I discovered that it went like the clappers only moments before I found out about the brakes. It was a seriously interesting experience, but redemption took a hand, and both car and somewhat terror-stricken driver returned safely to base.

It sounds implausible but, struggle as I might, I could not get off the screws that held the drums and so the problem was never solved. After several attempts it was finally sold to a man who wanted the engine for a rally car he was building. I made a £2 loss, not counting the cost of the adverts. Whenever I see material about historic Skodas in magazines or books I always look for a reference to that particular model, but I have never seen one. The funny thing was that the body was totally rust free, and everything, apart from the brakes, worked as it should.

My next transaction was lucky and unlucky in almost equal measure. One of the fellows in my office was a big, blustering Australian who lorded it over the junior programming staff mainly because he had been on the course a week ahead of us. His other reason to feel superior was that he had bought himself a Jaguar, a 2.4 litre Mk 1. I think he paid £120. He came in sullen faced one day and said he had problems. "You wouldn't read about it but the clutch's buggered," he declared in his best 'Strine. We sniggered.

A mechanic came to look at the car, and apparently the diagnosis was confirmed. The Aussie immediately starting offering the Jaguar around but, at the asking price of £50, he found no takers. A few weeks later when it came down to £30, I perked up and questioned him more closely about the symptoms.

"When you put your foot on the clutch, there's nothing there," he told me. "You can't get the stick into any gear. If you push really hard, it makes a grating noise. Like I say, the clutch is shagged."

Now this description of the fault was interesting. If it really was

The very elegant Jaguar Mk 1, This is the 3.4 litre and not the more numerous 2.4. The car got a bad reputation for its tapered chassis when Mike Hawthorn was killed in one on the Guildford bypass. The Mk 2 corrected this perceived shortcoming.

the clutch then the car was probably a write-off, since rectification would have required the removal of engine and gearbox; not a job for a young lad with no facilities. But the description he gave didn't sound like a clutch problem. Even with my limited knowledge, I recognised the symptoms of a failed master cylinder.

I threw caution to the winds and bought the car sight unseen for £8. I splashed out on a reconditioned clutch master cylinder and went back to his flat with him after work one evening. I also took along my bag of tools. I told him that reason for the visit was a recce before arranging recovery. I swapped the clutch master cylinder, and my Australian colleague actually helped me bleed the system. The look on his face was worth quite a bit when I started up his car and drove off happily into the sunset.

In a way, though, he had the last laugh because, when I got the car home and examined it closely, the body turned out to be in very bad shape. The dreaded tin worm had been on a ravaging expedition. Some bright spark had repaired the front wings with cement. I know it's hard to believe, but they had actually packed cement into the inside front wheel arches, let it set and then, I assume, shaped it with a Surform tool. The outer sills had been stuffed with paper and cardboard before the application of copious plastic filler. My dream of picking up £100 profit was dashed. It wasn't a total loss though, because Marty took it off my hands for 35 quid.

There followed a couple of "do it up and flog it" projects when, in effect, I sold my time cheaply. One was a 100E Anglia with a duff motor. A complete exchange crank with rods cost £7.10 shillings over the counter. (As late as the mid-50s, Ford side valves still came with metalled ends, although the price of the replacement set included a conversion to shells.) I never bothered with new pistons, just cleaned up the bores and stuck in some new rings. By the time I sold her she was running as sweetly as could be. Out of the £30 profit I had to deduct the price of parts and all my time so it was hardly coining money, but it was fun and at least put something in my rather shallow pockets.

For a while I got a bit cocky and saw selling second-hand cars as a way of making easy and regular money. I did a bit of trade with a dealer in Catford who specialised in buying fleet vehicles and selling them on to the trade. This was a bit up-

NEW FORD ANGLIA

This is an artist's impression of the Ford Anglia. The model was slightly less luxurious than the others in the range (hard to believe). Even harder to believe is that Ford sold so many of these awful little cars, I suppose because they were cheap.

market for me but I was led on by an acquaintance who claimed to be making a handsome living. I borrowed some cash and paid, for me, a massive £410 for a Fiat 124. I wasn't greedy, but sold it to the first person who answered my ad for £455. A nice clean profit. With the same advertisement still running I went back to Catford and bought another. This one looked OK but had a slight but persistent misfire. I couldn't sort it out so I spent a tenner having it looked at. When the chap failed to fix it but diagnosed burned-out valves I feared for my 400 quid and was relieved to get shot of it for £435. The experience unnerved me, so I paid back the loan and stayed in the lower echelons of the market.

I thought I had struck lucky when a work colleague announced he was selling up and moving back to Ireland. I immediately went sniffing around his very smart TR3A. Ian's TR

This rather odd shot of a Fiat 124 was part of a publicity campaign by the manufacturer. If the car looks a bit familiar, don't be surprised, it was reincarnated as the Lada which was made in the USSR. Believe it or not, the 124 was car of the year in 1966.

was one of those fabled cars that everyone at work spoke of in respectful tones, the accepted wisdom being that it was a "lovely example". The prospect of getting my hands on it seemed too good to be true. He couldn't make up his mind whether he wanted to sell or not but in the end we did a deal at £200 and I reckoned on a substantial profit. I drove the car home in the pouring rain, and by the time I turned into my drive my feet were awash. Investigation revealed the complete lack of a floor. The carpets were laid directly on some pieces of crudely cut ¼-inch steel plate, which weren't even bolted down. Further examination yielded a complete catalogue of absolute horrors. I had been comprehensively conned. I got to work with fibreglass mat and Cataloy paste and produced a work of art, even if I say so myself. I got £255 for her and considered myself lucky.

I can't help loving the TR2/3 series cars. They are everything wind-in-the-hair, flies-in-your- teeth, British sports cars should be. Basic and rugged, they are fun to drive, with adequate performance and good cruising capability. I'd own one again like a shot.

There were lots of cheap deals yielding small profits, or sometimes none at all. I would often attend Dingwall car auctions in Croydon, where the standard fare was ex GPO vans and general

cooking saloons. Sports models did particularly badly, and I was able to buy a raft of Spitfires, Spridgets and the like.

I spent my time with spray cans, adding racing stripes and go-faster flashes. I became quite adept at tarting-up scruffy old sports cars to look presentable. Dented and rusty bumpers could be discarded to give a racier look. If the ends of the bumper were OK, I'd cut out the centre section and move the overriders to hide the butchery. The resulting quarter bumpers usually enhanced the overall look. I'd get wire wheels steam cleaned and make up masks so that I could paint them to look like new without removing the tyres. Questionable sills and nether regions in general could be sprayed with underseal and then painted body colour. I even resorted to sticking on racing roundels and numbers to mask unsightly paintwork on doors, boots and bonnets. Plastic and leather paint did wonders for interiors, and re-trimming with domestic quality black carpet always gave acceptable results. I found a source of cheap hoods and could transform a car by renewing the soft-top for very little outlay.

I sometimes feel guilty about my antics, but in my defence I'd point out that I was dealing with very cheap motors and was, in effect, just selling my labour and basic restoration skills. I genuinely made scruffy old cars look a lot better. I sold them cheaply, so I think that their new owners got reasonable value for money.

It wasn't long, however, before my

Writing Advertisements for the *Exchange & Mart*

Nearly all my cars were moved on through the *Exchange & Mart*. I developed a set of rules to be applied for best results. They went something like this:

● **Never use ono** (or near offer). If you do, it merely sets a price that you will never obtain. If an ad says £100 ono nobody in his right mind would pay that, it is simply an invitation to offer less.

● **Slightly undersell.** Ideally both the ad and the telephone pre-sales spiel should set the potential buyer's expectations slightly lower than the vehicle warrants. Nothing sells a car better than a first viewing that is a pleasant surprise.

● **Always include the price.** Buyers shy away from ads without a price. The accepted wisdom is that, in general, no price means that the vendor wants too much.

● **Never include "excluders".** You're better off attracting all the potential buyers and then doing the weeding on the phone when they respond. Phrases like "no offers", "no time wasters", and "expensive" are to be avoided. Only include descriptive information if you think it is positive. This particularly applies to things like colours. Don't advertise that your car is puce or beige. If you have to, reveal the turn-offs on the phone and then only after you've given the callers something positive to get them hooked.

● **Get the volume of text right.** Too few words are as bad as too many. Both are a turn-off.

● **Consider what your advertisement will look like on the page.** It doesn't have to have the most eye appeal but you should ensure that it's not buried by the ads around it.

● **Remember, an ad won't sell a car.** Its objective is to get people to call. The sales process starts on the phone.

● **Don't mislead people.** Nothing is more irritating than travelling to a prospective purchase and finding that the owner has deliberately misled you. Never lie (but of course, you don't have to volunteer absolutely everything).

The cheap and cheerful MG Midget

insurance company began to get edgy about all these changes of vehicle. I tried for a while to get a trader's policy but, without premises, that just wasn't possible. As my finances improved, my self-image was increasingly at variance with low-end trading activities, and my forays into the trade gradually petered out.

Over the years, given my interest in historic cars, I've often considered starting some sort of classic car business, but it has always come to nothing. The problem with selling cars is that one has to buy them first, which can be a very time-consuming activity. I know traders who spend a good part of their lives attending auctions all over the world, trying to buy fine cars in good condition at the right price. It's all too much like hard work.

CHAPTER 8

Out of the Trough

For six months after Norma's death I didn't do a great deal, and certainly didn't have the heart to get involved with motor cars. I still had the Alpine and continued to use it as a work hack driving up and down the motorway between London and Manchester. At the same time as our temporary move north, Norma and I had also moved out of rented accommodation into our own home in Forest Hill.

As the shock of what had happened wore off and I began to emerge from the gloom, my thoughts returned to cars. The Alpine was showing signs of serious wear but I was still incurring monthly payments and I had very little spare cash; nonetheless, I needed a change of wheels. A friend of the family had a Ford Corsair 2000E and was so keen to sell that he offered me a deal I found hard to refuse. Foolishly, and without the benefit of a constraining influence, I obtained a second mortgage on my house and bought the car. It was a daft thing to do for a number of reasons. The first was that I got a lousy deal from the finance company, which tied me up so tightly that when I came to repay the loan it cost me almost twice what I had borrowed. The second was that the Corsair, nice as it was, just wasn't my sort of car.

It was in excellent condition however, a '67 model with silver coachwork and a black vinyl roof. This was in late 1969 when Ford was in the throes of inventing the "executive" car market.

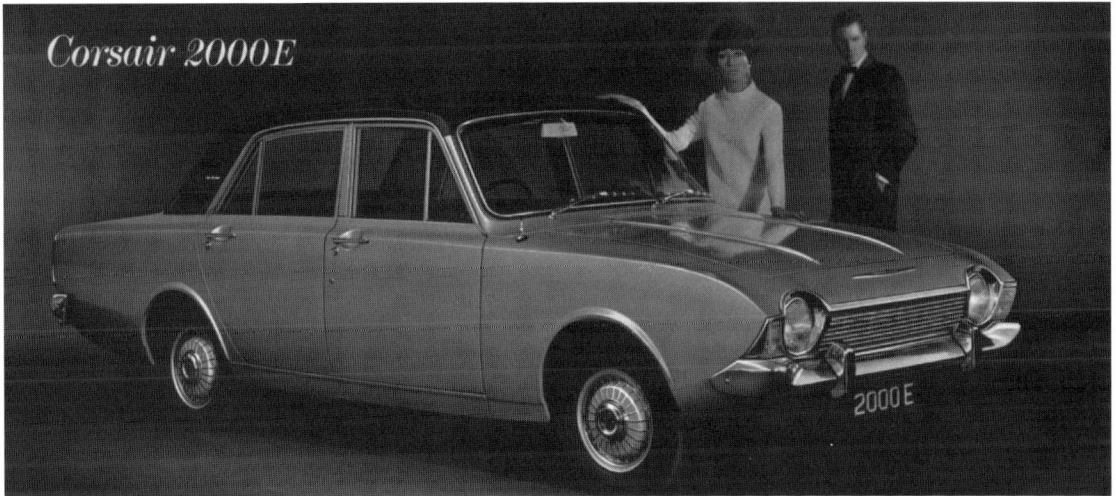

Corsair 2000E

The rather disappointing 2000E, looking surprisingly attractive in this Ford brochure shot.

They had set the ball rolling with the hugely successful 1600E, which was nothing more than a glorified Mk 2 Cortina with the 1600cc, GT version of the inline four-cylinder, cross flow engine. The interior was poshed up with extra gauges and wood on the doors and dash. At the time everyone (including me) seemed happy enough with the acres of shiny black vinyl that was the stock material used to upholster up-market models. For the discerning executive, Ford created a dark purple body colour that became a big hit. All the smart young men of the day aspired to an "aubergine" 1600E. My first tenant, with whom I shared the house in Forest Hill, turned up in a brand new one within days of moving in. But more of that anon.

The 2000E was a less happy attempt along the same lines. Based on the larger Corsair body shell, the interior treatment was very similar to that of its smaller cousin. This time Ford used the 2000cc V4 engine, which was never as smooth as the in-line 1600. The suspension wallowed a lot more and didn't seem to have the same degree of lowering and stiffening. (I remember doing a series of road tests around the block one Saturday afternoon with my housemate. I frightened him to death in his 1600E, which I found altogether more chuckable and easier to drift.) I suppose the Corsair was an ideal car for a family man but not for a young tearaway, perpetually on the limit whatever the road conditions.

Over Christmas 1969 I went to visit Norma's family in Ireland and took the Ford over on the ferry. It drove as it should, but on the way home from Liverpool the alternator failed five miles out of the docks and the red light lit up on the dash. There was no way of getting it fixed at that time of night, so I decided to try to drive the 200 miles back to London on the battery. Unfortunately, I ran into a blizzard on the M6 and, with the wipers going full tilt, I knew I had to conserve power so I doused the headlamps and tucked in behind a Triumph Stag. He did everything to lose me on the journey south (except slow down) but I clung to his tail tenaciously until we picked up the streetlights of outer London, where I let him outgun me. When he finally got away we were doing an indicated 110 miles an hour. The Corsair wouldn't turn over next morning, but at least the old girl got me home.

I am now forced to admit that, while sharing with my new housemate, Chris, I was consumed by gross, indecent and unadulterated envy. Whenever I looked at our Fords sitting in the kerb outside the house there was absolutely no doubt that Chris's 1600E, with its deep, lustrous shine and trendy good looks, was the better car. Every time he and his very lovely ballet dancer girlfriend drove off, I felt the little green-eyed monster give my scrotal sac a twist. I suspect that it had very little to do with his car.

My financial situation was dire. As a young computer professional I was now on a reasonable salary but I had a sizeable mortgage to pay. I was also still paying the hire purchase on the Alpine (oh yes, I still had the Sunbeam), and was now coping with the repayments on the loan for the Corsair. To make matters worse, my efforts to sell the Alpine were thwarted when a drunken truck driver out on a spree swung wildly into the back of it and rearranged the original design. He had no insurance and no resources (the lorry had been taken from his former employer), so at the worst possible time I was forced to carry the loss.

For a while I considered selling the house and taking advantage

The wonderful Ford GT 40. I wish I owned one. This is a MK2 version.

of the hike in property prices to clear my debts. It almost happened, selling the house that is, certainly not clearing my debts. On my way to work each morning I went along the Walworth Road and past Grindley's, a run-of-the-mill Ford dealership. It was a pretty lack-lustre outfit and I paid them little heed, until one day my eye caught a sleek, ultra-modern sports job that stood out rather sharply against the common herd. It turned out to be a GT 40 of the Le Mans winning variety. They were asking £5000, and for a short time I flirted with the idea of ownership. I went as far as putting my house on the market and showing round a prospective purchaser or two. Even with the sale of the house I wouldn't have been able to afford the Ford super-car. Mercifully, before long it disappeared from the showroom and so put paid to my absurd delusions. Of course it was just as well but, if I had bought it, what tales there would have been to tell!

Driving though Peckham one day, I passed a showroom with an utterly gorgeous, metallic blue MGC GT in the window. It was 20 months old with very low mileage and was keenly priced at £965. A wise man would have driven by. A sensible one would have taken a quick look and moved on. A merely sane one would have examined the figures and realised it was not for him; but I went in and did a deal. I was allowed a modest profit on the Corsair and a few days later drove home in my new toy. It was to be a while before I managed to extricate myself from the financial mire into which I had leapt, but it was a terrific car.

Best of all was the look on Chris's face when he went outside and saw his purple Ford eclipsed by my Rivera Silver Blue MG. I came back to life and started to live again with that car, but my appalling driving style didn't improve. I remember going across Westminster Bridge one evening and really winding her up as I approached the roundabout at the end. "Boy," I thought, "she really goes like a bomb." When I glanced at the speedometer even I was surprised to see 90 on the clock. Going into the roundabout necessitated a lot of wheel twiddling and a bit of opposite lock but, as usual, I survived.

And the MGC was Born

As the popular big Healey 3000 came towards the end of its life, mainly because of US safety and emissions legislation, an impoverished BMC began to consider a replacement. A cheap option seemed to be stuffing the 3-litre, series C engine into an MGB body shell. Donald Healey, still very much involved with the company, would have none of it and favoured a revised version of the original car using the 4-litre Rolls Royce unit. But the wise heads at BMC saw the shoehorn job as a relatively inexpensive way of getting a Healey replacement, and went ahead anyway. What had looked like a straightforward engine swap didn't turn out that way. First, the Healey unit was too long for the B shell, so a redesign was undertaken with the additional objectives of refinement, more power and lighter weight. Emission legislation was also a consideration; the coming need was for a cleaner engine. Contemporary commentators slated the MGC when it first appeared and criticism continued throughout its life. Most of it was probably due to the failure of the engine redesign project.

Although the final result was a bit smaller, being less than two inches shorter than the Healey unit, the MGC still required a bulge at the front of the bonnet. The most disastrous shortcoming was the failure to lose the excess engine weight; it was a scant 20 pounds lighter than the Healey unit. Refinement meant a seven-bearing crank but this in turn sapped power (an emissions oriented cylinder head didn't help either), and the MGC unit ended up five horsepower down on the Healey. All in all, not too impressive.

When BMC engineering had completed the job, the C shared few mechanical components with the B. The gearbox and the braking systems were quite different. In order to get in the tall 6-cylinder mill, the bottom cross member of the B was discarded and the C was fitted with torsion bar front suspension. The C did share the Salisbury axle of later Bs, although it had 15 and not 14-inch road wheels.

The overall effect was a disappointing, nose-heavy car that understeered quite severely. Perhaps BMC's biggest mistake was letting it look so like the MGB. The main external differences were a more aggressive bonnet with a bulge and a blister (to clear the rear carburettor), larger diameter wheels and a very discreet boot badge that proclaimed MGC and not MGB. Having said all that, I've owned two and liked them both. As a classic car it's a lot more characterful than its more numerous, 4-cylinder cousin.

For the first time I had a smart car, and I wholly enjoyed the experience. I have never believed the nonsense about girls being attracted to men because of the cars they drive but my social life certainly picked up. I spent a lot of time ferrying a car full of young women around town. Five in an MGC GT can be very cosy.

Norma's sister came over from Ireland and, on an impulse, I booked some leave and we took off for Italy. We drove from Calais through Geneva to the Mont Blanc tunnel on the first day: the "C" was a great highway cruiser. At that time the tunnel tariff was based on cubic capacity and when we got to the payment window the man behind the counter queried the model.

"MGB," I told him, quick as a flash.

He looked a little puzzled then shook his head. "Non monsieur," he replied, "MGC." He charged me the full 3-litre toll.

We wandered around the Mediterranean coast for a while doing the full economy bit by camping out (I was damned near

A rear shot of the MGC GT. Although panned by comtemporary critics, it makes a better classic car than one might think.

bankrupt). We crossed the mountains and by the time we got to Rimini I, for one, had had enough of sleeping on the ground. We went into a local tourist office and made enquiries about a cheap hotel for the night. The price they quoted was not quite as bargain basement as we would have liked but I decided we could manage one night of relative luxury. Happily we discovered we had misunderstood the tariff and the rate we had been quoted was the weekly and not the daily one. What was more, it included demi-pension. It seemed unbelievably cheap and we signed up for three nights. We drove around to the establishment expecting the worst but were pleasantly surprised. It wasn't the Waldorf Astoria but it seemed OK, even the hasty dinner they shovelled into us was acceptable. We sank thankfully into some real beds and were soon asleep.

What we had neglected to notice was that less than 20 feet from our window ran a railway line that was intersected by a level crossing 50 feet down the track. We were later informed it was the Rome Express that had woken us as it thundered through the crossing, siren blaring, in the wee hours. The expression "rude awakening" simply doesn't come close to describing the panic-stricken terror with which we slipped the arms of Morpheus and leapt from our beds. But it was a very inexpensive hotel, their beds were very comfortable and of course, on the second night the experience was a lot less terrifying.

Before setting off for home we swung north and took a look at Venice. We parked the MG in a huge car park on the outskirts and went into the city on the waterbus. We got back in the late afternoon and we decided to head for Milan. It wasn't until we were in line for the Autostrada toll that Vivienne started looking for her handbag. We turned everything upside down, but it was nowhere to be seen. Then it slowly dawned. We remembered that after our sightseeing we had returned to the car and, because it was a hot day, we had sat discussing the route with the doors open to let in some air. At this point Vivienne also recalled putting her handbag on the roof before getting in. When we had decided on an itinerary, we shut the doors and off we went.

Needless to say, after covering the 30 or so miles from the car park the bag wasn't still sitting on the roof. It was not our happiest moment, for in that fated handbag were not only Vivienne's passport and money but also my passport, traveller's cheques, lire and all my UK cash. I had left upon my person some 3000 lire (about £2) and a handful of petrol tokens, which wasn't a lot for a couple stuck in the middle of Italy with a car full of luggage.

I turned the MG round through a gap in the central reservation while varieties of policemen screeched and gesticulated. We roared back to the car park as fast as our wheels would carry us. After two hours of furious searching we called it a day. It was getting towards dusk and suddenly none of our Italian hosts could speak a word of English, and understood even less. I figured the only hope was the British Consul. When I made enquiries, the city police were completely unhelpful, couldn't understand a word I said and, to get rid of us, sent us off to the Carabinieri. In utter desolation we made our way to the militia post, our holiday ruined, our future uncertain and an uncomfortable and unpleasant homecoming in prospect. I tried to make myself understood. "Passport gone, money gone. I British, need British Consul, where is here in Venice?" I resorted to pidgin gobbledegook.

The officer behind the desk looked bemused, as well he might. Suddenly he brightened. "Ah, passport!" he exclaimed. He stepped into a back room and returned with Vivienne's handbag. Everything was still inside. He pulled out a bunch of forms for us to complete, then changed his mind. He dug into the bag, took out my passport and checked the photo, then he thrust the bag into Vivienne's hands. "OK, you go now," he said, wisely avoiding the paperwork. Despair was turned to joy, disaster had been avoided, God was in his heaven after all. It turned out that some kind-hearted and honest tourist had seen the bag slip from the roof and had handed it in. I hope she had a lifetime of good luck. In high spirits we headed back to the car and got on with having a good time.

I arrived home to a nasty letter from my bank and financial problems piling up around me. To add to my woes, my tenant, who owed me two months' rent, had done a moonlight flit. Worse, he had left me with a 'phone bill that took my breath away. It was Vivienne who helped get me back from the brink. The light of my life, the beloved MG, the car I couldn't afford, would have to go. A bitter pill to swallow, but necessary if financial viability was to be restored. I advertised for a while, but found it difficult to sell an expensive car privately. I ended up taking a 1964 Jaguar

The S-type was a delightful car in every way. My first real luxury vehicle.

The ubiquitous MGB

S-type saloon in part exchange.

I was sorry to see the MG go, and terrified that something awful and expensive would happen to the Jaguar before I could unload it. It turned out to be a wonderful car. For the first time ever my driving became sedate as I wafted around in the quiet luxury of that lovely limousine. It was completely unlike anything I had experienced before, and it sold to the first man that came along with an MGB and £200.

The MGB was a 1964 roadster that wanted some TLC. It got a new hood and a tidy-up. Someone had resprayed it in the fashion colour of the day and, with aubergine coachwork and a white top, it looked like a tart's breakfast. But quarter bumpers and sparkling wheels made it pleasantly eye catching. I enjoyed smoking it around for a few weeks and developed a real fondness for MGs of both the B and C varieties. There was no doubt that the B handled better than the C, although the steering on both was heavy and slightly dead. The C was the quicker car, but not by as much as the 1200cc difference would suggest. The B's performance was really quite adequate at the time and it held its own in traffic. Years later, when I acquired another, later model B, the performance hadn't improved one iota but by then the other cars on the road were a lot quicker. I was forever being outgunned by hot hatches. (I am proud to say that I have never owned a hatch, hot or otherwise.) The B, when it finally sold, made good money. Some dear soul took it away for £485, which left me with a very handsome profit on the triple play out of the MGC.

Vivienne and I were married in 1971 and we moved from Forest Hill to a smart, modern town house in Upper Norwood. Just the thing for an up-and-coming young computer professional. Our first child, Joanne, was born at the end of the year.

Vivienne took me severely in hand, and soon the debts were paid off and I was once again solvent: my bank manager even stopped writing me letters. But financial rectitude had its price and there was no cash in the kitty for smart wheels. I bought a very clean and tidy Vauxhall FB Victor at auction for £175. It was in every way what my earlier FA had not been. Rust-free and mechanically excellent, it had an as-new interior and did everything that I asked of it. It was also unutterably boring.

When I could stand it no longer, I sold the Victor and found

The FB Victor, an altogether more robust effort than the earlier F-Type.

a Rover 2000 in a dealer's yard in Bell Green, Sydenham. The car was extremely cheap, purely, I was assured, because the colour was not to everyone's taste. The exact shade might best be described as metallic pinkish lilac. Not a standard colour, I hasten to point out, but attractive nonetheless. I rather liked it, but when I got it home I was persuaded that my taste was somewhat on the bizarre side and I began to consider repainting it a more conventional hue. I had heard tell of one "Nobby" Lambert of

The Rover 2000, a revelation when first launched in 1964

Forest Hill who was reputed to "blow-over" a motor for 100 quid, so I went to see him. I loaded up the car with infant daughter in her carrycot in the back and Danny, my parents' Labrador, in his usual position on the front passenger seat. We set off for chez Lambert in good order.

The FB Victor

Vauxhall's FB variant Victor was very different from the earlier F-Type. For a start it became noted for the longevity of its bodywork. (One is likely still to see FB Victors at classic car gatherings, particularly the sportier versions.) The design, although much less flamboyant than the F-Type, was cleaner and neater. A sportier VX 4/90 (4 cylinders and 90 horsepower) had go-faster flashes along the sides and a different rear lamp cluster. It also featured a floor-mounted gear stick, unlike the column shift of the standard car. Vauxhall, following Ford's lead, promoted sales by regular and radical changes in model styling and the FB was quickly followed by the FC. Called the Victor 101, it featured curved side windows (a first in the UK) that had the effect of distorting views of the interior. It was not uncommon to see families of monsters with strange, elongated heads driving around in them.

Ideas on safety were more relaxed in those days and it was common practice to waft around with carloads of kids and animals bouncing about free and untethered. The journey was uneventful until we pulled into Nobby's road and neared his yard whereupon his dog came leaping out into the street and attempted to tear the head off mine even though they were separated by the window glass. They got into a shouting match and Danny, no lightweight, leapt into the back right on to the sleeping baby. In my panic to stop him as he leapt crazily all over the carrycot, I veered across the road and slammed into the back of a stationary Jaguar. In a frenzy I leaped from the car and wrenched open the back door. I was convinced that some awful tragedy had occurred. The dog, sensing disaster, went meekly back to his front seat. Lambert's cur had wisely quit the scene. I peered into the carrycot. The baby was still and lifeless. I felt the blood drain away from my brain as icy fingers grabbed my heart. I felt for a pulse half expecting there would be none. My cold hands must have woken her. Clearly cross at being roused from her warm and pleasant sleep, the little tyke began to roar her head off in rage. Relief flooded through me. Close examination revealed that she was completely uninjured; the commotion and the dogfight hadn't even woken her.

I went in to face Mr Lambert a very happy man. The £125 for the paint job, the extra £100 to repair the damage and a further £100 for the dent in his Jaguar didn't faze me in the least; at that moment it would have been cheap at a ten times the price.

I had the Rover painted maroon, and it looked terrible. Whereas the lilac had hidden a slightly uneven body, the maroon accentuated every fault. I soon sold it on to a chap who seemed happy enough with it and I almost scraped back my investment. Vivienne now had her own car, a woody Mini Traveller (she had started lessons in the Victor) so it was altogether easier to go in search of a replacement vehicle.

I am still not sure whether the Mustang was intended as serious family transport or as a final fling at trading. I got her

Lee Iacocca's pretty Mustang. The 289 cubic inch V8 is still one of the most popular American classics.

In an effort to grab attention and promote business, Hertz Car Rental in the US equipped themselves with a fleet of Shelby tuned Mustangs. These are now much sought after by collectors.

from a fellow in north London who had done a lot of work before running out of cash and selling her cheaply. I paid £500. It was my first American car and I was mightily impressed with the sturdy build. It was a 1965, 289 cubic inches, V8 convertible. She had the "Rally Pac" option with disc brakes and an oppressive, black interior. The whole car was in excellent condition. Unusually, it had a four-speed manual gearbox, and at the time I was pleased, but now I know better. These cars cry out for automatic transmissions.

Getting her back up to scratch was an interesting exercise. A new white hood (she was my first car with a power top), wheel trims from a Rover 2000 and contrasting, offset racing stripes running from nose to tail really set off her mid metallic blue coachwork. It all sounds in revoltingly poor taste but given the genre she looked the part. I generally cleaned and tidied, touched up some paint blemishes and made her look desirable.

I had finally left Colgate and had taken a job with a computer services company based near Heathrow. Given that I lived in Upper Norwood this may seem not to have been a particularly smart move, but my expectation was that, as a consultant, I would be required to work at locations other than my base. I often drove the Mustang up to the office through the rush hour traffic and she went faultlessly without the slightest hint of overheating or temperament. She was one of those cars, like the earlier Jaguar S- type, where one was always expecting trouble but none ever came along. She certainly gave me a very positive perspective on American tin. I have subsequently always hankered after a '67 Fastback, ideally a Shelby 350 or 500. I imagine they are great cars for long-distance rallies.

More because I wanted to see what she would fetch than because I wanted to be rid of her, I advertised the Mustang; I then did a deal with a chap who offered me a Triumph TR4A with a busted wing in part exchange. Fortunately, I was able to acquire an original Stanpart item from a main dealer. (Manufacturer's panels were already getting in short supply and the reproduction replacements, available at the time, didn't fit.) It was a good deal because I ended up with a delightful Triumph sports car for very little money. Once I had fitted the new wing and had it painted, the TR was an excellent car in every way. Vivienne took to it as soon as she discovered that a carrycot fitted very neatly behind the seats. Unfortunately, she enjoyed driving the car as much as I did.

It proved a faithful and reliable work-horse and we took many trips *en-famille*. It was another example of a tough little British sports car that, with a modicum of care and attention, handsomely repaid its owner. We had that car for quite some time, in fact until I was offered the "ultimate" sports roadster at a knockdown price.

Vivienne and the Triumph TR4A

A pal of mine who had started work as an estate agent in his parents' firm had flown the coop early in his career, and had set up a garage business with a friend. He had developed into a first-class mechanic, and it had been he who had sold me one of my early XKs, (one of the good ones, that is). Mike now offered me his E-type, on which he had lavished much care and attention.

I went down to view the 1962, 3.8-litre

Jaguar's glorious E-type. This is the early 3.8 litre roadster version of the fixed-head coupé that stunned the motoring world in 1961.

beauty and was immediately hooked. It looked magnificent. Mike had probably started with a wreck, and worked miracles. It had a brand-new factory replacement engine that came complete with plugs and distributor. The ex-factory price in 1972 was £190 plus a £100 core charge, which was returned if the components of your trade-in proved re-useable. The exchange engine was so tight that the first thing I needed was a new battery just to turn it over. Although I was supposed to be running her in, I just couldn't resist making her perform and golly, how well she went! At £480 I still maintain she was a bargain, with great potential for improvement.

The whole of the bonnet was virtually new and the body sparkled and shone in new, bright paint. I guess it was another case of tart's breakfast, because Mike had once more gone for a fashion statement and had painted her Ford's ubiquitous aubergine. I had stuck on a white top. The interior was a less happy affair but I had future plans in that department. I quickly disposed of my wonderful little Triumph to a pleasant RAF type, and I took delivery of the Jaguar.

From the start the car didn't get off on the right foot. Unlike in the Triumph, there was no place behind the seats for a carrycot or anything else, so strike one. She was loud, noisy and attracted a lot of attention (more than a Mustang?) The perceived wisdom was that she was better suited to a boy racer than a respectable married man, strike two. She was not without her faults and she was likely to be a significant drain on resources if I was to get her completely up to scratch, strike three.

I have to admit that even I became a little worried when, while cleaning her one day, I pushed my finger though the body under the rear bumper. What looked shiny, solid metal was no more than a brittle carapace of iron oxide. Although the rest of the car looked sound, I wasn't man enough to start poking about. I stuck her in the paper at £599. (The magic 99 that fools no one. Why do so many vendors do that?) The first chap that came around took her off my hands without a murmur, and so my E-type departed. The car I had so long lusted after had come and gone in the twinkling of an eye. It was to be more than ten years before I got another. It was probably just as well, since little Sarah was born soon afterwards.

There followed a Triumph GT6 Mk 2, which I remember with affection: a sort of miniature E-type in signal red with the customary black vinyl interior. Much maligned by the cognoscenti, these little cars were extremely good once the rather unhappy rear suspension arrangement had been sorted. With overdrive, these pint-sized but hugely practical cars could do anything asked of them. The rear compartment offered moderate load-carrying capability and there was even room for a carrycot on the vestigial rear seat. 100-mph cruising was certainly an option. The one-piece bonnet and wings allowed unrivalled access to the engine bay.

My mother, Danny the Labrador, my Mk 2 GT6 and me.

This period in the history of the British motor industry always seems to me a terrible watershed. Standard-Triumph was still producing what, in my opinion, was a world-beating range of cars. On the saloon front they had the fabulous, 16-valve Dolomite Sprint as well as the wonderfully quick and comfortable 2500 PI. For those with more conservative tastes, the Triumph 2000 was also an excellent car, as was the innovative, front-wheeled drive 1300 (later the 1500). The small sports cars ranged from the cheap and cheerful Spitfire to the GT6. The bigger sports cars were the very rapid and stylish TR6 and the brilliant Stag. It is popular these days to denigrate British products of the time, but to my mind no other manufacturer anywhere in the world produced as good a range for the price. Of course all of these cars had their faults, mainly as a result of under-funding and general lack of development. We have all heard the stories of foolishness and mismanagement, but it's sad to think of all that potential being so needlessly wasted. That's my whinge over, at least for the moment.

My move to Management Dynamics had been something of a disaster. The computer services industry went into serious recession almost as soon as I left Colgate. The three months between being offered a job and finally taking it up had seen a huge downturn in my new employer's business. I stayed with

The MK 2 Triumph GT6 in all its glory. A sort of mini E-type.

them just over 18 months and in that time I saw my department shrink from forty to just one – me. Almost as soon as I arrived, the dreaded redundancies began. It was a harrowing and nerve-racking time. At one point my manager, with whom I got on particularly well, was given the job of pulling us out of the mire and appointed Sales Manager. He asked me to join him in the sales department and, as the alternative was probably the unemployment line, I jumped at the chance. My reward was the use of a company car, but it was nothing to get excited about, just a 1600cc Cortina Mk 2. I took the opportunity to dispose of the GT6, because the axle had become a little noisy.

My manager and I were the only two left in our department and this got even worse when he announced his resignation. My bacon may have been saved when I finally secured a big sale, but within days of the deal I got another job so was able to hand in my notice, together with the Cortina. I remember that before I went I was paid a signing commission for the sale. They were not obliged to give me anything, and it was a characteristically generous gesture.

With the money from the sale of the GT6 and some of my commission, I was in the happy position of being in the market with cash in hand. I went to look at a Triumph TR5 that was advertised as being in good condition and only a couple of miles from home. The owner was asking £750, which was a good deal more than I was able to pay, but one never knows what deals may be done.

The chap lived in a smart flat in a desirable area but turned out to be the most supercilious and condescending man I ever had to deal with; we hated each other on sight. He could hardly be bothered to discuss the car with me and quickly became irritated by my questions, as though asking about condition was some sort of personal affront. He made it clear that he wasn't prepared to show me the vehicle personally or take me out for a test drive. I was about to leave when he suddenly tossed me the keys and told me to drive around on my own. I found the car in the lock-up

*Triumph's very rapid TR5.
Its fairly uninspired OHV
engine was transformed by
mechanical petrol injection
and a hairy cam.*

garage to which he had directed me and was pleasantly surprised.
The TR was a late '68 in Valencia blue with a black interior. It
looked in excellent shape. I almost didn't bother going out in it;
based on what I saw there seemed little prospect of getting it for
what I had available. She started up well enough but then, almost
with delight, I discovered the fatal flaw: the gearbox had all but
given up the ghost. Second gear was impossible to locate and it
made the most frightful racket in all the others. I got her warm and
tested everything else as best I could, then I stuck her back in her
garage and went back up to do battle.

The nasty little chap did a lot of shrugging and lip curling

*My Valencia blue TR5.
She was a very nice motorcar
in every way and one of a
handful of my old cars that
I remember with special
affection.*

and finally conceded that the transmission needed a bit of attention. He offered to reduce the price by £25. I decided I was on a hiding to nothing, and made to leave. The lady with him (I assumed she was his girlfriend) suddenly piped up and asked me what I would pay. In sharp contrast, she was as nice as pie. I was cross and fed up with the bad-mannered oaf and told them £500. He snorted and hurrumphed and dismissed my offer out of hand. She was more conciliatory and tried to get a discussion going but pally was having none of it. I bid them good day and left. I was about to drive off when the nice lady appeared in the doorway and motioned me to stop. We did a deal at £525.

One of the great things about those Triumphs is that the gearboxes can be changed without having to lift out the engines and it was less than a day's work to swap transmissions. I got a TR4A unit from a specialist for £40. What a great car she turned out to be! For the period, she was also very quick. I kept her for quite a while and changed the springs and shocks, which made a massive difference to the ride and handling.

Triumph did a better job than BMC
When it first appeared, the TR5 was the fastest production car that Triumph had ever produced. Still using the handsome Michelotti-designed body, Triumph did a sort of MGC trick and stuffed in their six-cylinder, two-litre motor, but not before they had stroked it to 2500ccs. Unlike the MG there was no weight penalty in converting to the six and the 5 outperformed the 4 in every department, (except fuel consumption.) The new motor even sat neatly under the bonnet. The increase in power came from the use of Lucas mechanical petrol injection and a fairly hairy cam. There is much discussion about exactly how much power the TR engine put out. The normally quoted figure is 150 bhp but the measurement used was the old SAE system that was later changed to DIN, which, if used at the time, would have indicated a lower figure. Whatever the truth, it was a good deal more powerful than the 104 bhp (SAE) of the TR4A and went like

the clappers with 0 to 60 coming up in less than nine seconds. With better brakes and a slightly beefed-up chassis it was an altogether better car. Unfortunately, there were always problems with the fuel injection and the cars got a reputation for poor reliability (due mainly to lack of experience in the trade). In my opinion the TR5 is still one of the most desirable British sports cars of the post-war period.

When the 1973 petrol shortages came along, I was working on a project with Green Shield Stamps at Edgware and went up every day in my TR. She wasn't the most fuel-efficient car around and I was kept on the road only by the good offices of my client. Green Shield had their own garage and closed it to the public, using their limited stocks to keep the reps cars going. They were very kind to me. I think it was during this period that the government introduced odd and even day petrol sales based on car registration numbers.

When things got really tight on the petrol supply front, I used it as an excuse to acquire a 1966 Mini Cooper that turned out to be good fun but didn't give much better gas mileage than the TR. I hung on to the Triumph, awaiting better days.

In 1975 Vivienne and I separated and I went off to live in a flat in Beckenham. She and I are still the greatest of friends. In recent years she has caught the historic rallying bug and we often come across each other on various European events. She is a devoted mother and a fine person. I owe her a great deal, not least for helping me control my spendthrift urges and assisting me out of the financial mire that threatened to engulf me.

CHAPTER 9

Transition

This chapter covers a long period when a lot of changes occurred in my life. The fact that some of my actions resulted in people having their lives disrupted is a cause for regret and genuine remorse. When this period began, my personal life was a mess and got messier, but, by the time it was over, things were more settled and I had finally started down a worthwhile and more responsible path. Fortunately, this is predominantly a story about motorcars and not people so I can leave most of the unflattering detail in the shadows of other events.

Financial settlements of one kind or another necessitated the sale of my much-loved Triumph TR5 as well as the Mini Cooper.

This is a Cooper S; mine was the basic model in red with a black roof.

I suppose the Cooper had some sort of sill problem, because it had a habit of flooding inside when driven in damp conditions. It was nonetheless a fabulous little car and enormous fun to drive. The rather charismatic duo were replaced by a cheap but not very cheerful Mini Clubman. As usual, it had been inexpensively acquired and was a little rough around the edges. I used it as a daily hack until I had scraped together enough money to replace it. I have always hated boring cars so, when the chance came to trade it for something with a bit more dash, I was delighted. With just one car and needing the cash from the sale before I could buy another, I concentrated my search on dealers that might be prepared to take the Mini in part exchange. I looked at a number of sports cars and ended up with a very nice 1970 MGB from a forecourt in Streatham.

This was my second B and, apart from being a little wanting in the acceleration department, she was an excellent car in every way. Abingdon, for all the faults of the parent company (now British Leyland), had put together a creditable product. The fact that these cars continued in production until about 1981 without significant modifications to the design (if you ignore the addition of rubber bumpers and the raising of the ride height) is a tribute to the faithful following they had generated. My glacier-white car had the customary black interior, although I think by that time leather had given way to vinyl. She was five years old but looked new. The panel fit and shut lines were excellent and the doors closed with a solid and resounding "clunk". The engine was oil-tight and always maintained admirable oil pressure. In overdrive top she would cruise endlessly at 90 miles an hour and felt as solid as a rock.

I met a lovely German lady, and the two of us were frequent visitors to her parents' home in Elze near Hanover; the little MG would do the journey without a murmur. It was the sort of car you could jump into and confidently set off on an unscheduled trip to Timbuktu. At least, that's how she felt. Apart from some minor work on things like kingpins and a rear oil seal, she gave no trouble.

On one of the trips back from Germany she refused to start after a short stop and my diagnosis of battery failure was more or less correct. In fact, a terminal post had snapped. I tried to solve the problem by drilling down through the post and securing the break with a self-tapping screw, but the fracture was too low down for this to be effective. We were in Belgium at the time and we toured the garages for miles around without finding the requisite six-volt replacement. We eventually came across a proprietor who confidently predicted he could get one within the hour. In the event it was more like three before the thing finally arrived. All that time I had kept the engine running because my friend Regina didn't drive and wasn't quite strong enough to push start the car unaided. I was cautious because I wasn't sure how helpful the Belgian would be if we decided to leave without purchasing his offering. I imagine the chap thought he was on to a good thing, as we had hung around so long and, it seemed, had no option. We were a bit surprised to be told he wanted £120 for one six-volt battery. My strategy paid off because I told him what to do with it and we got in the car and drove away. We only stopped the engine when the MG was safely tucked up on the car deck of the return ferry. She had run non-stop for about seven hours and had been stationary for much of the time but there was

The MGB in Germany with Regina's brother at the wheel.

never a sign of overheating or temperament. The briefest of push starts by the crew at Sheerness, and we were on the homeward leg.

Disaster finally struck one Easter on the way to Elze. The weather was particularly foul, with deep and drifting snow even on the journey down to the ferry at Sheerness. At one point on the M2 we hit a patch of what looked like newly fallen snow but was really ice barely covered with a light dusting. I lost control, as the steering went feather-light. At the last possible moment the front wheels found some grip and I was able to steer out of trouble. It was nonetheless a close call, and I took it very carefully after that. We struggled through Holland in near blizzard conditions and it was only when we got into Germany that things improved. I was keeping to a steady 50 mph in very poor conditions, when the engine suddenly started behaving erratically and the car lost and regained power several times in the course of a few seconds. One moment we were going along steadily and the next we were bucking and stalling as I struggled to maintain control. It was as though the throttle had developed a mind of its own. We hit a patch of ice and went spinning wildly across the autobahn, crashing the nose into the Armco barrier. The force of the impact sent us spinning the other way. We veered across to the opposite side and this time struck the Armco protecting the central reservation. We ended up with the boot of the car wedged firmly under the barrier.

Regina's stepfather with the B in the background. This was taken on a visit after repairs had been carried out.

We had two pieces of good fortune. First, we were not struck by another vehicle (even in those conditions drivers of big Mercedes cars were roaring down the fast lane at 100 mph plus) and second, neither of us was injured. The poor old MG was an awful mess. The police arrived and proceeded to scream at me in German. I spoke very little and understood even less, so their admonishments were rather a waste of time. They did, however, help extricate the car and, once on the hard shoulder, I was able to find the reason for the erratic running that had presaged the crash. For some reason the points had all but closed up. Once they had been readjusted the car started and ran perfectly, the battering having in no way impaired her driveability. We stopped for the night in a gasthaus and, after a good German dinner of wienerschintzel and a few beers, I began to feel less as if the world had ended. Regina, a battered MG and, from the point of view of pride, an even more battered driver made it to Elze the next day.

I carried out most of the repair work myself; luckily only the outer panels had been damaged. I obtained a new wing from a fellow a few doors away who had started the restoration of his BGT before it had been written off by a hit-and-run while at the kerb. (Shades of my old Alpine.) I found a steel bonnet and a rear bumper in the spares section of the *Exchange and Mart* and actually splashed out on a new boot lid and badges. I cut the middle section out of the damaged front bumper and made up a snazzy set of quarter bumpers. I repainted only the newly fitted items, and the whole project came to less than £150. The finished version looked better than original.

The children were getting bigger, and carrying them in the back of what was essentially a two-seater became uncomfortable as well as unsafe, so my thoughts turned to acquiring something with room for four. As always, there wasn't a lot of cash. I advertised the MG and ended up with two couples coming to view at the same time. They all but got into a fist-fight about who had telephoned first. In the end I was forced to make an arbitrary decision. One very disgruntled pair went off cursing and spitting: the other got a very nice MGB.

I answered an advertisement for an inexpensive 1973 Triumph 1500 saloon. It turned out that the car was being sold by an Australian who was on his way home and wanted out quickly. I took a test drive and, although everything seemed basically all right, there was definitely something wrong with the gearbox, which gave trouble when selecting second gear. He was asking £750 but I got the car for less.

The Triumph 1500 was in many respects a mid-sized version of its bigger 2500cc cousin, except that, unusually for Triumph, it had front-wheel drive. For its size it was extremely well

The 1500 had a very similar body shell to that of the Dolomite but featured front-wheel drive. My car was a mechanical disaster, but attractive and well appointed.

appointed, with lots of wood and thick, deep pile carpets. I suppose BL quality issues were beginning to manifest themselves because she was only just over three years old and, apart from the gearbox glitch, there was also a problem with sluggish oil pressure build-up on cold starting. I had a pretty bad time with the car but most of it was my own fault.

A week before its first trek to Germany, I went to my parents' home for dinner. We turned out at about midnight and I casually mentioned to my father the problems with the gearbox as he walked with me to the car. He was resolutely in favour of my fixing the problem before my departure and suggested I should use his facilities to do the job. I pointed out that, as the car was front wheel-drive, any attempt to get at the transmission internals would necessitate removal of the engine. I was reluctant to take on such a big job before our imminent departure. Being an optimist and a "go get 'em" kind of guy, he didn't see this as a problem at all. So convinced was he that the job could be easily accomplished that he persuaded me to drive into the garage and put the car over the pit there and then, so that we could take a look at what I faced. Mother naturally thought we were nuts and went off to bed, leaving us to our own devices. By 4.30 in the morning the engine and gearbox were on the workshop floor and

I spent what was left of the night in the spare room. That's the kind of man my father was: crazy, but absolutely marvellous if you needed help with a problem. Now he is now longer around I miss him more than I can say.

Father - Crazy but Irrepressible

About this time my father was bitten by the aeroplane bug and, having qualified with a private licence, went on to own and run a small light aircraft business based at Biggin Hill. He ended up with a motley collection of aircraft, which he hired out to people wanting budget flying. I was visiting him one evening when he got a call from an airfield somewhere in Cornwall informing him that one of his planes had crash landed during the day. After making enquires, it became clear that although the damage wasn't too serious the craft would not be flying out under its own steam without extensive repairs. Now, Dad wasn't a man to spend unnecessarily, and he soon decided that repairs could be more economically effected at Biggin than in Cornwall. What utterly incensed him, however, was the fee the airfield proposed to charge for storing the wreck until he was able to arrange collection.

The only vehicle he had at the time was a Mini Traveller, so he decided it would have to do. He spent the rest of the evening

It's not a great photograph, but it does record a piece of family history

making up a huge roof rack that spanned the full length of the Mini. He also fabricated and fitted a special tow bar. Father and the part-time gardener set off for the West Country at the crack of dawn the next morning.

They arrived after about six hours driving. The two of them, under my father's expert direction, proceeded to dismantle the damaged plane. They removed the engine and put it inside the van; then the wings and tail plane were taken off and lashed on to the roof rack. Father rigged up the fuselage with the towing bracket he had made the night before and fixed it to the rear of the car. The process took quite a long time but, not wanting to spend on overnight accommodation, 20 hours after leaving home the two men set off on the return journey. They were stopped by the police seven times on the way, but on each occasion Father's charm, sheer cheek or bullheadedness got them through. I suspect it had much to do with the reluctance of the various officers to fill out the paperwork relating to apprehending a Mini towing an aeroplane along the A303. They arrived home exhausted mid-morning on the following day. Luckily, on this occasion a camera was on hand to record their feat.

In the course of the next week I obtained new synchro parts and put the gearbox back together. I also decided to fit a new oil pump and new main and big end shells. It was while replacing the end caps that I made a disastrous error. For some reason, while tightening one of the big end nuts I must have become distracted and I tightened it down too much. The result was that I subjected the bolt to almost twice the proper torque. The right thing to do would have been to junk the bolt and fit a new one, but I was in hurry to finish the job so I just backed off the thread and re-tightened to the recommended setting. A disastrous and costly piece of bad judgement.

With the complete assembly back in the car, I was delighted to discover that all the problems appeared to have been cured. The gear change was like a hot knife through butter and the oil pressure came up swiftly and stayed there. The car was transformed. We set off on the Christmas trip full of enthusiasm and she went like a bird most of the way there. But not quite all the way: barely 20 miles from our destination and cruising happily at 80 mph, the over-torqued bolt snapped and made a bit of a mess of things. We ended up with a rod through the block. Scratch one engine.

We contacted Regina's parents, who mercifully weren't far away. They came out and towed us in. It wasn't the jolliest Christmas I can remember, with the prospect of fixing the blooming Triumph hanging over me. Once again, Father came to the rescue. He managed to locate a replacement engine in a breaker's yard for £50 and, as he had an aeroplane at the time, he flew the acquired engine to Le Touquet. On Boxing Day, Regina's brother Hardy and I took the rear seats out of his Fiat 128 and drove down from just south of Hanover to collect it. We stopped overnight in Belgium and got back late on the 27th. I started work as the day dawned next morning.

Regina's parents had a tumbled-down garage of sorts but, since it was filled with junk, it provided virtually no cover, so most of the work was carried out in the open. I chocked the garage doors and used an old roofing beam as a crossbar. I rigged up a pulley, block and tackle and lifted out the broken mill, leaving the gearbox and driveshafts in place. Fatal mistake number two. I did my best to get the swarf from the blown engine out of the transmission but I guess a really thorough clean-up just wasn't possible without removal, dismantling and professional equipment.

Conditions were particularly bleak and, when it started to snow, I began to feel a little sorry for myself. I remember Regina's bemused family at the window watching as I worked alone in the gathering gloom with snowflakes blowing around me. I looked up and there they were, fixing me with baleful stares, half sympathy and half-utter disbelief. Wondering, I suppose, why their only daughter had taken up with an impecunious and eccentric *Englander.*

It was not with any feeling of accomplishment that we loaded up the Triumph and set off for home. Regina's sceptical relatives wished us bon voyage, clearly surprised to see the car running again but apprehensive of our prospects. The journey was uneventful until a few miles from home, when we suffered comprehensive bearing failure on the Sidcup bypass.

I took the engine apart for the third time in as many weeks and this time had the gearbox and diff unit thoroughly cleaned. I put it all back together with a reground crank, new bearings and a rebuilt oil pump. I was very, very careful. "This time," I said to myself, "it has to be perfect." But it wasn't. On cold starting she would still rattle until the oil pressure built up; so I gave up and sold the damn thing.

I suppose this tale of woe seems somewhat at odds with my previous comments about Triumph and their range of cars but it has to be admitted that most of my grief with the wretched car was mainly self-inflicted. I made too many stupid mistakes and, on that occasion, didn't get away with them as I usually had. On the positive side, I learned a lot of useful lessons that have since stood me in good stead.

My next car was the complete antithesis of the Triumph. Still

Bertone's (Giugiaro's?) very pretty GTV. This is the 2-litre version

needing child-carrying capacity and being short of cash, I was introduced by a neighbour to a handsome 1970, Alfa Romeo 1750 GTV. This was another car I remember with great affection. In all the time I had her she never let me down. On numerous continental trips she ran sweetly and cruised at 100 mph for hours on end without fuss or bother.

Designed by Giugiaro when he was employed by Bertone, the little two-plus-two is, in my view, a perfect example of the stylist's art. Some cars are very much fashion statements of their time. The problem is that fashions change and the statements lose their relevance. What was yesterday's icon becomes tomorrow's plain old fashioned. That is why the Bertone GTV is a masterpiece; the perfectly proportioned body seems timeless and always looks right. The engine, an all alloy twin cam, is another work of art, with twin Webers and about 130 horsepower. GTVs are noted for their prodigious and trouble-free mileage. The car had the first five-speed gearbox of my acquaintance and I was initially put off by the strange angle at which the gear lever protruded from under the dash. But I need not have concerned myself, for once warmed-up the box was a joy to use. I suppose I sound a bit effusive in my praise of the car but this model and the subsequent 2000 GTVs really are outstanding.

My eldest daughter Joanne helping to pack the boot before a day out in our Alfa 1750 GTV. One of the best cars I have owned.

As with a lot of Italian cars, rust was the enemy. Poor anti-corrosion design and lack of pre-delivery treatment, not helped by poor quality steel, meant fairly horrendous problems as the cars put on a few years. I was forever patching and doing running repairs around the edges.

I found the car very comfortable to drive (I'm only 5 feet 6 inches), but tall drivers often complained about the lack of accommodation for longer legs. Handling, road holding and balance were excellent and, although testers' reports all show fairly unspectacular 0 to 60 times, these Alfas can be hustled through country lanes with great rapidity. These days, whenever I see excellent, right-handed examples for sale at prices as low as £4500, I'm tempted to buy one for use as everyday transport. By now I suppose, everyone has got the message: I like Bertone Alfa GTVs.

While I owned SWM 92J (I doubt she has survived, I suspect the tin worm did for her some time ago), Regina went back to Germany and I met and married Shirley. I also quit my secure and well paid job and, with a work colleague, set up on my own. After a shaky but nonetheless solvent first three months, business began to flourish and I sold my Alfa to buy another. There was nothing wrong with the car, and my main motive was to move a bit up-market simply because I could.

The Alfetta 1750 GT and Shirley, who very kindly sent me this picture after I had written the chapter. I had completely forgotten about the boat. It was extremely scruffy and a lot of fun. This was taken at Putney.

The replacement Alfa was a more up-to-date version of the earlier car, referred to as an Alfetta GT. So called because, like its famous pre-war namesake, it had near 50/50 weight distribution as a result of having the transmission located at the back. It was nowhere near the car its predecessor had been. The linkage between the box and the lever was never the happiest piece of engineering, lacking the precision of the earlier model. However, apart from a small incident on the way to a client one day, when

2-litre Alfetta GTV Strada

the transaxle assembly decided to shake loose, I experienced few problems. Business seemed on the up and, one day, while driving through Sundridge Park in Bromley, I spotted a brand new 2000 GTV in a main dealer's showroom. She was bright red with a smoke grey velour interior and I was immediately seduced. My accountant gave me the thumbs up and the Alfetta was sold and the new GTV Strada given pride of place.

In between the sale of the Alfetta and the delivery of the GTV there was a short gap and, just for the hell of it, I bought a lime green MG Midget for £190 from a local ad. The immediate reason was that I had arranged to go camping at the weekend and didn't want to disappoint anyone. The car really was a little horror, and what I thought would be an enjoyable and nostalgic experience turned out to be purgatory. It was a boiling hot day and before we set off I thought I'd better look under the bonnet. To my horror, I discovered that nearly all the core plugs had almost rotted away. They were covered in clagg, with water seeping through at every point. It wasn't the kind of thing I wanted to know just then, so I quickly closed the bonnet and got on with the journey. The wee beastie held together and the weekend passed uneventfully, in the automotive sense anyway. When I got back I disposed of the Midget for a very small profit and never again experienced the pleasure of driving an old banger as regular transport. At the time, I think I failed to shed a tear.

The red Alfa Romeo was my first brand-new car. I had waited 15 years from my acquisition of the Morris Ten, with which I had never turned a wheel, before acquiring my first new vehicle. It also marks something of a turning point in this chronology, because from then on my everyday transport became much less characterful and idiosyncratic (except for a short time in the US). I had clambered onto the bandwagon of prosperity and developed the habit of acquiring new cars when replacements were due. My love of old motors remained, however, and it wasn't long before my thoughts turned to classics.

There's not a lot to be said about modern, particularly new, cars. They start, they stop and they go, which is very nice if you actually need to get somewhere, but they are not the stuff of tall tales. I can't remember much about the red Alfa apart from the fact she was very pretty and went tolerably well. The car was basically a slight update of the earlier Alfetta and, although the gear linkage was a little better, it suffered from the same basic weakness. I stayed with the car until early 1980, when I took delivery of a new Mercedes Benz SL.

I had that Merc for about four years and, although she was an acquired taste as a driver's car, I grew to value her a great deal. I waited 20 months for delivery, resolutely refusing the blandishments of the dealership, who were keen to have me pay a premium and jump the queue. I think I put in the order almost as soon as I got the Alfa, partly because I was keen on the prospect of getting my mitts on a seriously up-market motor, but also because the corporate accountant had a hand in the decision. At the time the model was so popular (helped, I think, by the Ewing family in the TV soap 'Dallas'), that it was not possible to buy a second-hand example for less than it would have cost when new. (I think an element of inflation helped.) I believe the statistics showed that it had one of the lowest depreciation rates of all the quality vehicles on the market at the time. So not only was it a rather swanky carriage, but it was also a "good buy". It is rare that one is able to combine avarice with prudence.

Our 350 SL somewhere in France.

I ordered a 350 SL in a colour they called "champagne", with a tan interior and a brown hood. I also went for the alloy wheels option. In those days radios were an optional extra and I irritated the dealer by refusing the expensive Becker Mexico option, and went instead for a much cheaper one, which worked fine. It took a while to get used to the heavy controls and massive steering wheel, but she was an extremely restful car and could cover long distances without effort.

The problem with new cars is that there isn't scope for tinkering. Once you've read the handbook and inwardly digested the content (something, incidentally, I never do), that's about it. So it wasn't long before I was hankering for the opportunity to get

The now classic SL 350 complete with removable hardtop. These are really beautiful cars and today make wonderful classics.

This is the end result I was after with the proposed rebuild of the TR4As. It never happened.

my hands dirty again. A chap offered me two TR4As for restoration at £1200 for the pair, and I took up the challenge. I rented a lock-up garage not far from home and started planning the project, which was doomed from the start. The plan was to make up one out of two, which sounded plausible in theory but turned out to be hopelessly unrealistic in practice. Both cars were in an advanced stage of decay. One of them was still taxed and on the road, while the other was an overt basket case. In the course of dismantling, it became clear that the road-going car was actually the worst. The weakness of the "one out of two" notion is that, given the same type of wear and tear and the same basic

design, the two are always likely to suffer from similar problems. The chassis of the road-going car was found to be beyond economic repair and the other one was almost as bad. Being right-handed examples, the worst corrosion on both was on the right, where over the years the road grime thrown up by oncoming vehicles had wreaked corrosive havoc.

The outer panels were mostly beyond hope, and the inners were also in a terrible state. One of the problems of restoring old cars that have been used as regular transport, usually on a shoestring budget, is that over the years they are likely to have been repeatedly bodged. Once the plastic filler and crude patches have been removed, there is often very little left to work on. So it was with my two TRs. Matters were not improved by the fact that my lock-up garage was of the pre-cast concrete variety and suffered from horrendous damp and condensation. Within weeks everything that wasn't already rusty when it went in was covered in the stuff; even the aluminium started to corrode. I learned a lot from the process, however. Looking back on it, I think I made a wise decision to abandon the restoration and sell off the bits for spares. I hung on to the new inner body panels I had purchased but got rid of everything else. This was before the "classic" movement really got underway and virtually everything, however ratty, was in demand. People still wanted cheap bits to keep the cars going. I more or less got my money back, and certainly whetted my appetite for getting into a proper restoration project.

I paid £1400 for a TR5 in shabby, but what appeared to be restorable, condition. The engine was on its last legs and the gearbox didn't have overdrive, but mechanical reconditioning and upgrade is always the easy bit. As usual, after purchase and detailed inspection, the body proved to be in worse condition than I had realised. The outer wings were repairable, but as replacements were available I went for that option.

This led to a big row with a supplier and one very disgruntled customer. I made an inventory of the bits I wanted and went down to a well known TR specialist to discuss my requirements.

He absolutely assured me that the outer panels he supplied had been made on the original presses and that all would be well. When it came to fitting them, however, they were nowhere near the right shape and size. In some cases the curves were all wrong, so there was no way they would ever have matched up with the general bodyline of the vehicle. I was as cross as hell and took them back from whence they came. Did I get an apology? Did I, hell! Instead, I was subjected to a tirade by the trader, who accused me of the basest ingratitude. The gist of his argument was that he, poor lamb, had slaved away to make it possible for me to keep my TR on the road and all I did was complain because the goods weren't up to scratch. The fact that he was in business, taking my hard-earned cash in exchange for his tatty produce, hadn't, it seemed, occurred to him. It wouldn't have been so bad if each panel had borne a large, red label stating, "Warning! Don't expect these items even remotely to fit." Needless to say, not a single such word had been mentioned during the sales process. He gave me my money back, however, and when I left he was still muttering about how unreasonable some people could be. Anyway, another valuable lesson learned: always repair rather than replace panels if it is at all possible. On later projects I have gone to enormous lengths to reclaim rusty and damaged bits of bodywork, and have always been rewarded for my trouble.

I did a lot of work on the TR and found secure, dry storage before I went off for what was billed as a short visit to America. It was at this time that I left Shirley and set up home with my beloved Kathleen. It was particularly harrowing, because by then my third, delightful little daughter, Siobhan, had arrived. I'm not proud of what happened and there is no doubt that I caused a lot of unhappiness. It was entirely my own fault and Shirley behaved with great dignity and generosity throughout this difficult period. There is nothing to be said in my defence except that Kathleen and I have been together ever since. This all happened the better part of 20 years ago, so there may be hope for us yet.

CHAPTER 10

America

We started doing business in America in 1980 and it became increasingly obvious that sooner or later we would have to establish a local presence. The city we selected was Houston in Texas. Today, this may seem a curious choice, but at the time we had among our clients seven of the world's top ten oil companies and most were headquartered there. In the early '80s, with oil prices high and forecast to go higher, it was the fastest growing city in the US.

In 1982 the man we had stationed in Houston went on an adventure holiday to Haiti and came back with an ugly case of Blackwater Fever. Hospitalised for nearly six months, he left our Houston operation somewhat rudderless. As things had been going fairly well up until then and we saw the US as a crucial market, Kathleen and I were shipped out to hold the fort. The plan was for us to stay for six months, or at least until the Blackwater man was back in harness. As it turned out we were there for nearly seven years, but that's a tale that will gradually unfold. The Mercedes was mothballed and the TR restoration project put away to await our return.

We took a year's lease on a condominium near the office, sight unseen (actually it was recommended by someone we had learned to trust). On a Wednesday evening in November, the day before Thanksgiving, we arrived at Houston Intercontinental, hired a car and drove with some trepidation to our condo. When

Kathleen with my daughters Joanne and Sarah in Houston for a visit. The Condo complex and Kathleen's Mazda RX7 are in the background.

we finally tracked it down we were as pleased as punch. It was very comfortable, nicely appointed and very American. We loved it. We hadn't a clue that Thanksgiving was such a major American holiday (even bigger than Christmas) and that everything would be shut (except the restaurants). We woke up next morning to appalling weather and spent the entire day in our California, king-sized bed, mesmerised by forty-channel cable TV. In the evening we went to a huge, barn-like restaurant and ate incredible seafood at bargain prices. It was a nice way to begin our American adventure, and right from the start we loved the place and the people.

After 30 days of hire cars, we took driving tests, which included a written section, and got our Texas driving permits. A car is a total necessity in Houston, which has little public transport worth mentioning and in many places no sidewalks. Of course it meant we needed a car each and so, with economy in mind, we started looking at the second-hand market. Kathleen, who had passed her test in England just weeks before leaving, was much taken with the Mazda RX7. Although she had qualified on a manual, she had immediately graduated to driving the Mercedes with its auto box, so in unfamiliar territory she felt more comfortable with an automatic. We found her a 1979 model RX7 with less than 20,000 miles on the clock. It was the first Japanese car I had experienced and I was impressed. Apart from having a prodigious thirst, the rotary engine was a marvellous thing. The more it revved, the smoother and quieter it became. I thoroughly enjoyed driving it and it is still one of Kathleen's all-time favourites.

I remember an occasion when some friends invited us to dinner soon after we arrived in America. They lived to the east of Houston near Beaumont, not far from the Louisiana border. They gave us detailed but, as it turned out, totally inaccurate instructions on how to get there. We set out in the Mazda and drove about 100 miles before we were roughly in the right area. There was virtually no traffic and the only dwellings were sparsely located trailer homes. All around was swamp, and you could almost sense the alligators in the undergrowth. There was no moon, but an amazing sky full of stars; we got completely and hopelessly lost. There was no one to ask. Occasionally, as we drove by a darkened trailer, a hound dog would start howling disconcertingly. At one point we stopped the car and sat looking out at the bleak terrain. As we gazed into the night a huge shooting star suddenly blazed across the sky and seemed to fall into the bog somewhere in the middle distance. It was like one of those '50s sci-fi movies where the courting couple park in the woods and see what looks like a flaming meteor, but is really an alien space ship, fall into the swamp. It only takes the space monsters a few minutes to nip out, cover the couple with green slime and have them for tea. A little unnerved, we quickly started the car and moved off.

After a while we began to worry about ever getting out of the area again, let alone finding our friends. The first vehicle we had seen in an hour came past heading in the opposite direction, so I quickly turned us round and followed him in the hope that he was actually going somewhere. Perhaps he would lead us back to civilisation. After about five miles he turned into the drive of a big trailer home and we followed him in. People told us afterwards that it was a dangerous thing to have done. "Coulda git ya darn fool heads blowed off," they said. Well, they didn't say it exactly that way, but that was certainly the gist.

The chap in the pick-up got out very cautiously and so did I. Once I'd explained our predicament in my best English accent he was as nice and helpful as anything. With the prospect of gunplay out of the way, his little son came out to take a look at us, still very suspicious.

The little fellow listened for a while, then piped up. "Where yous-awl from?" he asked.

"We're from England," we told him. He thought for a while, trying to place us on his mental map.

"Hell, that's outa state, aint it?" he finally responded.

They turned out to be a nice American family who called our friends for us, explained why we were two hours late and set us on the right road. We found our way after that, had dinner and drove the 120 miles home. That's Texas for you.

Foolishly, still craving a British classic, I came upon an advertisement in the *Houston Chronicle* for a TR8 convertible. These cars were made in very small numbers and, apart from a handful of right-hand drive models that escaped onto the UK market, nearly all went to the US. The car was actually in stock at the local British Leyland dealership and was in appalling condition, considering it was only two years old. The previous owner had illegally removed all the emission control equipment so, technically, the dealer should not have being selling it at all.

Kathleen making the TR8 look positively desirable. Note the aftermarket Minilite wheels.

The car had 37,000 miles on the clock. When I gave it its first road test it was running on about six of the available eight cylinders. The dealer was covered in confusion and promised to get it tuned and running properly before I tried again. I went back a week later and this time it was running on no more than five. I suppose he wanted shot of it and, being a fool, I was keen to get my hands on this rarest of TRs. From the moment I bought the damned car it never ran properly, although I did everything that a devoted and caring owner could do including shipping it back to the UK for a complete rebuild. It was pig when I got it and a pig when I eventually sold it.

The TR8 was the final incarnation of the once proud TR series. After the debacle of the TR7 (which no one really believed was a TR at all) with it's unimpressive four-cylinder engine that couldn't even come close to the TR6 it replaced (at least not the European version of the 6), the TR8 looked promising. Leyland first offered the car in the US but, by the time they got around to thinking UK, the whole TR tradition had come to an end forever. For some reason, it seemed that Leyland had the notion that performance was not important in the American market. I find it hard to comprehend the thinking that prevailed during the product planning process.

"Let's build a V8 version of the TR7," someone must have said. Perhaps they had in mind the very successful TR7 V8 coupé which had been campaigned in international rallies on Leyland's behalf and looked as if it might be a world-beater.

"We'll sell it like hot cakes in America," some switched on-marketing man will have observed.

"Great idea," a top manager must have confirmed.

Who then, for goodness sake, came up with the notion of equipping it with the lowest performance Range Rover engine they had available? From an engine that has been known reliably to develop 200-plus horsepower (Leyland's own Rover Vitesse produced 185 bhp), why, oh why, were we given an anaemic 130 bhp version? If, in 1980, 130 horsepower from 3.5 litres, emission control notwithstanding, was the best Leyland could manage, then they deserved all they got.

Anyway, build quality must have been at an all-time low, because everything that could fall off, apart, asunder and into disrepair, did so on my TR8. The electrics were the worst I have ever known, with inexplicable failures that would mysteriously correct themselves the moment you set about serious investigation and then malignantly reappear in the fast lane of the freeway. It was a nightmare, but I persevered for all of seven years until I finally threw in the towel and sold the pile of junk. I suspect I will offend a lot of people, but I have to say it really was a bloody awful car.

Our initial selection of vehicles proved a problem, because we both ended up with what were essentially two-seaters. When the children came out for visits we resorted to hiring family saloons. Of course I wasn't going to give up my TR, so Kathleen traded in the RX7 for a Mustang convertible. Not Lee Iacocca's legendary creation, but a new, 1984, 3.6-litre convertible. It had only one

Not the best shot of the Mustang but it provides a general impression

crucial virtue, which was that Kathleen really liked it. I suppose it was pretty but it had some weaknesses: little things like handling, road holding and ride quality. In the wet it was the nearest thing to committing suicide (and I suppose murder if you carried passengers) that I have experienced.

On one occasion, Kathleen was driving down one of the main roads in Houston in a torrential downpour. At the time, my parents were on a visit and were with her in the car. She was a fairly new driver and her version of the tale (it's the only one we have) is that she braked for some traffic lights and the car did a perfect 360º, coming to rest correctly positioned in the outside lane with the front wheels on the white line. Now Kathleen is not given to unladylike language, but on this occasion a single expletive escaped from what must have been a store held deep in her subconscious. "F**k," was all she said as they came to rest at the red light. We will never know which my parents found more shocking, the balletic pirouette or the foul language.

The white Mustang, with its powder-blue interior, was a nothing sort of car, with not much power and feather-light steering; a single sneeze at the wrong moment could have you careering across several lanes of traffic. To be fair, we had the car for about three years and it gave no trouble at all. On one occasion we came out of a shopping mall and couldn't find it. Our initial thought, naturally enough, was that it had been stolen. There was however, another virtually identical Mustang parked very near to where we had left ours but it definitely wasn't our car because the licence tag (registration number) was completely different. The wheels were also different but it was a white convertible with a blue interior, so we took a closer look. It was then we noticed that the front and rear licence plates didn't match, and that the wheels looked different because the mock wire covers had been stolen. It was our car after all. We had to get new licence plates and ended up with some rather nice alloy wheels, so it wasn't all bad.

For business reasons, while negotiating a big contract it

became necessary to help a client out by taking over the lease on his Mercedes 380 SE. I didn't need such a car at the time but, as they say, business is business. I was already a Mercedes fan and the big limousine confirmed my opinion of Stuttgart's finest. From a style point of view she was a bit of a bus, but from a driving and engineering standpoint she was a masterpiece. Solid wasn't the word. If you had got fed-up with driving to work, you could have mounted a gun and retaken France. When it became time to give her back, I was heart-broken.

After two years in Houston, it began to look as though we were in for a somewhat longer haul than initially planned, so we began to consider moving from the condo into something with a few more amenities. I have to admit that our good friends Bill and Jenny provided the initial impetus. We met them first when Jenny was a neighbour in our condominium complex and it wasn't long before Bill, at the end of a messy divorce, moved in with her. Bill was a wild extrovert who didn't know the meaning of self-consciousness. He would get up to incredible antics and we had some great times with them, they were a very fun couple. The story of the acquisition of their new home demonstrates many facets of life in America.

Mercedes 380 SE, not the most stylish carriage but a lovely piece of automotive engineering.

When the Houston boom began to slow down, speculative builders found themselves with property on their hands, and devised all manner of means to unload it. Jenny had owned her

flat for a number of years and had built up a small equity. At the time it was worth about $70,000. Bill had just started a new business and, true to character, was wildly optimistic about his prospects. They went to a seminar organised by the builder of a very smart town house complex and were sold a dream. By Houston standards, the new properties (there were six in an enclosed courtyard) weren't cheap at $350,000 each, but the builder was able to sweeten the deal. First, he offered to buy Jenny's condo for 95% of its market value. Second, he assisted with a 100% mortgage on the new property, (as Bill worked for himself, I assume he wrote what he liked on the application form and no one looked at it too closely). Third, the couple were allowed to make their own selection of décor, curtains and carpets (they selected some very nice stuff). Fourth, the builder handled all the legal fees and the removal costs. Fifth, the terms were $1 down (no, that's not a typo) and no more to pay for two years. Sixth, because the mortgage was 100%, the builder gave the couple the equity value of Jenny's condo in cash. It came to about $25,000.

When they first explained the deal I, with my British caution, detected a number of potential hazards and pitfalls. Not the least of them was that, although there was nothing to pay for the next two years, the interest was still accruing and the debt, at some 12% per annum compound, was growing rather alarmingly. (This happened before Texas brought in a law banning negative equity plans.) Bill brushed away my objections and assured me of his confidence in the future. It was the perfect deal, he told me. It would give his fledgling business an opportunity for growth and, based on his two-year projections, the financial burden would be no more than a breeze. We attended their house-warming and it was indeed a wonderful place. With the equity cash, they made a substantial down payment on a new S class Mercedes. In one easy leap, with virtually no income, Bill and Jenny had made the transition from modest condo and slightly battered old Audi to luxury town house and a new Mercedes. The total outlay was $1.

What a country!

A few months later, we moved as well, to more modest quarters than those of Jenny and Bill, I hasten to add. We were delighted with our purchase of 6007 Previn Court (aren't those big numbers amazing?) in a leafy north-west suburb of the city. We began to live the real American life with a pool, a jacuzzi, and neighbourhood barbecues.

The Corniche at Previn

When it became obvious that we weren't going home for a while, I decided that keeping the SL in storage in England wasn't a very sensible course of action. On one of our trips to the UK, a dealer with a convertible Rolls Royce Corniche offered me a trade. Although it was a right-hand drive car, the idea of swanning around America in a fancy Britmobile seemed like fun. So we did a deal and had the Rolls shipped directly to the Port of Houston. I have to admit that owning the car was not a success, although we had all of the federalisation work done at some expense. For one reason or another it was rarely used and, given my time again, I wouldn't have bothered taking it over, but hindsight is 20-20, as they say. One of the things that the Rolls demonstrated, however, was the big difference between US and UK attitudes in some areas of life. Battered old Chevrolets would pull up beside us on the freeway and gangs of rough-looking men would enthusiastically gives us the thumbs-up. If I had a dollar for every time I heard "Love your car," from an ordinary working person in America, I'd be doing OK. Sadly, this contrasts badly with my experiences of

We did a wedding for a good friend.

owning a similar vehicle in England.

We never had to pay valet parking fees when we went to brunch or dinner at the swankier establishments. It never went to the lot, but was always left right outside the entrance. The problem was that we weren't the kind of people who enjoyed the attention and we began to hate the circus aspect of owning a Rolls. We started to use it less and less and, in the end, it spent nearly all its time in the garage. On balance, we were a lot happier using the Mercedes. When we were due to leave we found it difficult to sell however, and ended up shipping it back with us to the UK.

Our Mercedes 380 saloon was replaced by a Jaguar, but I've rather leapt on with the tale of our everyday cars at the expense of the classics so I'll back up a little.

The classic revolution started one day when Kathleen and I were returning from a rather splendid brunch, (how I miss some things about America). We were cruising our way home when we spotted a sign for a British swapmeet. Loosely translated, it meant that there was a gathering of British classics and a sale of old car parts. As we had nothing better to do, we followed the signs and dropped in on the fun. It was a local and informal affair but there, in all their splendour, were a pair of glorious E-type Jaguars. It may be remembered that ten years earlier I had owned an E-type of unusual hue and suspect coachwork, and I decided then and

*The XK 120 in primer chez
Mr South America*

there that I would like another. Kathleen was, as usual, very supportive and so the search began.

The cars I turned up were either too tatty or too expensive and so it went for a couple of months, until one day I saw an XK120 advertised in the antique cars section of the *Houston Chronicle*. Not the E-type we craved, but nonetheless desirable and a blast from the past. It was owned by a flamboyant South American who had obtained the car with the objective of restoring it to its former glory. Unfortunately (for him at least), he had made a bit of a mess of things and the car was now for sale. He had bought the XK in primer as a partial restoration project and, rather than leaving repainting to professionals, he had insisted on preparing and priming the bodywork himself. I suppose, when he stood back and looked at his handiwork finished in matt undercoat, it hadn't looked too bad. Sadly, when the car was finally painted, the woeful lack of proper preparation resulted in a pretty awful finish. He'd put a lot of time and effort into the work and the out-turn knocked the stuffing out of him. When we met, he had lost his enthusiasm and

*The XK 120, painted and
looking a little more
respectable*

wanted no more of the car. As soon as I saw it, however, memories of my earlier XKs flooded back and I just had to try and re-live my youth.

I didn't say a word to Kathleen, but bought the car for $6000 (about £4000). It sounds cheap by today's standards but in 1985 it wasn't such a bargain and it wasn't such a nice car. Its saving grace was a rust-free body, but everything else was a disaster. The original interior had rotted a long time before and a monstrous plastic approximation had been substituted. The chromed steel bumpers had been replaced with strange aluminium replicas and even the grill was a cast aluminium copy of one from an XK 140. Although I didn't know it at the time, it was completely worn out mechanically. Since acquisition I have replaced the engine, the gearbox, the back axle and the suspension, as well the entire braking system and the complete steering assembly. I guess that's about as comprehensive as you can get.

My first mistake was not bringing it home and living with the car for a few months, so that I could evaluate everything before having any work done. In my eagerness to present the acquisition to Kathleen in the best possible light, I had it shipped directly from the seller to a paint shop for a respray. The end result was hardly any better than it had started out, and I was so disappointed that I had it done again. On this occasion something went wrong with the paint and it had to be done a third time. It still had its awful interior and mock chromeware, but I was moderately proud of it. I was persuaded to show the car at the annual Jaguar Club of Houston show. They had on display a lot of truly stunning examples that showed up my car for the terrible mess it was and for a while I was as depressed as hell. (I knew how my South American friend must have felt.) But the experience motivated me and, better informed, I set to work on improving my XK. I'm still working on it and one day she will be a beauty.

We found our E-type by the merest chance during a business visit to Dallas. After dinner at our hotel one evening, I happened

The XKE at the 1986 Jaguar Club of Houston Show

to glance through a copy of the local Dallas rag and, lo and behold, there in the old car section was a small ad for a Series 2 E-type. Kathleen was with me at the time and, having nothing better to do, we went to see the car. It turned out to be nicer than expected, with what seemed like a very solid body, a re-trimmed interior and a nice new paint job. It had good oil pressure and drove extremely well. The chap selling it told a convincing story about restoring it for his own use and then being forced to sell in order to finance a business venture. I paid a deposit and we returned a week later to drive our acquisition the 240 or so miles back to Houston.

Before I drove it off, being a careful soul, I popped the bonnet to check the oil and water. I don't know what prompted me but, for some reason, I also checked the front engine mounting bolts (an odd thing to do). They were finger loose. A socket was produced and the previous owner, after a few turns, declared that all was well. However, now suspicious, I checked for myself and found that they were still loose. Investigation revealed that they were totally the wrong thread and size and I was able to lift them out. Not a good way to start a long journey in a strange car.

We spent an hour or so touring the local DIY motor parts stores trying to find the right bolts, but without success. When we got back, the chap suddenly remembered that he had some of the correct size in his shed at the end of his garden and, asking me to

wait, he went off to retrieve them. Again, I'm not sure why, but I
decided to follow him through his house to the end of the garden
where he did indeed have a shed. It was a big shed however, big
enough for six cars and by a surprising coincidence it was filled
with E-types. It turned out, of course, that he was a dealer in the
business of buying E-types, giving them a cosmetic once-over and
then selling them on while posing as an enthusiast.

One very cross and stupid buyer, and an exposed and
embarrassed dealer, whipped the bolts out of another E-type,
fitted them in my car and I was on my way. The journey was
thankfully uneventful and the car behaved beautifully. After this
somewhat inauspicious start, my yellow roadster proved to be an
excellent all-round car and we spent several happy years together.
I gave it no more than a thorough clean-up and took it along to
the Houston Jaguar car show the following year, where it won
second place in the "driven" class concours. In the meantime I had
also slaved over my '120, and I was delighted when that too won
second in class in the same category.

At about this time, we attended a classic car show back in
England and met a man whose company specialised in converting
TR7s into V8-engined TR8s. We struck a deal on the restoration
of my Triumph and, when we got back to Houston, I had the TR8
shipped to the UK. It was to be quite a time before I saw it again.

We now had two old Jaguars, which should have been
enough for any reasonable person, but we've already established

*The XK 150 undergoing
serious restoration*

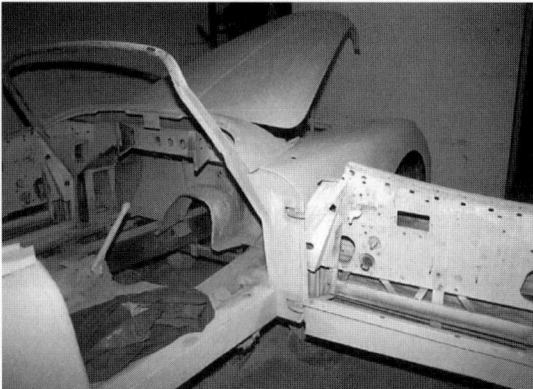

that I'm not one of those. An acquaintance I knew through the Jaguar Club called me one day to say that he had been asked by a customer to dispose of an XK150. The car turned out to be a mixed bag: a quite rare 3.4 "S" roadster with an officially quoted 250 horsepower output (but don't believe a word of it: it was just Jaguar publicity hype of the '50s). The body was as original and near perfect as one could hope to find. Apart from some corrosion in a headlight nacelle, there wasn't a trace of rust anywhere. Surprisingly, even the big steel doors were in excellent condition apart from worn-out hinge pins. The engine had been recently rebuilt but didn't show the kind of oil pressure one would expect. The paint was dull and faded and the interior was the usual plastic disaster area. The brakes, also reputed to have been rebuilt, weren't up to scratch either. It stood on rusty chrome wires with a different type of tyre at each corner. Most of the body chrome was in poor shape, and the rear bumper had a dent. All in all not a very prepossessing package, but a real '150 S roadster nonetheless. I think in dealer terminology it would have been described as a basically sound car with lots of potential.

The owner was a pleasant Texan who had owned the XK for thirteen years. Following a recent remarriage, he had been persuaded by his bride to fall out of love with it, principally, I believe because she needed the garage space for the new boat she was intending he would buy them. We settled on $11,000 (£7,500) and he kindly agreed to deliver the car to my home. He and his wife, after quite a longish trawl through the city, parked the car on our drive and we all went off to dinner together. There he regaled us with stories of the '150 and its past glories. He was clearly quite upset to see her go. When we got back it was too late to deal with the car that evening, so I left her where she was for the night. She must have decided she didn't like me and planned her revenge, because she never went under her own steam again for several months.

The next day, when I tried to start her, I discovered that the clutch had stuck to the flywheel. I did everything thing I could think of to free it off, but nothing worked. I was faced with the prospect of having to remove the engine and gearbox. In desperation I towed her to a slight incline and started her in second gear. It was an odd feeling, bowling along without the option of disengaging the engine. I stamped up and down on the throttle but to no avail, she still wouldn't free up. I took my life in my hands, pressed in the clutch and accelerated hard; with a mighty bang, the clutch plate came away from the flywheel. Relieved, I parked her back on the drive and went to make space for her in storage. (With a couple of old cars to house, I had rented a big lock-up garage, which at the time was dirt-cheap.) A day later I pressed the starter button and . . . nothing. I checked every electrical connection a dozen times but could find no fault, but, when I finally got to it, the starter appeared to be defective. Once that was removed the trouble was clear: the brushes had worn to nothing. As there also seemed to be a weakness in one of the fields, I had the unit rebuilt. With the starter now bright and shiny and back in place, I was confident of success, but it was not to be. She started, coughed and then died. (I began to get superstitious about XK 150s and me, remembering my luck with the first pair.) Two SU petrol pump rebuild kits later (the S variant has dual fuel pumps), she was running, but only just. Three SU carburettor rebuild kits, a coil and a set of points later and she finally spluttered into life. I suppose I showed so much determination and good faith that she forgave me the change of ownership and learned to love me instead. I stuck her away into storage to await refurbishment.

It's a funny thing, but on the occasions I have lent that car to a close friend he had persistent problems. First with a petrol pump and the second time with carburation. The moment he returned the car it behaved perfectly and I couldn't reproduce the faults. Nonsense I'm sure, but it makes you think?

The story about Bill and Jenny came to a rather odd conclusion. Unfortunately, their business venture didn't go as well as expected and, when the two years were up, Bill found himself with a big overdraft and a sizeable debt on the property. Houston's economic crash was in full swing and the their house was probably worth about half the value of the mortgage. In deep trouble, he wrote to the mortgage company hoping to arrange a stay of foreclosure, and discovered an interesting twist. The six townhouses within their courtyard setting had been numbered from "A" through "F" and Bill and Jenny lived in "B". When the mortgage firm replied they mentioned, almost in passing, that Bill had quoted the wrong house letter. They pointed out that their records showed he was the owner of house "D" and not "B" as he had claimed. It's worth backtracking a little to explain that, some time after the couple had moved in, the builder had gone belly-up and house "D" had never been completed. As far as Bill was concerned the mortgagor's claim was arrant rubbish; he had purchased and had always lived in house "B". As negotiations unfolded, however, the mortgagor produced irrefutable documentary evidence, much of it signed by Bill himself, showing beyond doubt that he was in fact the legal owner of house "D" and definitely not the house the couple had occupied for the last two years. It was an amazing oversight, and no one had spotted it.

We had dinner with them a few days after they received momentous news from their own lawyers confirming the mortgagor's assertion. In effect, Bill owed some $450,000 on an empty shell. His only recourse, they told him, was to sue the builder. But as the firm had already been declared insolvent and was long gone, there didn't seem much scope for relief in that direction. Bill said a lot of strange things that night but we were too dim to realise that they were giving us oblique hints about their future plans. Jenny was tearful when we parted and there was little we could say; for all their misplaced optimism and imprudence, it seemed a harsh outcome. We never saw them again. We were subsequently told that two nights later they had secretly packed up and moved to California to restart their lives. I like to think it went well for them there and that they are now prosperous and happy.

The New XJ6 sitting on the drive at Previn

By the time we handed the Mercedes 380 back to the leasing company, I owned three old Jaguars and was something of an aficionado so, when the factory announced the new XJ6 (XJ40) range, I decided to take the plunge. Delivery, I was assured, was at least six months away, but within three I got a call from the dealership informing me that our car had arrived. Kathleen and I went downtown with great excitement. But the car presented to us by the salesman was nowhere near the spec we had ordered. He checked his paperwork, apologised and then set off with us on a trek around the extensive premises looking for our car. He kept muttering, "It must be here somewhere." We finally gave up and he admitted that it have been a dreadful mistake. On our way down through the building, I spotted an Old English White XJ6 that was having Daytona chrome wire wheels fitted. And that's the one we had. It was nothing like the colour scheme we had ordered but it looked great, and the leather inside smelled even better. (Why is it that only British-made leather interiors smell so good?) We got a big discount on the wheels and we were all happy. Kathleen disposed of her Mustang and virtually took over the new Jaguar.

One of our close neighbours, Ron Oglesbee, became a particular pal. Ron was an old car buff like me and an incorrigible Anglophile, even down to owning a delightful Mulliner bodied 25/30 Rolls Royce. He actually bought the car in England when he and his wife came over on business. He was determined to find the car of his dreams and spent a long time looking without success. He was eventually introduced to a man who had started collecting old Rolls Royces before the war and had amassed over 100. Ron was very specific about his requirements. It had to be a 25/30 with Mulliner coachwork, Marchal headlights and twin side mounts. The man had the very car. It had 37,000 miles on the clock and even the paintwork was original. Ron bought it on the spot and had it serviced by a specialist in readiness for shipping. The couple finished their business early and had time for a tour around Britain, so they took the Rolls, which ran perfectly all the way. The itinerary included Scotland and Wales. I learned recently that dear Ron had passed away. If there is a heaven I'm sure Ron's is filled with old British cars that he drives with relish on long and

Ron Oglesbee's amazingly original 25/30 Rolls

winding roads. Some day, maybe I'll join him.

In all we spent six very happy years in Houston, with a seventh year spent flitting between the UK and the US. At one point our schedule was an alternating three weeks in each location. Towards the end of our time in Houston we purchased our home in Kent. By American standards it's an old house (built in 1593). When we showed Ron the estate agent's details he went into raptures, he just loved all those old oak beams. He persuaded us to loan him the very pictorial brochure so that he could show it to a friend who lived in Conroe, a little Texas town 40 miles outside the city.

Ron showed his pal the pictures of our proposed new home and was surprised by the reaction. The friend insisted it was a joke. He took a bemused Ron into his dining room and there on the wall was an oil painting of the very same house. Now there is nothing particularly unique about our property, it must be one of tens of thousands of surviving Elizabethan or Jacobean country homes in England but there, on the wall of a house in a backwoods Texas town, was a painting of the very house we planned to buy. Now that's coincidence for you.

The painting on the wall in Conroe

This was the contemporary styled house we bought in north-west Houston. Kathleen's Mustang can be seen tucked away at the side.

The truth of it turned out to be quite prosaic. Pat and Janna, the Conroe couple, had been stationed in England by Pat's former employer some years before. They had decided to spend their last year out of London and took a house near Tunbridge Wells. One day while driving through the country lanes Janna's car conked out in front of the house (so there is a car connection after all). Janna got assistance from the owner and they became firm friends. Taken by the old-world charm of the house, Janna commissioned the picture that now hangs on her dining room wall. Funny old world isn't it?

Some months before we quit America, I had taken the E-type into a workshop for a new clutch. While the car was on the ramp I was able to get a good look underneath and discovered a few nasty rust spots in the floors. Not certain whether repair or renewal was the right course of action, I stripped out the interior for a better look and found things were a lot worse than expected. At the time I decided to go the whole hog and renew the floors and the inner as well as the outer sills.

I gave the car to a body man who came highly recommended, and we agreed that three months would be a reasonable time for getting the car back on the road. Unfortunately, it was to be the last I saw of my car for quite a while. One night the body shop, and with it my car, disappeared. No one I spoke to in the area had a clue about its new location, or even if the business had started up again. By that time we had moved back to the UK but during my return visits to Houston I spent a lot of time searching for the E-type, and perseverance paid dividends, I did eventually find it in its new location some six months later. Naturally I was as mad as hell when I went there, but the painter just greeted me as though nothing had happened. Apparently, he'd been just about to call me, and I believed him. He was a bit dilly but he wasn't a crook. Of course it was nowhere near finished, so I collected up the bits, shoved them in a container and shipped it all back to England.

The Jaguar S2 E-type and the Triumph TR8 on the drive at Previn. We created a little enclave of old British iron. It was nice to fly the flag in America.

We finally came home in 1988 and by then the prices of classic cars had begun to rise sharply. Just before we left, I was offered a dazzling canary yellow XK 140 roadster. The man selling it was a well known lawyer (I say no more). He told me that he had overseen the entire project personally and that the restoration had been meticulous. It certainly looked in almost concours condition; with a black interior and wire wheels, it was near perfection. I paid a fortune for it and was comprehensively and totally taken to the cleaners. There wasn't a single panel that didn't, in due course, have to be repaired or renewed. It was an unmitigated disaster, but I'll leave that painful tale for the next chapter.

Together with the contents of the house, we put all our cars in boxes and shipped them home to England. It was a sad day when finally we said goodbye to the country that had greeted us so warmly and had treated us so well. There are still times when,

Life could be pleasant in Texas, although the weather in Houston was pretty awful a lot of the time. But everything was air-conditioned, so it didn't matter. The pool temperature reached 90° Fahrenheit in the summer. The house was decidedly strange, with weird angles and an atrium garden in the living room, but we loved it.

filled with nostalgia, Kathleen and I become maudlin about those happy days spent in that vibrant country.

CHAPTER 11

Home Again

More than a year before we were scheduled to come back to England, we started thinking about housing. Although we had kept our small home in Beckenham, we had by now collected a slew of possessions and needed somewhere a little larger to stow ourselves and our gear. Kathleen began a series of house hunting expeditions, usually on her own, while I beavered away in the US.

She saw all sorts of properties many of which, had we bought one, would have made us rich on resale many years later. One of the criteria was garaging for a bunch of old autos, and Kathleen saw some amazing properties. One in particular, situated in a Kensington mews, offered extensive space for about ten cars, most of it underground. The only drawback was the fact that in order to get any motors out to the light of day, one had to move the drawing room furniture, haul back the carpet and bring the chosen vehicle up in a marvellous old lift. The car would then have to be driven through the very ornate windows that had been constructed in place of what originally would have been huge garage doors. She saw more than 50 houses of various types and it became clear that, given the finances we had available, we could acquire either a London abode with lots of car storage, or one that was nice to live in, but not both. Kathleen not surprisingly, was heavily inclined to the latter.

When we finally arrived back in the UK, I found myself with a gaggle of old cars. The partially restored TR that I had left tucked away was still in hiding and there was the TR8 that had now been comprehensively restored. The Rolls was also back home, as were the XKs. Last, but not to be forgotten, was the E-type. Most of my friends and relations had me down as a lunatic and there were times when even I doubted my sanity. A positive aspect (apart from the fact that I had a collection of moderately desirable tin) was that it was 1988 and prices were rising sharply, so I could at least claim some investment prescience. (All nonsense, of course, as I have never bought cars with an eye to investment.)

I'll come clean at this point and admit that while in the US I did make the odd foraging raid over to the UK and had, in the course of events, added a couple more bangers to the list.

By late '87, the idea of putting together a small collection of Jaguar sports cars had sort of established itself. I was well enough served in the XK area but had only one E-type. As there were at least five series and three body styles, the permutations could have led to financial ruin, so I settled for the notion of being satisfied with one each of the six and twelve-cylinder cars.

I was still in investigation mode one weekend, when Kathleen and I visited Stratford on Avon on a corporate jolly. With the intention of idling away the time between tea and dinner, I bought a copy of a classic car magazine. In it I found an advertisement for a V12 roadster. The car was standard in all respects apart from a special exhaust and a Forward Engineering Weber carburettor conversion. With time on my hands, I called the number and the description of the car sounded interesting. I told the owner I was away for the weekend but promised to call again on my return to London. I chatted on for a bit and by chance mentioned we were in Stratford. It turned out that the car was in Moreton-in-Marsh, less than a dozen miles away. I persuaded Kathleen, much against her better judgement, that we had time to see the car and make it back before dinner. (She was right as usual and we were horribly late. As I was the principal speaker, this was particularly unfortunate.)

The car turned out to be one of the last 100 E-types made, with less than 40,000 miles on the clock. The man selling it was the second owner and he had had it for eleven years. The sight of the 5.3 litre V12 with its six, twin-choke Webers was awesome (a much misused word). With its straight-through exhaust, it sounded like a Spitfire in full flight, and I don't mean a Triumph. Its major faults were what appeared to be a little surface rust on the sills, a less than pristine interior and a very tatty hood. The owner had been in Iran for most of the eleven years he had owned the car and, now home with his Iranian wife and small child, he was finally coming to the conclusion that his pride and joy would have to make way for more family-oriented requirements. The fact that I was a fellow enthusiast created an immediate bond between us. We settled on a price and I gave him a cheque as deposit. He had accumulated a mass of spares and, because I had a big hire car with me he insisted that I load everything there and then.

I sent him the balance by wire transfer and two days later Kathleen and I went up by train to collect our new acquisition. We loaded up the last few remaining bits and pieces and, with Kathleen in the car beside me, we said our final goodbyes. He and

The V12 has a rather nice registration number - 492 D. It is not how the car started out, however, and was bought by the previous owner because he couldn't refit the original rear plate, with its seven-digit number, when the straight-through exhaust conversion left too little space. For years I couldn't bring myself to sully the bonnet with a stick-on plate, until MOT regulations forced me to.

Six, twin-choke Webers produce a neater result than the original quad Stromberg arrangement.

his very charming wife were standing arm in arm on their front step watching us leave. I started the engine and the wonderful twelve-cylinder wail filled the air. It was too much for his wife who suddenly turned to her husband and burst into floods of tears. Up to that moment he had managed to control his feelings but his wife's anguish and the loss of his cherished E-type overcame him and tears began to course down his cheeks. Kathleen, surprised and overcome by the show of emotion around her also started to weep. That seemed to be my cue; I gunned the motor and shot out of the drive. It was only moments before they were lost in the rear view mirror. The journey home was one of the most memorable drives I have had. With the top down we enjoyed the power and thrilled to the roar of that lovely engine.

I had the bodywork checked over very carefully as I was particularly concerned about the rust on the sills. Expecting the worst, I was delighted when informed that she was as sound as a bell. In the course of the next few months I retrimmed the interior and had a new hood fitted. Today she has less than 50,000 miles on the clock and is still on the original clutch. The clutch slave cylinder is the only part that has had to be replaced in 25 years, although I have fitted new shock absorbers and rear springs. She was first registered in January 1975 and was produced in the bad old British Leyland days when the Jaguar factory was referred to as Big Car Plant No. 2. On this car, however, the build quality has proved exemplary and there can be no doubt that she was put together with care and attention. The car is as tight and composed as when she left the factory. The controls are light (the steering is too light but a 14-inch Motalita wheel helps) and the synchromesh is perfect. 492 D is one of my most cherished possessions.

As it turned out, I was lucky to get her, because it seems I had managed to jump the queue by getting my hands on the magazine when I did. The previous owner later told me that after I'd paid my deposit and left he had had at least 20 other calls. Some people even offered more than he was asking if he would change his mind and renege on our deal, but he was an honourable man and stuck to our arrangement. Only a few months after my limited refurbishment the market went stark, staring mad and I was offered three times what I paid. I'm glad I didn't sell, even though now the market has cooled and the car is barely worth what I gave for it.

1987 was a momentous year. It was the time when we floated the company on the London Stock Market and, in celebration, I decided to treat myself to a vintage car. I would really have liked a Bentley but resources wouldn't stretch that far and, on a visit to a garage in Wandsworth, I saw a big green Lagonda that was priced a lot more reasonably, so I bought that instead. It was basically a nice car but we never got on together and I learned a lesson about acquiring cars without first doing my homework. I bought the Lagonda for all the wrong reasons, mainly because it looked nicely vintage, a sort of poor man's Bentley. I didn't drive the car before buying, and if I had things would have been different. I had the mistaken notion that just owning such a handsome car would be enough, but it wasn't.

It was a 3-litre with the T7 body normally associated with

The 3-litre waiting outside my parents' home in Beckenham en route *to the Bromley Car Show*

the more powerful Meadows engined 4½-litre M45s. Being a 1933 model, it wasn't actually a vintage car, but to all intents and purposes it was a '20s throwback. It was just the sort of vehicle that vintage enthusiasts love but I don't enjoy at all. Of course, I didn't discover that until I had owned it for a while, so I suppose there was a sort of inevitability about the whole thing. Don't get me wrong: I'm a great respecter of Lagondas, it's just that the ancient feel of much of their pre-war output doesn't appeal to me. (LG6s and V12s are altogether another matter.)

My car had lots of features that made it difficult to drive. There was a central accelerator pedal, a right-handed, crash gearbox with reverse gate, and muscle-ripping steering that brought out beads of sweat at low speeds. There was no idler assembly to mirror the action of the steering box, so guiding the vehicle was more about general aiming than precise direction. A lot of people do very well with this type of car and become highly skilled; I didn't. Every journey was a heart-in-the-mouth

I always feel guilty about the 3-litre Lagonda. I can't help but feel that if she had been an M45, I would have tried harder to get to grips with her. I hope she found a good home.

experience. The sad thing is that she was really a lovely old girl that deserved a better and more understanding owner. I hope she got one. I ended by selling her back to the dealer I bought her from after she had been standing around for too long.

As prices of everything, including property, began to rise, we started to panic and decided to buy a house we had seen in Hampstead. Having spent months searching for a home with significant car space we now settled on one with only a small, single garage. The cars, when they arrived from America, would have to go to storage. It was a formula for dissatisfaction and was coupled with what amounted to a protracted war with a firm of crooked builders, who went bust and disappeared as soon as we had secured a court judgement against them.

During these transition months we flitted between Houston and London until a new firm of pricey but competent artisans were appointed and a liveable home finally delivered. The right-hand drive Rolls was repatriated from the US, but London living didn't suit it so it was disposed of quite quickly. Another car over which I shed few tears. Some you love and some you don't.

The TR8, which had also been shipped home, was months behind schedule when I got a call to say that it was finally ready. I went up to Worcestershire to collect it and I was pleasantly surprised with what had been achieved, cosmetically at least. The customised interior had been retrimmed in attractive grey velour and certainly looked the part. The car was now right-hand drive, with a very quick power rack that needed fewer than two turns lock-to-lock and required considerable care. The paintwork, in the original metallic blue, looked excellent and the mock Minilites I had fitted in America had been retained and set the car off rather well. The engine had had the full treatment, with a reputed 200 horsepower on tap. It was now 3.9 litres with 10:1 compression pistons, a hairier cam and a four-barrel Holly carburettor. I couldn't wait to get behind the wheel.

It was a gigantic disappointment. For all the time and effort, not to mention money, that had gone into her, she still lacked the

The dreadful TR8

zip and sparkle that I expected. I know that the problem was specifically with my car and not the breed in general, because while I was at the workshop I road-tested a TR7 that had been fitted with a bog-standard 3.5 V8 from a cooking Rover. It went like a bomb and was altogether more responsive than my car. I was bitterly disappointed, but was sold the line that I needed to let the engine bed down before making a final judgement.

Another bone of contention was the gearbox which, unlike everything else, had seemed fine when the car went in for restoration. The bill, however, included a substantial charge for a transmission rebuild, which the proprietor assured me had been necessary. Disgruntled and generally fed up, I set off for home with the TR. On the M40 the plot unravelled. I can't be absolutely sure about my diagnosis but I'm fairly certain I know what happened. At about 90 mph the car suffered a complete electrical failure. Everything went dead; it was as though the battery and the alternator had been unplugged. The engine cut out of course, but the car was still in gear so the load in the gearbox was instantly shifted from being driven by the engine to being propelled by the rear wheels, effectively reversing the load forces. The rebuilt box that had just cost an arm and a leg, blew to bits. (I suspect someone had left out a spacer or two.) An hour's wait for the AA (I was actually a member of the US triple A at the time but the British organisation sportingly honoured the reciprocal arrangement), and I was unceremoniously hauled off the motorway.

The restoration firm, to give them their due, picked up the car and replaced everything without a quibble. It went back to them several times after that but they never did make it go worth a damn, so I finally gave up and sold it. No one can accuse me of not making an effort. My mistake was not realising that I was flogging a dead horse and cutting my losses sooner.

This seems to be building into a catalogue of woe, which isn't completely representative of the period because there are some positive stories, but I'll get the bad ones out of the way first.

Having retrieved my series 2 E-type from its incarceration in Houston, I finally received it on the back of a truck one miserable, rainy English day. I was too busy to deal with it at the time so I shoved it away in the garage and forgot about it for a year. Finally, re-motivated by a magazine article about someone else's shiny restoration, I restarted the process of getting the car back on the road. I began by sorting out the bits and pieces that needed refitting and started acquiring the necessary replacement parts. I spun this out for bit while I converted the car to right-hand drive. I did the work myself and found it an interesting and educational exercise.

When I finally came to fitting up the shell, however, I noticed that the paint appeared to have developed the automotive equivalent of ringworm. The entire body was covered with lines of little blisters under the paint. There was no point in putting the car back together in that state, so I contacted a friendly neighbourhood garage who said they could correct the problem relatively cheaply. (I've learned that low-cost options are rarely the cheapest.) While the job was with them they discovered that the welding done by our friend in Houston had been little more than a joke and, instead of fitting the new sills I had supplied, he had just used plastic filler over the old ones. So a programme of extensive re-welding and fitting new sills was carried out. When the car finally came home I was again too busy to get on with it so it stood around in the garage for another year until I was able to get started again.

Over rather a long period I worked in a somewhat desultory fashion, re-fitting some of the chrome and the trim as well as working on the electrics. It finally got to the point where quite a lot of work had been done and the project began to shape up quite nicely. Flushed with new enthusiasm, I rolled the car outside and set about cleaning off the accumulation of dirt and grime that had collected over the months. To my amazement and absolute horror I discovered that the "ringworm" had returned. Gloom and despondency descended and I shut up the stricken motor in the depths of its garage and stomped off to other projects. I had made every mistake in the book, wasted a lot of time and money and was left with a complete lemon. It was some time before I could even bring myself to think about the project again, but I finally decided to have one last shot at getting it right. I undid all the fitting up I had done and my old friend Brian Stevens (more of him anon) stripped off the old paint to reveal bare metal. We were pleasantly surprised to find that the bodywork was mercifully rot-free and with the exception of some poorly repaired accident damage was in good order. Brian etched, primed and painted the car in its original primrose cellulose. I also took the opportunity of replacing the old, damaged bonnet with a new one at a time when Jaguar were running a half-price sale. Fitted up, with sparkling new chrome and many of its original parts, the car was a nice balance between restored glitter and charming patina. Almost six years to the day I first tore out the interior to deal with a few rust problems, the car passed its MOT test and was back on the road.

Whenever I drove the E-type, she always behaved impeccably and, although I rarely used the car, I had somehow developed a special feeling for her. But everything changes and, as my garage began to fill with newer acquisitions and space was at a premium, I was approached by my good pal and rally co-driver John Lockyer, who inquired if I wanted to sell. And thus my dear old six cylinder

E has gone to a better home and John loves her more even than I ever did, so in a way it's a happy ending.

Once the Rolls had been sold I went looking for a replacement and, partly because of my classic Jaguar connections and partly because it was an outstandingly pretty car, I acquired a new XJS convertible. I owned it for almost four years and had no cause for complaint. It did everything we asked of it and, apart from a woefully inadequate turning circle, it was a good enough car. I can't quite put my finger on why I'm not more enthusiastic, but I suppose I was always disappointed that I was never able to

At the docks on the way to somewhere in the sun. Kathleen drove the XJS a lot and got on better with it than I did.

hustle the car along as I would have wished. She was big and automatic and that may have had something to do with it. I never really got the hang of her, certainly never achieved the feel of man and machine in harmony. On twisty country lanes, Golf GTIs could run rings around me. Kathleen enjoyed driving the car but also found manoeuvrability a problem. We had a number of continental holidays in her and, although the petrol bills made my eyes water, we had a jolly time. It was eventually passed on to a colleague at work who, unlike me, was thrilled with the car and, to the best of my knowledge, has it still.

Slightly out of sequence, but a happier tale (at least for me), was the affair of the DB1 Aston. I visited the Wandsworth showroom from where I had acquired my Lagonda and found, to

My DB1. At the time, one of the best examples in the country.

my amazement, two examples of a car I had never seen before. The official designation was Aston Martin Sports 2000 but the model has retrospectively become known as the DB1. It was the final fling of the old Aston Company before being taken over by David Brown. They only built 15 cars, and the one I bought was probably the best available at the time. The body styling was very period (late '40s) but quite handsome albeit a little bulbous. The car was the work of Aston engineer and designer Claude Hill, who was responsible for virtually the entire development process. It was definitely not a great car but it had a certain presence. It was let down by its pretty awful four-cylinder engine, which just wasn't up to the job. In contrast the David Brown gearbox was a joy.

By now it must be clear that I am addicted to old cars, and that whenever I have a spare bit of cash I tend to squander it on a set of ancient wheels. Bonuses and windfalls were usually wholly or partially converted to automotive tin of one type or another. And so it was with the Aston. I saw it in the showroom at a time when I had some cash and was at once taken with its racy good looks. Beguiling though it was, it didn't perform well enough to hold my interest for long. It was another of the classics I bought on looks alone and with which I was subsequently disappointed. Although it was the time of the rising market, for a while I had the dubious distinction of having paid a record price for one of these cars. I experienced the uncomfortable sensation of reading a press report in which, although I wasn't mentioned by name, the author made it clear that he thought the purchaser a fool for having parted with so much cash for so little car.

Maybe it was the article that sowed the poisonous seed of doubt, but I was soon anxious to discover if I could get my money back. I talked with a number of dealers and, although the market was still generally buoyant, things seemed to have gone into recession as far as DB1s were concerned. About a year later however, at the height of the boom, I read a report of a Philips' sale where a similar car had reached the dizzy heights of £106,000 at auction. I couldn't believe it, here was I worrying over my £25,000 outlay and there was an auction house achieving great things. I called them at once and was very impressed with the service. They came, collected the car and sent it to their next big sale. I set a lowish reserve and waited with bated breath. It didn't attract a single bid. It was all very much an anti-climax. Philips behaved like gentlemen: they returned the car and never charged me a penny. Alas, after the false dawn it seemed that I was stuck with a bit of a white elephant. Then the market turned bear and

The car had a beautifully trimmed blue interior. With the top down you could just squeeze in four people.

Almost a really beautiful car. There is always, it seems, something about '40s styling that just misses.

car prices began to tumble. I decided that, if I couldn't sell it, I would convert it into something more desirable. At any rate something I would find more to my taste, and to hell with originality.

In the chronology of Aston production, the DB1 had been followed by the DB2, which under the skin was a very similar car except for its wonderful six-cylinder, WO Bentley-inspired engine. This isn't intended as a history lesson, but it's worth quickly picking up some background. When the Bentley firm went to the wall in 1930, the company was bought up by Rolls Royce, and WO went to work for them. By all accounts he and RR were not the best of chums and he soon left them to join Lagonda where, among other things, he is credited with designing the famous 4½-litre V12. After the war it was obvious that smaller-engined cars would be the order of the day and WO, still at Lagonda, directed the design of an outstanding Willie Watson-produced 2.6-litre, twin overhead cam six. It is said that David Brown bought Lagonda in order to get his hands on it. It was this engine that became the motive power of the DB2 and later Astons.

I began to consider converting my DB1, with its anaemic four pot, into a much better car by fitting the Lagonda six. Surely Claude Hill would have strongly supported the idea, I thought.

Since there were only 15 such cars in existence, when I disclosed my intentions to the cognoscenti, a number of them berated me for my philistine tendencies and urged me not to "ruin" (their words not mine) a piece of automotive history. But I pressed on regardless. (I later discovered that Claude Hill had resigned from the David Brown company in protest at the decision to use the 2.6 instead of his four-cylinder engine in the DB2.)

The strategy was to acquire an old Lagonda 2.6 saloon, examples of which could still be found relatively cheaply. I began the search in earnest and even followed up a possible donor. The project was cut short, however, by the agent of a Japanese collector who on behalf of his client was putting together a set (what is the collective noun for Astons? I rather like "Clutch") of Aston Martins. As luck would have it, a DB1 was the missing link. We had a very matter-of-fact telephone conversation about price (I never actually met the man). Frankly, I would have let it go for £20,000 so I was quite ready to accept the £77,000 he offered. I had to pay a big slice as commission to the dealer who set up the deal, but there was still a handsome profit: certainly the most I have ever made from the sale of a car.

We shall never know if the 2.6-litre engine will fit into a DB1 or if it would have transformed the car as I had imagined. I wonder if anyone has done it since?

The XKs came home with me from America and sat untouched in the garage at Roundsditch, the old house we moved to in Kent. The plan was to complete the refurbishment of the '120 and the '150 and to use the '140, as it was in excellent condition, or so I thought.

I started getting my hands dirty with the conversion of the XK120 to right-hand drive. It took a long while because, at the time, it was nearly impossible to find the correct bits. I sort of started, and then one thing led to another and I found other projects to occupy me. It took someone else's lovely XK 120, seen at a car show, to re-motivate me. I've got one of those languishing in a dusty garage, I told myself, so I took a couple of days off work

The XK 120 converted to right-hand drive. In my opinion it's one of the finest pieces of automotive styling ever.

and started making 'phone calls. By the end of the second day I had sourced everything I needed. I completed the work in two weeks. Once the conversion was done, correcting the mechanical deficiencies became the next priority. I decided that in order to speed things up, I would put the engine rebuild out to tender. I wrote to a dozen specialists asking for guideline prices and timeframes, as well as customer and trade references. I had three responses, and Brian Stevens of Basingstoke got the job. (This was how I first met Brian, who later worked on the E-type as well as the XK140.) The car came home a few days before Christmas and went beautifully. I took it for a run on Boxing Day, but by the time I got it home the engine had developed a nasty clacking noise. I called Brian next morning and, although the workshop was closed for the holidays, the call was switched to his home. Brian was out, but his wife answered and told me that the workshop would reopen early in the New Year. I assured her there was no urgency, and whatever it was could wait till then. Within half an hour Brian was on the telephone. I explained the symptoms and he immediately had an idea about what might have gone wrong.

"I'll be over in an hour," he told me. I tried to remonstrate with him, suggesting that the first week in January would be time enough. But he was having none of it.

"No, I'll come over right away. I think I know what's wrong

Brian Stevens, ace automotive engineer, with the author at a vintage race meeting.

and I won't be able to enjoy the rest of the holiday until the problem is fixed," he insisted. It actually took him two hours to get to me, half an hour to find and correct the problem and three hours to get home through the M25 holiday traffic. I was impressed with what was surely service above and beyond the call of duty. Since then Brian has worked on all my cars and we have become good friends.

The XK 140 that looked so good, proved anything but. It was when I was converting it from left to right-hand drive that I started to notice little areas of shoddy work. Things like the edges of the front wings that seemed not quite the right shape, and inner sills that were suspiciously knife edged. But it was hard to be certain: the car looked good, it even won first prize at a classic show.

I finally confirmed she was a wrong 'un when I started

My daughter Siobhan and my mother in the XK140. This was before we stripped her down to find the true extent of the bodged restoration. She looked much better in the flesh than she does in this rather poor picture.

removing trim panels. What I found underneath wasn't pretty. Could it be that instead of a potential concours winner, the car was no more than a rusted hulk stuffed with plastic filler? Soon traces of micro blistering began to appear over the body. Brian came round to have a closer look and to some extent even he was taken in. Although he quickly spotted the obvious problem areas, he felt that on balance it was probably a fairly sound car. In his view, it was likely that the final stages of the restoration had been rushed in order to get the vehicle to market. In any event, we agreed that the only way to find out for sure was to strip off the paint and see what was underneath.

The words 'artistry' and 'travesty' both come to mind when I think of what we found. My assessment, and Brian agrees, was that the Houston restoration process had started with a car that had been left standing in less than ideal conditions for many

years. My guess is that they started work on a derelict hulk. When we got to it the basic, unadorned body shell was bordering on scrap. There had been no attempt to repair the car properly. What had been attempted, and with outstanding success, was a recreation of the original car from rotted out steel and copious quantities of plastic filler. If the *Guinness Book of Records* had an appropriate category, the work would be at the top of the page. We took about a hundredweight of filler from various rust holes, cracks and crevices. For a while I kept it in boxes, intending at some point to stuff it slowly into the man who had sold me the car. When we were done, what was left looked like a colander. Luckily, it was possible to purchase the body panels we needed, including a lot of very useful repair sections. I kept the "A" posts

The XK140 after the body renovation but a long way from completion. She's been sitting in Brian's workshop for the best part of four years.

for quite a time to show as examples of incredible bodging. We counted five layers of patches on one post where successive knife and fork merchants had gone crazy with a welding torch.

The amazing thing is that the car won prizes. It is hard to imagine the amount of effort that must have gone into the fibreglass work. I honestly think it would have been easier to repair the car properly in the first place, than to produce all that plastic sculpture. Having said that, Brian has had to do a great deal of work in order to get the body back into metal. Sadly, other projects have muscled their way into the schedule and she still awaits the final touches. However, the bodywork is now complete and painted in pale primrose, which I think looks better than the canary yellow that, I am told, is the correct XK colour. She now awaits her new, straight port 3.8 engine and rebuilt Moss overdrive gearbox. The interior will be two-tone black and tan. I look forward with enthusiasm to completing the restoration and finally bringing her back from the dead. Somewhere, I have an effigy of a Houston lawyer stuck with pins; I add one each time I see the car.

The XK 150 was a completely different story. Although it needed a lot of work, the bodywork was in truly excellent shape and it was given a fastidious rebuild in record time. I'll leave that story until the chapter on my attempts at historic motor sport.

CHAPTER 12

More Old Motors

For a while Kathleen and I lived an odd life, based in London but still having our Houston home. We continued two-centre living for some time. Eventually it had to end, and we threw in the towel on London living at the same time and settled for a house in the country that didn't really have enough garaging, but a lot more than the place in Hampstead. We moved to Roundsditch in late 1988 and began thirteen very happy and settled years.

The XJS was replaced with a Mercedes 300 CE, which was a wonderful car. It had little arms that would come out and give you seat belts when you started up. It was extremely well built and solidly engineered. It passed my "special" test with flying colours. Over the years I have devised what I call the chamois test. It is very simple and consists of washing a car and then drying it off with a chamois leather. On the XJS it would catch on lots of places such as light surrounds, bumpers and the grill. The Mercedes was completely different, there wasn't a sharp edge anywhere, the chamois just flowed around the bodywork without a hitch. I think the contrast shows the respective amounts of care and attention to detail that went into the two designs.

I enjoyed the 300 CE from the start and, although she wasn't a super-fast car, her road manners were impeccable. I particularly marvelled at the automatic sunroof sensor. I first noticed it when travelling quite quickly with the roof open. It started to drizzle, and the mechanism triggered and closed the roof automatically.

On another occasion it closed when it wasn't raining, but within a few minutes the heavens opened up. Dashed clever, these Germans, I thought. A week later, driving in an absolute downpour, the sunroof opened all by itself! Of course, there was no automatic sensor, it was just an electrical fault. Closing when it had rained had been a coincidence: the blooming thing was defective. Silly me! However, it only took the service department a few minutes to correct the fault, with no recurrence.

During a pub session one Saturday lunchtime, I got into a discussion about the practicality of using old cars as everyday transport. I was firmly of the opinion that, if one chose wisely, a classic could be an interesting alternative to modern iron. To prove my point, I decided to put my money where my mouth was and use a car that was at least 20 years old as my regular hack.

Given that regular use included the winter months, none of my Jaguars was a practical prospect. Frankly, even then I was too long in the tooth and stiff jointed to subject myself to side screens, approximate hoods and risible heating, so XKs were out. E-types with their long, albeit elegant, snouts were not a proposition for supermarket car parks or kerbside parking. It was clear that the car for me was either a Triumph or an MG. (Was the whole scheme an excuse for another old car, I wonder?) If I am honest, my first choice would have been a TR5, with its impressive

My MGC roadster, sporting her mock Minilites. She was a really delightful car and totally reliable.

performance, but the car that presented itself at the opportune moment was a mineral blue MGC roadster. On a beautiful sunny day, when I first saw her with top down, standing provocatively with her wheels at a jaunty angle, I just couldn't resist.

I picked her up from her previous owner and my journey home included a bit of M25 as well as some suburban stop-and-go traffic. She behaved impeccably through it all. I was surprised at how quickly I became used to the feel and how well the car went with that nice, roarty exhaust note from the torquey six. The steering was a good deal lighter than I remembered from my earlier GT. I determined to keep my speed within the legal limit which, bowling along the M25 on an uncongested day, was hard to do. Keeping a wary eye on the instruments, I enjoyed a pleasant and trouble-free drive. It was when I thought I had got the feel of the car, that I experienced the dreaded understeer along the winding country lanes near home. Going into a bend a little too quickly the steering seemed suddenly to stiffen and the car very definitely did not want to make the turn with me. But once you know about odd behaviour, you learn to cope and in general I found the overall handling acceptable for normal road use.

I suppose, looked at objectively, the MGC in its basic form is rather a poor sports car, but I liked it a lot. It seems perfectly to sum up the old British Leyland: under-developed and without the punch you would have expected from three litres. It was also very Spartan, with its rubber-lined interior, tin dash and amazing pack-away hood. On the other hand, Abingdon's heritage shone through; for a 25-year-old car it proved amazingly reliable, willing and gutsy, with an undeniably "enjoyable" character. The engineering was basic but solid. Everything worked and went on working. In the two years I owned her she had very few days off the road. There were some faults, but none too serious and all easy to fix. The car had its original engine, which was approaching 94,000 miles and still held excellent oil pressure. The outer panels had all been extensively renewed, but the basic structure was completely original and rust free. The engine bay let

I did a lot of work to make the interior particularly nice including fitting head restraints and a leather rim Motolita. I was sorry to see her leave.

the car down, with its ages of accumulation of grime, and the mess left by an earlier hydraulic leak, but the thought of lifting out that huge, iron lump for a clean-up was too daunting to contemplate.

I did a lot of cosmetic work on the car and, by the time I had to dispose of her, she was a honey. I retrimmed the interior in piped leather and went for a later seat design that incorporated head restraints. I fitted my favourite Motolita, 14-inch, leather rim and replaced the rather tatty wire wheels with a set of centre-lock, replica Minilites. I had the hood made in black mohair, piped blue to match the body colour.

This was no mollycoddled souvenir: since there was no room in the garage, she spent all her spare time sitting on the drive, rain or shine. Most mornings I used her for the station run and left her in the car park all day.

I finally sold her to a charming young man who wanted her as a cherished classic, which was as it should have been. I had an enormous lump in my throat when he drove away in her. Kathleen told me I was very quiet that evening and spent a lot of time gazing into the middle distance.

Would I again consider using a classic as everyday transport?

Probably not. Modern cars, for all their lack of character, are superb at what they do. You take them out of the showroom and just drive them between services. No topping up the water or the oil, no breakdowns and no hassle. Then there are all those mod cons like climate control, ABS, power steering, stereo, centralised locking, power hoods; shall I go on?

Moderns are great for using and forgetting about. Classics are – well, classics. Mind you, if I could get my hands on a really nice Alfa Bertone 2000 GTV . . . .

My business had gone through a number of difficult years, and I didn't much enjoy having to present bad news to the world at large. Worst of all was the necessity of having professional advisers vet every word. All public utterances had to have the right, what is now referred to as, 'spin'. When things got better and we were on the up again, it seemed a heaven-sent opportunity to leave what I had helped build to other, more eager hands. For me, it wasn't a difficult decision, but it caught everyone else by surprise. I will always be grateful to our American investors for letting me out so graciously. (I can't but feel that if my boss at the time had been Clement Attlee, the old Labour Prime Minister, he might well have described me as being "not up to the job".) Although I stayed on in a part-time capacity as a non-executive director, my involvement was minimal.

So, overnight I suddenly had a lot of time to indulge my passion for cars, and indulge it I did. To celebrate my new-found freedom, I allowed myself a wild extravagance. As everyone knows, I have been a Jaguar aficionado for a long time, and the car I had always craved was an SS 100, so I set about searching. Actually, I had flirted with the notion of acquiring an SS on three previous occasions. Once, in the US, I was offered a really beautiful car at a very good price but, being me, I tried to bargain it down and lost it. The second occasion was at a Coy's auction, when the famous Appleyard car came up for sale. I knew that particular SS would make a lot of money, given its provenance, but they also had a 2½-litre with a less illustrious pedigree which

I hoped would be available at a more reasonable price. In the event, the Appleyard car made £165,000 (I think I remember correctly) and the other, carried along on the wave, sold for somewhere near £80,000. (I heard that the Ian Appleyard car later sold privately for £275,000.)

Many years later, another 2½ came up at a Sotheby's sale. This car had been the property of a Kentish farmer who had used it in competition and later for picking hops. The car was what auctioneers call a "barn find", which is usually a euphemism for derelict old wreck. In the case of this particular SS 100, that's exactly what it was. I telephoned the auction house before the sale and was assured that the car was basically sound. "It needs a good clean-up and putting back together," the gentleman told me. I got a bit of shock when I went to the preview. I suppose it was all there but it was exactly how a car that had been cheaply made in the first place would fare if abandoned to the elements for 30 years. The most valuable item was, without doubt, the chassis plate. I actually went along to the auction because I felt that the wreckage might possibly be bought cheaply. I had in mind a figure of between £10,000 and £15,000. If I could secure the car for that sort of figure, I planned to take my time over a slow and careful reconstruction.

Following my usual practice, I stayed out of the bidding and waited for the other protagonists to exhaust themselves. When the bidding finally gave out, some lunatic had paid £63,000 and loose change. That's the trouble with auctions: people get carried away.

That's not quite the end of the tale because, a year later, the man who had bought it offered to sell it for the equivalent of £70,000. He had spent a fortune and all the bits had been restored. On the face of it, it looked like a good buy but I was put off by the way the owner had approached the project. I was uncomfortable with the fact that a different specialist had restored each major component. I was offered, not a finished car, bolted together and up and running, but one with a lot of the components yet to be slotted into place. I later saw the car when it was back in England

Ian Stewart driving my car at a Rest And Be Thankful hill climb meeting in 1951. Note the other interesting machinery in the background, including what look like J2 Allards and an XK120.

at the workshop of one of the country's leading SS specialists and, to be honest, it looked pretty decent, so maybe it would have been a good buy after all. (Some wag made the comment that it would have been good-bye to £70,000 but who knows?)

I was so keen to get my hands on a car that I made the mistake of potentially stirring up the market by talking with too many people in the trade although, perhaps fortunately, nothing came of it. Many months into the search, a pal who was a member of the Rolls Club saw an advertisement in the club magazine for an SS100. It was being sold by Hoffmans of Henley, the Rolls and Bentley specialists. It turned out they were selling it on consignment for a customer, and a few days before Christmas I went to see it. I took Brian Stevens along to give it the once-over. The chap selling had owned the car for a number of years and also had quite a collection of other very nice vehicles. The SS turned out to be a 3½-litre and possibly the 1938 Scottish Motor Show car. The owner took us to his extensive garage and, although I knew exactly what I had gone along to see, my heart still skipped a beat when he removed the covers. She was absolutely gorgeous, and in lovely usable condition. From the moment I saw her, I knew I just had to have her. We played around for a while in mock negotiation and I threw in the bargaining chip that I had another car to see before I could finally make up my mind. This was actually the case, as I had unearthed another SS in Wales, but I suspect the owner knew I'd buy his car. It was probably a worthwhile ploy, because I got a few pounds off the price and we closed the deal then and there.

SY 6684 is a particularly interesting car, because she came with an enormous history file. The first owner, a Scot, hence the Scottish registration, is reputed to have bought the car from the SS stand at the last Scottish show before the war. He obviously loved her to bits, because the record shows that he had her only three months before disposing of her to Noel Bean, the Scottish hill-climb champion. Noel kept the car for ten years and used her for all manner of competitions. I have a lovely old picture of him competing at Bo'ness in 1946, in the first motor sport event in Scotland after the war. He got fastest time of the day, incidentally. In 1949, he sold the car to one Ian Stewart who, I believe, was associated with Ecurie Ecosse. Ian converted the car to a replica of the works racer, with a boat tail and cycle wings. He was quite successful and I have a number of old photographs of the car competing in various events. Its next change of ownership was in 1955 when it went through a series of hands, all of them it seems connected in one way or another with motor sport. I suspect it fell into poor repair, and there is some mention of it being involved in a tree fall. Restoration back to original condition began in 1974 and was continued by Barry Forster, a one-time chairman of the Jaguar Driver's Club, who acquired the car in 1977. Barry was a great publicist for his SS100 and the car appeared in several advertisements, including the Varta Batteries campaign as well as Jaguar's launch of the XJS in Canada. My most prized picture is one of the car outside the front door of Sir William Lyon's home. He and Lady Lyons are standing and admiring his handiwork.

It's nice to get so much recorded history with a car. Needless to say the SS 100 is one that I plan to keep until they take me away in a box. The thought of someone else driving off in her is almost more than I can bear. It's not possessiveness, it's just affection.

Varta Batteries ran a whole series of advertisements featuring the SS 100. Barry Forster, the owner at the time, was also chairman of the Jaguar Drivers' Club and seemed to get the car featured in lots of promotions for various products. Revell used the car to launch their SS 100 plastic model kit, and Jaguar Canada featured it in a very glossy brochure for the XJS. The vast history file that came with the car contains lots of photographs of Barry and SY 6684 getting involved in all manner of sporting and civic events. Apart from regularity rallying, the car leads a much quieter life with me. I like the look of the girls on the horses; sadly, they didn't come with the car.

The SS from the rear. The delicate upsweep of the rear mudguards is very subtle but adds so much to the aesthetic appeal. I guess I'm in love with these beautiful cars, and so hopelessly biased.

Kathleen and I competed on the 1996 Norman Conquest Rally in the SS. The car ran faultlessly and we came first in class, and fourth overall.

SS 100

The SS 100 was a development of the SS 90, which was similar in design. One of the main differences was the change from a 2.7-litre, side valve six to an overheard valve version of the same engine. The car was originally offered in 2½-litre (2.7) and then in 3½ litre form. When it first appeared, it was by no means well thought of by the upper echelons of the motoring public. Because it was fitted with a Standard Motors engine, it was not considered a thoroughbred and, had it been used, the original side valve in the SS 90 would have done it no favours in terms of performance. William Lyons is reputed to have investigated a number of ways to get more power for his flagship sports car. The options considered included fitting a Zoller supercharger and even an American Studebaker unit. The solution finally adopted was a Westlake-provided, overhead valve conversion to the Standard engine. The modified unit provided the required zip and the 3½-litre car, tested by Motor magazine in 1938, was found to have a sub-11 second 0 to 60 time and a top speed of 107 miles per hour. The price of the larger-engined version was just £445 when announced in 1937, which was about a third of the price of an equivalent Alfa.

Beauty is, of course, in the eye of the beholder, but to my mind the SS 100 is the archetypal British, '30s sports two-seater. The whole thing is perfection from an aesthetic point of view. There isn't a bad angle; it looks wonderful from wherever you view it. The subtle touches like the complex upsweep of the rear wings and the special headlights are the work of genius: Sir William got it absolutely right. Some people have tried to improve on the design by playing around with it in a number of ways but they have all been dismal failures by comparison with the original.

It's not all good news; there has to be some penalty for that incredible price-performance ratio. The truth is that the SS 100 is a cheaply built car and it shows if you take a close look. Quality marques of the period like Alvis and Lagonda all have wonderful cast aluminium scuttles that provide not just chassis stiffening but also excellent body support. The SS has a plywood scuttle that provides nothing like the structural integrity (or longevity) of metal. Performance, to some extent, was achieved by lightness, (it weighs just 23cwt), and the relatively flimsy build quality is evident. The ash frame is basic and the aluminium body quite delicate.

On the positive side, one of the car's great strengths is its mechanical simplicity. The engine is a straightforward push-rod unit developing about 120 bhp from 3½ litres, so it is nicely under stressed. The Girling brakes are 13-inch drums all round with *mechanical rod operation. Once set up, all they need is regular but simple adjustment.*

Although not in the same league as some of the considerably more expensive continental sports models of the period, SS 100s were regularly used in competition. Today, many examples have a competition history and this is particularly true of the bigger engined cars; most · 3½-litre versions have been involved with motor sport of one sort or another. Bodies were frequently stripped, and boat-tailed to improve aerodynamics. Modifications like bronze heads and special exhausts were fitted to boost performance.

As values have risen, most cars have been returned to their original state. The once rather déclassé SS 100 has become a much sought-after classic.

A week before I left my job, I read an account of a competition for which the prize had been a Rover Mini Cabriolet. The eventual winner didn't drive and didn't want the car but there wasn't a cash alternative, so the dealership was looking to unload it on the winner's behalf. The details were none too clear but I eventually tracked the car to a main dealer in Stratford on Avon. I got a substantial discount and had a Knight Development 5-speed gearbox fitted, which transformed the motorway cruising capability. I have never considered selling my Mini, because she is

The Mini Cabriolet in the French sunshine

such a cute, useful little car and takes up very little garage space. If I didn't have her I wouldn't be able to cram in another car anyway. A few years ago we took her down to the South of France on vacation and she attracted more attention on the Côte d'Azure than the Ferraris. The initial intention was to use the car as everyday transport, but for various reasons she has got mixed up with the classics and gets an outing relatively infrequently.

The Rolls Royce Corniche II

Six months after I retired, the Mercedes went back to the leasing company, although I gave serious thought to buying the car from them. I spent a lot of time considering my options. When you are paying for your own car, as opposed to driving a company vehicle, it somewhat concentrates the mind on financial considerations. I finally rejected the Mercedes and decided instead on a late model Rolls Royce Corniche convertible. I reckoned that I could buy a lot more car for the money and, although the maintenance would be higher, the resale value would result in an overall cheaper deal. The car I eventually found was a 1988 Corniche 2 in metallic larkspur blue with a red interior. Although it was considerably more than the Mercedes, I

The Corniche had a particularly sumptuous interior.

still thought the economics made sense. The leather interior was in unmarked condition and the chrome looked new. The carpets had been replaced, as had the lamb's wool rugs. A thing I dislike about many convertible Rolls Royces is that they so often look like a tart's breakfast with magnolia interiors piped in garish, contrasting colours. This car however, was nicely understated. Before I took delivery I had a blue mohair hood fitted, together with a set of Rolls Royce alloy wheels.

The mention of garish Rolls Royces brings to mind a Corniche that used to stand on the main road when we lived in Hampstead. I passed it most mornings on my walk up to the tube station. Apart from the fact that it held up the traffic that was trying to get up and down the busy artery, it was a prime example of bad taste. Like the car I eventually bought it was also metallic Larkspur blue, but there the similarity ended. The hood was cream and the interior was trimmed with shaggy sheepskin and the carpets were cream shag pile. The final touch was the chrome, which had all been gold-plated. Each time I saw it parked in the curb with cars, buses and trucks held up and only just managing to squeeze by, I was reminded of what an unfortunate piece of exhibitionism the car represented. I have to say that the selfish parking incensed me (there was an ancient statute that allowed residents to block the road with their carriages) and I wouldn't have been sorry to see a bus write off the monstrosity.

I found the contrast been the two cars illuminating, and I patted myself on the back and thought what a clever fellow I was for acquiring such an elegant example. Frankly, I never noticed the reversing lamp rims. It was the service garage manager who queried why only the reversing light rims were gold plated. I had no idea but I suddenly experienced a moment of disquiet. Further investigation revealed that the Hampstead car and mine were one and the same!

When I found this out, I wrote to the previous owner, and he replied with a very nice letter telling me that he was keen to sell the sheepskin seat covers that I had so despised. He offered to let me have them at a bargain price. He added that when he sold the car it had been replaced with a new Corniche IV and he had arranged for the gold plated bits to be swapped over, (hence my new-looking chrome). The red interior looked new because it had never seen the light of day, having spent its life covered with fleece. The carpets had been replaced before I bought the car and the hood had been renewed on my own instructions. So, in a few easy moves a complete transformation had been accomplished. I don't know why the reversing light rims hadn't been swapped but, if they had, I suspect I would never have discovered the truth. I rather think I would have preferred it that way. Another one of those odd coincidences that life so often throws up.

I had the Rolls for five years, and there were a number of reasons why I eventually sold it. (If you don't want to hear me whinging about how our country is today, please move on to the next paragraph.) The main one is that it has become impossible to drive this type of car without being absolutely certain about the circumstances in which it will be used and where it will be parked. Public car parks and kerbside parking are out of the question if you wish to avoid returning to keyed paintwork or a slashed hood. I also found the level of hostility I met from other road users, particularly the drivers of commercial vehicles, to be disconcerting. (I know it is not politically correct to make these comments but I'm just telling it like it is.) I was usually in trouble if I needed to be let out at a busy crossing or change lanes in traffic.

I started to use the car less and less and, with garage space at a premium, I wanted other cars more than I wanted the Rolls. Did it prove an economic purchase? It's hard to say. I sold it for only a few thousand less than I paid, but the maintenance was high, mainly because I used a top specialist and kept the car up to scratch. When it went to a new home after five years it was better than when I first acquired it. I haven't done the detailed sums but, when everything is taken into consideration it may be that the right kind of Mercedes would have been a more economic option. I enjoyed the car, however, (it was much nicer than my earlier

Corniche), and I somewhat regretted its passing.

The story of my Sunbeam Tiger really belongs in the next chapter but I'll cover it in this one anyway. The whole project started when I competed in an historic rally and was so enthused that I decided to have another go the following year with a more suitable car. For a number of reasons, I decided on a Sunbeam Tiger. First, Tigers are small and relatively nimble (they're really Alpines on steroids). Second, with a large American V8 engine in a small body they can be made to go extremely quickly. Third, they are relatively inexpensive. I found a car in Sussex that looked good and seemed to go well enough. It was a slightly garish blue, with an expensive cream-coloured interior.

Driving it home, I was fairly careful but noticed that the handling seemed a little peculiar. I managed to spin it twice in the dry, going into roundabouts. At the time I thought I was being stupid, but subsequent investigation revealed other reasons for the phenomenon. Driving into the first junction I was going moderately quickly and the car seemed to behave quite predictably, with the big iron engine causing noticeable understeer. I wanted to make the turn, but the car wanted to go

The Tiger in rally dress

straight on. The moment I put my foot on the brakes, however, the behaviour completely changed and understeer was translated into immediate oversteer, with the car religiously following the front wheels. As I wasn't expecting that to happen, it rather caught me out. On the second roundabout I went in much more slowly but I was still surprised by the reaction. I took it to one of the country's leading Tiger specialists, and his work revealed some very nasty modifications that had been made to the suspension in order to fit in a Mustang 302 cubic inch engine instead of the original 260.

The Tiger had all the gear, including full harnesses.

To cut a long story short, I decided to use the car as the basis of a seriously competitive rally/race car. The Scottish rally was in April and work began in January. We rebuilt every bit of the Tiger, including a high-performance 289 engine. I changed the colour to red and retrimmed the interior in black. The performance was positively scary. We worked like Trojans to meet the deadline and, for a while, it looked as though we wouldn't make it. I ran everyone ragged, harrying and chivvying them along. With two weeks to go I knew we would be ready, but probably without an interior, but who cares? Tough hombres like me don't need cosseting.

All the people working on the project did magnificently and then the rally organiser cancelled the event with just a week to go! It was a bitter blow, because the car had been specifically built for the Scottish Highland Fling rally with its unique blend of hill climbs, auto-testing and regularity. Sadly, the event never ran again, and with it went the main purpose of that rather special Tiger.

In May of the same year, I was scheduled to take part in the Tour of Ireland rally in an XK. A friend of mine expressed great interest in having a go and persuaded me to lend her the Tiger. She formed an all-woman crew and the two ladies got down to Dublin without mishap.

In the rush to finish the car, there were still one or two areas that needed attention. One small problem was the ignition key which, being the original item, was very worn. On hard acceleration it had the unfortunate habit of falling out of the ignition lock, so it was sometimes the case that, in order to kill the engine, one was forced first to scrabble around on the floor and find the keys.

My co-driver and I got down to the hotel in Dublin in the XK with time to spare and, keen to show him the Tiger's spellbinding performance I borrowed it back and took him for a spin. Approaching a straight bit of road I accelerated hard and the throttle jammed open. We were doing about 100 mph and still putting on speed when we came to a roundabout. As luck would have it, on this one occasion, although the ignition key had almost come out of the switch, it had hung on precariously with the tip still in the slot and I was able to push it back into position and switch off the engine in time. My blood ran cold at the thought of what might have happened if the girls had been driving the car. The throttle jam had been caused by wiring that had ridden up between the carpet and accelerator pedal and was easily fixed. Before I handed the Tiger back, I obtained a new key that stayed put in the lock. The difference between redemption and disaster is often so slight. I would never have been able to forgive myself if the ladies had come to harm. In the end they did

tolerably well and for the most part handled the Tiger like experts. The driver, incidentally, was my ex-wife Vivienne. If she hadn't dropped it into a ditch right at the end of the last day she might well have been among the prize-winners.

It was a great car but, without an event on which to use it, I decided to let it go, and strangely enough it was bought by an Irishman who telephoned from Dublin and bought it sight unseen for exactly the asking price. He came over with his son to collect it, and it gave me an awful pang to see them drive off in it.

Kathleen and I, who had been together for thirteen years and were almost in our dotage (well, I was anyway), decided on a final round of families, and our daughter Elizabeth was born in May 1995. As one might expect, she is the apple of her daddy's eye, fairly effortlessly winding me around her little finger. Small children change one's perspective and, as we had no family-sized classic, I immediately set about rectifying the situation. (I had the perfect

This isn't my MK V; I wish it was. They are really elegant cars that retain a very pre-war look. I suppose the heavy-handed frontal chrome was intended to please the American market, which the car failed to do, unlike the later Jaguar sports cars.

excuse for buying another old car.) Given my predilection for Jaguars, I successfully bid on a MKV drop-head at a Sotheby's auction. The restoration started at once but, as usual, other projects got in the way and the work is as yet incomplete. One day, I hope in the not-too-distant future, we will be able to travel in her *en famille*.

The Jaguar MK V

The MK V Jaguar, made between 1949 and 1951, is possibly the most underrated Jaguar produced. It is a big car, but not enormous like the MK VII that came after it. When Jaguar restarted production after the war they reintroduced the Standard Motor Company's pre-war 2½ and 3½-litre, push-rod sixes. Standard had no further interests in these designs, so Jaguar took over the tooling and made them themselves for the MkIV and the MKV. Built on the chassis that was later cut down for the XK 120, the MKV is a sturdily made car with a very stiff box section chassis and independent, torsion bar front suspension. They are extremely nicely finished inside, with acres of leather and wood trim. The three-position hood is held in place with sturdy, chromium plated cabriole bars that retain a certain pre-war elegance. Fewer than 1000 drop-head coupés were produced, and fewer than 100 remain, but as yet they have not been rediscovered. Cars in excellent condition still turn up for sale at bargain prices. (It always seems strange to me that convertible MKVI Bentleys command two to three times the price.) Performance of the 3½-litre car is respectable, with 60 mph coming up in about 15 seconds and a near 100 mph top speed, but these cars are not about going fast, they are luxury carriages made to waft along in and be enjoyed.

In the last few years I have had a major change of strategy with regard to old cars, but more of that later. Probably the last of my old-style acquisitions was an XK 120 fixed-head that arrived not long ago.

It may be remembered from Chapter 5 that I got my first XK,

a '120 fixed-head, when I was nineteen. I loved that car a great deal and have always harboured the desire for another. I also happen to think that the '120 fixed-head is one of the best pieces of automotive design ever, eclipsing even the '120 roadster.

The author prtetnding to smile. Much work was done on the rolling chassis, Note the '120 roadster under wraps in the background.

Frankly, with three XKs already, I never really believed that I would add another to the collection. That was until a friend of a friend, who had several times resolutely declined to dispose of a "project" car, decided it was taking up too much garage space. I went to look at it and made him an offer he couldn't refuse. The car had started life in America and evidence suggested it had come off the road as long ago as 1966. I now know that it had lain derelict, in less than ideal conditions, for quite some time. The interior had completely rotted out, although the body remained sound and the chassis perfect. Mechanically it was worn out. Someone had started work but had given up, mercifully not before moving the car to dry storage. There it languished until

Road testing the rolling chassis

acquired by a New York medico who resolved to finish the job. But life seldom goes as expected and, although the good doctor did some useful work, he also gave up and sold the car. He did, however, amass a pile of replacement parts, mainly the shiny bits. The car was eventually sold to a UK trader who passed it on to the man from whom I acquired it. I paid too much, but I hope over the next twenty years it will give me so much pleasure that the overspend won't matter (well, you need some sort of rationale don't you?). Luckily, the car came with its boxes of bits.

The plan was sensitively to update the car for use in everyday traffic. I intended to do most of the work myself, but farmed out the body repairs and painting to Brian Stevens. He picked up the stripped-down car and, after lifting off the body, returned the rolling chassis complete with engine and gearbox.

The US doctor had had the chassis shot-blasted and painted, and the suspension rebuilt. Unfortunately, the years between his efforts and my acquisition had taken their toll and, as I intended major changes, I stripped the chassis down once more and replaced all the bearings, joints and bushes. I also changed to servo-assisted discs at the front. The car had steel wheels but, because I had a brand new set of wires and radials hanging around the garage, I decided to fit them. I also took the opportunity of converting her from left to right-hand drive.

One of the disadvantages of the '120, in comparison with its later derivatives, is the lack of overdrive, which makes for less than comfortable motorway cruising. Unfortunately, on the '120 there isn't enough room between the engine and chassis cross member for the XK overdrive box. There are a number of options for installing a higher final gear, and I went for a Getrag five-speed gearbox from a 5 series BMW.

The New York doctor told me that he had had the engine rebuilt by a local restorer and, from the outside, it looked like a professional job. I was in two minds about taking it apart but in the end, to be on the safe side, I removed the head and sump. The head had been totally reconditioned: as fine a job as you will find. The timing gear had also been renewed and expertly put together. The block had been re-bored with new pistons and a rebuilt oil pump. However, although all the shells had been renewed, we

Non habeas corpus. *The chassis with wire wheels.*

were astounded to find that the crank had not been reground and that some of the journals were outside acceptable tolerances. Apart from that, all seemed to be in excellent shape. "Go figure," as our American cousins would say. After a regrind and new shells the motor was put back together.

The repaired body was returned beautifully painted in opalescent silver blue and sort of bolted to the chassis. Over the next week the body went up and down like a yo-yo as I tried various combinations of spacers to get it right. In the end I got fed up, chose a ride height that seemed about right, turned up a set of nylon spacers and bolted the whole thing down.

I had initially planned to get the engine running in minimal configuration, but in the end decided to fit the loom, instruments and everything else needed to fire up, so there was quite a lot to be done. Suddenly it all came together. I was, it seemed, within minutes of hearing the engine run; but alas! The best laid schemes of mice and men . . . .

Here's how the final leg panned out; I hope it provides an insight into some of the trials and tribulations of home restoration:

Almost there, but for some reason I can't get the distributor to mate with the drive. In and out, several times. Could there be a part missing? Visions of having to lift out the engine and start pulling it to bits. Several hours later finally confirm that it isn't a '120 distributor after all, even though it came in one of the boxes of spares. Relief mingled with irritation. Several days delay while Jeremy Broad, the specialist parts supplier, finds what I need and gets it to me.

Drop in the newly supplied Broad part; hallelujah! It fits. Static timing is a doddle. Check there's oil in the engine; fill the rad with water. Oops, it's flowing out through the carb mountings on the manifold. Damn, damn, damn! There's been a question mark over that manifold from the start. At some time it's been frost damaged and the repair weld is clearly visible. It looked OK but apparently wasn't. Drain the system and stomp back to the house in disgust. Call Jeremy (he knows my voice by now), and order a replacement.

Spirits rise over the next few days so I pull off the faulty manifold and examine it closely. Silly me, there's nothing wrong with it after all, it just wasn't tightened down enough. My wife Kathleen appears at the workshop door, the package from Broad's in her hands. Hey ho!

Finally water tight, holding fuel and statically timed. Luckily, I had a spare centre dash panel so I've been able to fit up the instruments without risking my beautiful new one. It does mean that I'm able to follow the progress of things like oil pressure and water temperature. Connect up the batteries and spin her over without ignition. Sorry, no can do, they're as flat as pancakes. Abandon the project? Sell the car? Instead, I stick the batteries on charge and decide to come back tomorrow.

Tomorrow's here, I don't expect much and I'm not disappointed: the starter whirrs, then nothing. Check the system but all seems well, power in all the right places. Front wheel off and remove starter. Tests OK. Replace and try again. Engine turns beautifully. I give it a good long burst on the starter without ignition. Oil pressure rises pleasingly. Check around the car to make sure all is well. It isn't, there's oil all over the exhaust and the garage floor. Expletive!

It's not serious. The copper washers on the oil feed at the back of the engine are shot and nothing I do will make them seal. I'm careful not to over tighten. Search around but fail to find replacements. Consider stripping down the roadster that is standing next to the fixed head but fight off the urge and decide to come back tomorrow with the right bits.

It's back together. Try turning without ignition one last time. Nothing! "I don't believe it!" It takes a while, but I find the problem. Removed the dipswitch bracket yesterday and didn't tighten it up enough when I replaced it. The bolts hold the solenoid on the other side of the bulkhead so it's nothing more than a bad earth.

Once fixed, the engine turns freely and seems oil tight. Time for lift-off. Ignition on, three turns and vroooom! She fires up for the first time in 30 years. Whoopee! Sounds sweet, timing's a bit off though, need someone to hold the timing light while I fiddle with the

Now recognisable as an XK 120 fixed-head coupé. Almost finished.

distributor. I need an assistant. "Kathleen. Oh Kathleen, my dearest!"

Would I do it again? Probably not: buying a car in boxes, that is. I had no problem working out where the engine and back axle went but so much of a motorcar is made up of tiny brackets, funny shaped bolts and oddly sized spacers. I suppose that patience is the main requirement, and that's not my strong point. Most irritating, has been finding out that so many of the boxed parts that came with the car proved not to be the right ones. Almost as bad was discovering, usually one at a time, that numerous bits weren't there at all. I was particularly driven mad by missing springs and fasteners of one type or another. When I went to look at the car I was most particular about ensuring that all the instruments were with it. I knew from experience that a '120 set would cost a bunch. I was confidently shown the gauges all neatly wrapped and boxed. It was only when I tried to fit them that I discovered they weren't '120 items after all and had to be replaced. And – they cost a bunch. I'll stop complaining. I enjoyed the work, learned a lot and eventually will have a very nice car to show for it.

CHAPTER 13

The Special Cars

A few years ago I took stock of the vehicles I owned and came to the fairly obvious conclusion that I had to stop accumulating old cars. Financial probity, lack of storage space and just plain common sense suggested that enough was enough. I hit upon the notion of having a major clear-out and replacing the cars I sold with a smaller selection of vehicles that I have always wanted. Good looks and performance were important considerations as, of course, was cost. Although I am in the fortunate position of being able to indulge my passion within reason, there is definitely a ceiling, and I have had to temper zeal with financial prudence. I make no claims about my judgement: my collection is a purely personal selection of the cars I like and has no particular theme or rationale.

I've made a good start on accumulating a fairly eclectic set of the cars I have always wished to own, but have not done quite so well in the clear-out stakes. Being committed to keeping one or two old friends that I could not bear to lose, I have a feeling that some of the XKs will be around for a long while and I just know I'll want to keep the MKV drop-head when the work is complete. And of course I'll hang on to the Mini Cabriolet and the V12 E-type, but a few of the others have already found good homes.

Part of the plan has been to include two fine British, pre-war cars in the collection. Why pre-war? Mainly because I think they are particularly interesting, with their extra gadgetry that has been obviated by technology or had its function automated in

An example of a glorious, special bodied Lagonda V12 Rapide. Several Indian potentates ordered these cars.

more modern machinery. I have in mind things like manual advance and retard mechanisms, Kigas pumps, four-wheel jacking and one-shot chassis lubrication. Why British? Because, I suppose, that is where my heart lies. I've owned few non-British cars (although, by and large, those few have been excellent), so to some extent my exclusion of foreign models is based on ignorance. When I began to consider what type of pre-war cars I wanted, I decided that one would have to be an archetypal two-seater and the other a big, four or five-seat family tourer. They both had to be open cars. There are a number of cars I'd love to own but, as I already have the SS, my requirements in the pre-war, two-seater department are already taken care of.

When it comes to acquiring a bigger PVT (Post Vintage Thoroughbred) there are some wonderful possibilities, particularly if price were no object. Which of course it is. I suppose the Lagonda V12 Rapide, almost in a class by itself, has a strong claim to the title of 'most desirable British PVT'. (Although essentially a two-seater, the car has an optional, sideways-facing rear seat for an additional passenger.) In my opinion the best are the few special-bodied V12 Rapides, usually built for foreign royalty, that really are perfection, but again these are one-offs and hugely expensive. When it comes to true four-seaters, many would claim that the 4½-litre Invicta is the car to beat, and I wouldn't argue, but here we are talking seriously expensive motorcars. I also have to admit that, although in general I'm not a vintage car man, Speed Six Bentleys appeal enormously, as does the wonderful 8-litre tourer. But these days, such cars are priced in the stratosphere and are, as far as I am concerned, completely out of reach.

When it came to looking for a big, pre-war, British drop-head coupé, I thought there were three options. Perhaps the most traditional choice would have been a Derby Bentley but, to be truthful, I've never been a particular fan of Derbys unless they were bodied by continental coachbuilders such as Franay or Kelner. I suppose these cars were essentially aimed at upper-class English gentlemen, who were notoriously conservative. There are one or two special-bodied examples, usually with art deco styling, that are to die for, but the respected and popular British body builders didn't much go in for flamboyance. Of the quality and engineering integrity there can be no doubt.

A car I would find hard to resist is a 4.3 Alvis, particularly a Van den Plas-bodied example. From a performance and engineering standpoint, Alvises are wonderful and the tourers are particularly nice, if a little windswept for back seat passengers. The styling is certainly elegant, although I've always thought the P100 headlamps a trifle overwhelming at the front. But an original Van den Plas 4.3 is a fabulous car.

When WO Bentley left Rolls Royce and joined Lagonda, he set about building "the best car in the world". Frank Feeley was the in-house designer at Lagonda who produced a masterpiece when he penned the V12 drop-head coupé for WO. The car is superb from all angles. The curves in the bodyline are amazing and must have been hell to produce. I imagine the panel beaters cursed Feeley up hill and down dale. It's a big motorcar, but the design is masterly, with an imposing grill framed by Lucas P100s that look just right. The twin side mounts also add a special touch. What I find unique about the car is the hood, which, unusually, looks as elegant and well shaped in the erect position as it does when folded. Bentley added all sorts of modern touches like torsion bar suspension and hydraulic brakes. The overhead cam V12 is reputed to be a lovely engine but easily misunderstood, and sometimes troublesome as a result.

Lagonda also offered a "poor man's" version in the form of the LG6, which was to all intents and purposes the same car, but with the tried and tested Meadows 4½-litre, six-cylinder engine. It is an odd thing but, in order to get in the Meadows, which was a few inches longer than the V12, Lagonda had to lengthen the chassis and bonnet, so the LG6 has a slightly longer snout than the V12. In their time, the LG6 and V12 Lagondas were considered a bit too showy by the English upper class, who stuck with their Bentleys; they were, however, much loved by theatrical types and Maharajas. These cars of the late '30s epitomise the end of an era when privilege and elegance were the order of the day. It was swept away by the Second World War, and when production restarted in 1945 such opulence was gone forever.

I first came across a fine example of an LG6 drop-head on a rally in Ireland. It was owned and driven by Stan Williams, an inveterate car collector and rallyist. Apart from the fact that Stan hustled his Lagonda through the country lanes as though it was a Lotus Seven, it was a very impressive motorcar in many other ways. So when I got a call one day from a respected dealer who was brokering an LG6 drop-head coupé, I couldn't help but be interested. The car was in Connecticut and, according to him, it was probably the best example in the world. I'm well used to dealers' hyperbole, but he was very convincing and so I persuaded Brian Stevens to go out with me and take a look. We grabbed a couple of Virgin Air cheapies and headed for Newark. Brian had never been in America before, and so we hired a limousine at the hotel and took a three-hour tour of Manhattan on the day we arrived.

The circumstances were typical of America. We got to the airport hotel in mid afternoon and I immediately called down to the concierge to enquire if it would be possible to get a car and driver to take us around the city. "When had you in mind?" he asked. I told him in half an hour. "I'll get right back to you," was his reply. He called within five minutes. "Your car will be waiting in the lobby in twenty minutes," he said. It was, and we were given a very enjoyable, three-hour tour at a reasonable price.

We had a pleasant dinner with the dealer that evening and he drove us to the Lagonda next morning. The car was as good he had said. Brian gave it a thorough going-over and, apart from a small snagging list, could find few faults. That evening we flew home. The only negative aspect of the acquisition was the fact that it took nearly four months to get the car to England but there is no doubt that it is a wonderful addition to the collection.

The car was first bought by a Mr C.G. Chaplin of Philadelphia. For a while I thought that it might have been the great "Charlie" himself, but I soon discovered that he was C.S., Charles Spencer, and not C.G. The original build sheet shows that Mr Chaplin ordered his car from the factory to be delivered directly to English Motors of New York. Although destined for the US from the start, the car is and always has been right-hand drive. One wonders how the owner got on with his English automobile in America. I have no record of how long he kept it, but the documentation shows that he returned it to the works in 1947 for a substantial rebuild.

My 1938 LG6, 4.5-litre Lagonda. A poor man's V12?

During the early '90s, it belonged to a one-time chairman of the US Lagonda Club, who had the car restored at enormous expense. His ambition had been to own the best example in America, and when the work was completed he succeeded in his aim. Sadly, he died soon after winning the coveted CCCA prize. The car is a typical example of "over the top" American restorations which are much frowned on by many, rather conservative,

The LG6 being restored in America

English owners. More than one member of the UK Lagonda Club has been rude about the tomato red coachwork. "Why don't you fix on a bell and mount some ladders?" I've been asked quite a few times. The chrome-plated wire wheels also make a lot of people snort with disapproval, but I think they look the part. At first I wasn't so sure of the colour myself, but over time it has grown on me and I think it well suits the character of the vehicle. It's the only example I have of what could be described as "show quality", which is not something I'm generally very keen on. But the 1938 LG is a very special motorcar and I've rather taken her to my heart.

I've always admired '60s Astons, although I have to admit that I've never been a dyed-in-the-wool Aston fan, but I do think the DB5 is one of the most elegant examples of the mark. Soon after I retired from business, I had the crazy notion of using a DB5 as everyday transport, although a lot of people who knew better warned me off the notion. I nevertheless found a very pretty convertible that seemed to be in good condition, at least to my uneducated eye. I was cautious about spending so much cash, however, and asked Peter Stratford of Goodwood Green, the

Aston specialists, to have a look at the car for me. After inspection he gave me his opinion, and I rather liked his style.

"Apart from the body, the chassis and the engine, the car is in excellent condition," he told me. He was unequivocal in his advice. "Don't buy it," he said. I was disappointed, but there wasn't much point in hiring an expert and ignoring what he said. In any event, nice as they are, '60s Astons are relatively fragile and not practical for everyday use, so it was probably for the best.

Peter called almost two years later. He had found a really excellent Aston and wanted to know if I was still on the look-out for a good one. Logistically it had a lot against it. First, the car was in Paris. Second, the owner had arranged for it to be rebuilt by a French classic car specialist which, on the face of it, didn't sound an ideal choice for restoring such a quintessentially English automobile. Third, the Aston Club, although confirming that the chassis number did in fact belong to a right-hand drive example, had no record of it in the club's archives. Fourth, the car had no history. The story was that the owner had bought it in England in basically good, original condition and thought it would be fun to have a British, right-handed car in Paris. Apparently it wasn't.

Given all of the above, I still thought it worth pursuing, partly because Peter Stratford went to Paris, saw the car and was very enthusiastic, and partly because it was no ordinary '60s Aston.

The rather handsome Aston DB6 short chassis Volante that I found in Paris. I have grown to appreciate the car more than I did at first.

When Aston Martin announced the end of the DB5 and the introduction of the DB6, by some amazing turn of events they had thirty-seven DB5 chassis still in stock. Quite how such an oversight could have occurred, or indeed whether it was an oversight, I'm not certain. The DB6, unlike the DB5, was designed as a very definite four-seater with an extra few inches in the chassis to accommodate proper back seats. It also had a less steeply raked roofline, to afford better headroom for rear passengers. The thirty-seven chassis were given the shorter DB5 Superleggera (meaning super light and originally made by Touring of Milan) convertible body, but also had some of the DB6 modifications like quarter bumpers, a slightly revised interior and some changes to the frontal treatment. Although it had the new DB6 rear light clusters (taken from the Triumph TR4A parts bin), it retained the very attractive DB5 hood line. Any other company would have allocated a DB5A label to the hybrids and sold them cheap, but not Aston; they badged them as DB6s and introduced the name "Volante" to differentiate the new convertibles. These cars soon became highly sought after and are known as "Short Chassis Volantes". The Paris car was one of the exclusive thirty-seven.

It was in exceptional condition in every respect and could, without a great deal of effort, be made into a show car, but that is not what I intended. I think it is an outstandingly pretty car and, like all 5 and 6 series Astons immortalised by 007, has a special place in the heart of the British nation. Without doubt it attracts more attention and gets me into more conversations than any other car I own. I once went to visit my mother in Beckenham in South London, and during the journey there were three occasions when people came up for a chat while I was stationary at traffic lights. I got to Mum's, left the car in the kerb outside her house and within minutes there was a ring at the bell. A lady, with her two young children on their way home from school, apologised for disturbing us but said she just had to know about the car. We talked for a good fifteen minutes; it was delightful to meet someone, particularly a lady, so enthralled with an old motor. The

name Bond was mentioned more than once.

I had often considered owning a Ferrari but usually rejected the idea for a number of reasons. The car I would have wanted, a 250 short-wheelbase Berlinetta, was just too expensive and the alternative 512 Berlinetta Boxer too modern. If I was going to own a Ferrari, it had to be a V12 two-seater with exceptional good looks, so the field was somewhat narrowed. Frankly, I would never have considered a 275 GT Berlinetta if I hadn't been given a ride in one by Brian Stevens, who was doing work on it for a mutual acquaintance. Brian had driven the car from the client's home in Geneva, and raved about it. It was certainly one of the handsomest '60s cars I had seen. Once you get used to the rather quirky gearshift, which has reverse where one would expect to find first, and first where second would normally be, one can make significant progress. The 275 is my first Ferrari and, unlike a lot of other owners, I haven't become a uncritical fan; well, not yet anyway. The Pininfarina design, built by Scaglietti, is a work of

The 275 GTB twin-cam is a classic V12 design. In the desirability stakes, it seems to have fared better than the later and bigger-engined 365 Daytona that in the last few years has lost some of its earlier popularity. This is a picture of my car arriving in Lloret for the start of the 2000 Catalunya Historic Marathon.

art but the build quality is anything but, and the spares situation makes ownership almost untenable if you plan actually to use the car.

Buying a 275 GTB wasn't easy, particularly as I wanted a very definite specification. First, it had to be right-hand drive; and second, I wanted a whole gaggle of rather specific features. To tell the truth, I did a bit of research, and much of the following comment is based on other men's wisdom. There are two types of 275: the earlier examples had engines with two camshafts and the later ones had four. A lot of people claim that the 275 GTB/4 (the 4 is for four camshafts) is arguably the greatest front-engined, road-going V12 that Ferrari ever made. They may be right, but the problem is that a good car will set you back a lot of money, particularly in right-handed form. Accepting that the four-cam

The engine of the 275 twin-cam showing off its six twin-choke Webers

may be the best thing since sliced bread, it seemed to me that for a lot less money one could have almost the same thing. The four-cam is desirable partly because of the twin cams per bank, but also because of other improvements that Ferrari made over the life of the 275 model.

All four-cams are what is known as "long nosed", a modification made after it was discovered that the front of the "short nosed" cars tended to lift above 150 mph on the Mulsanne straight when they raced at Le Mans. (For most owners this must surely be of no more than academic interest but it is generally accepted that the longer snout is also more aesthetically pleasing.) Then there were the vibrations, inherent in the front-engine, transaxle layout, that were sorted by the addition of a torque tube fitted between the bellhousing and the rear-mounted gearbox. The four-cam cars have six rather than three Weber carburettors to give them a tad more urge. The long-nosed cars also have a revised boot arrangement that allows practical use of the trunk as serious luggage space.

For some reason, probably because the literature on the subject seems so besotted with the four-cam, people don't seem

Pictures of my 275 extracted from the Italian book that Tom gave me. This car required very careful re-commissioning. When I got her, MOT certificates from 1983 showed the mileage at 53,024 so it seems that she had done only 800 miles in 15 years. A museum piece!

to have cottoned on to the fact that in 1966 Ferrari made all the main improvements to the twin-cam. So a 1966, long nose twin-cam with torque tube and six carburettors is, apart from the number of camshafts, every bit as good as the four-cam, and, what is most important, it will cost up to 40% less. What I didn't cotton on to, however, was that only nine of these ultimate spec twin-cams were made in right-hand drive form. One has since been crashed and written off, another has been converted to left-hand drive and one has been made into a convertible, which leaves only six cars. I'm glad I didn't know that before I started my search or I might not have bothered.

The car I eventually found had once belonged to an infamous nobleman who has spent a bit of time at Her Majesty's pleasure for attempting to turn some of his collection into hard cash through the mechanism of bogus insurance claims. On the positive side, I also acquired a lot of press cuttings of his Lordship gazing fondly at what is now my car and proclaiming it to be his "favourite" Ferrari. The car, once painted red to fit in with the peer's collection, has been returned to its original "argento" silver, a colour which suits it very well.

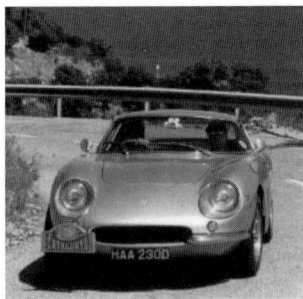

Action shot of HAA on the Catalunya. Not a trace of body roll!

I spent quite a bit of time looking for a 275 GTB, and made one or two unsuccessful forays to look at various cars with my friend and frequent rally co-driver, Tom Coldicott. Knowing of my interest, and while on a skiing holiday in Italy, he and his wife ventured into a book shop in the little village where they were staying and found a small volume on Ferraris. They thought it would make a nice gift and bought it for me. Produced by Alpi Editori, the slim tome, all in Italian and entitled *Le Ferrari da Leggenda*, loosely translated as "The Legendary Ferraris", was perused and then added to my library. Some time after I had acquired my car, I was idly glancing though the book when I noticed for the first time that the 275 featured on pages 40 and 41 and again in a frontispiece was, in fact, my own HAA 230D. Presumably photographed when in the possession of its previous, more illustrious owner, the car in its earlier incarnation is shown red, and bumperless.

If I ever get a bit full of myself in my classic Ferrari, there is always someone ready to bring me back to earth. While I was out for a recent drive, a fellow came up to me, making approving noises. "Lovely cars these Datsun 240Zs," he said appreciatively. I have to admit to more than a passing resemblance.

I needed to be even braver for my next car. It is generally accepted that the Mercedes Benz 300 SL is one of the truly great post-war classics. I have been a long-term admirer of these German cars but until recently too nervous to stick my neck out and acquire one. While its earlier Gull Wing sister is universally lauded, the roadster has somewhat languished in its shadow. I'll ignore accepted wisdom and say that, for modern driving, the open car is by far the better of the two.

A few years ago, feeling brave, I decided to try and find a good one. Most examples are now in America, so it was always odds-on that I would acquire a US model, although I think the European spec cars are marginally better looking with their one-piece headlamp lens. (Although I got my car in Germany, it was originally made for the US market.) In 1961 Mercedes went over to disc brakes and these later cars tend to fetch a premium. In mid 1962 the cast iron block was replaced with an aluminium alloy one, but rumour has it that these tend to be troublesome, although they still attract even larger premiums. I was lucky in finding a 1962 car with discs but with the older, iron engine. Only left-hand drives were made, so on this occasion I didn't waste my time looking for a right-hander, although I do find it strange sitting on the wrong side.

Developed from the fabled SLR in which Moss and Jenkins won the Mille Miglia, it is a highly acclaimed motorcar. It's made like a coach-built Rolls with doors that shut at the lightest push and make a satisfying "clunk". It is quality through and through, with a beautiful dry-sump, fuel-injected six that puts out about 240 horsepower. By any standards it is still a quick car, with an air of austere, Teutonic luxury. As with the Aston, I have not been

My 1962, Mercedes Benz 300SL roadster posing for its picture. It is one of only two left-hand drive cars I own.

able to trace any history, although the car has only 37,000 miles on the clock and is in outstanding condition.

When you set your mind on getting a particular car it often involves quite a lot of work and effort. The acquisition of the SL well demonstrates the point.

I began the search with a couple of abortive attempts in the US. One of the cars on offer was from a very reputable dealer and I was almost tempted to ignore my own advice and buy sight unseen, but at the last minute I saw sense and organised an inspection through the Mercedes-Benz club. The report was damning in the extreme and I saved myself a lot of grief.

Tom, on one of his visits to Hamburg (he is a Lufthansa pilot), came across a large classic dealership that had half-a-dozen SL300s on offer. None was up to standard, but the fellow in charge mentioned that he had a commission sale for a Roadster that was, at the time, still with its owner in Hanover. "It's a really beautiful car", he told us. "I haven't seen a better example," he added, whetting my appetite.

He promised to get the car to Hamburg, but it never materialised. For a while there was talk of us going to Hanover to view but that, too, came to nothing. I had just about given up when he called to tell me that he was no longer the agent. "The chap is going to sell the car himself", he said, "but If you buy from him direct, he has promised me a commission." He left me a number.

The American-bought Jaguar XK150S that I acquired in 1986 with some newer toys. In the foreground is the Mercedes 300SL roadster, with the Ferrari 275 GTB lurking at the rear. William Lyons' creation is in no way overshadowed by its more illustrious companions. All these cars did European rally duty in 2000.

The owner was less than friendly when I called: most uninterested, it seemed, in selling his car. Apparently he was very busy and this wasn't a good time for a visit. He said he would get in touch when things quietened down at his end. That really did seem like the end of the road, but he was back on the 'phone a week later. He had sent the car to another dealer, this time to a small town in a resort area, near Munich. He had arranged a clause in his agreement to allow me to buy the car without him having to pay their commission. "Get yourself down there", he told me, "you won't be disappointed."

Frankly, I would not have bothered if it had not been for Tom, who arranged a set of "Friends and Family" cheap tickets. We dragged Brian Stevens along with us. Going down was a pleasant experience. It was off-season but the weather was kind and we had an interesting flight. Well, I did, because Tom arranged for me to sit in the cockpit for the landing, which was quite exciting. We had a good dinner in a typical Bavarian beer keller and a made a slew of new German friends. It was quite a riotous evening. The next morning we set out for the dealership, which we found buried in the country. It was an amazing establishment based around a 17th-century barn. The building had been converted into the most striking classic car showroom I have ever seen, with 50 or more up-market cars, beautifully displayed. The SL we had come to look at was fabulous. They also had four other 300SLs on display, but the Hanover car was easily the best. A thorough inspection and a road test later, and I knew it was the one I wanted. But buying was going to prove difficult.

The dealer and his men were polite and helpful, but it was clear that my buying the car was not in their interest and they offered only the minimum of assistance. "You're on your own, pal," was definitely the message.

Unfortunately, there were a number of potential problems. First, I had not met the owner but I had conversations with a couple of UK traders who had, and their advice had been to proceed with extreme caution. Second, the car, although in Germany, was still on US plates and not European registered, although the owner assured me that import duties and VAT had been paid. Third, all the riveted-on identification plates were missing from the car. We were able, however, to find all the factory stamped marks that had been punched into the engine, chassis and body. "It's no problem," the owner told me, "the restorer failed to reattach the tags, that's all." I wasn't happy. To make matters worse, the numbers we found were decidedly disquieting. The car was a 1962 model, so one of the last produced, and indeed the chassis number seemed to confirm this. The body number on other hand was very early in the series, which suggested that the two were not necessarily matched. The owner's insistence that the money be paid into a Liechtenstein bank didn't help either.

I suppose a sensible man would have walked away and written the episode off to experience. But it was such an excellent car; it wasn't something one would easily find again. The only non-suspicious thing was the price, which although keen was certainly not cheap. The owner wasn't giving it away. Even so, having seen a few examples, this was the one I wanted. We went home and, based on a fistful of documents, copies of which were provided by the owner, I started the trail of investigation.

I began with the US title document, and got nowhere. All my best efforts drew a blank; so off to a bad start. I discovered that the car had passed to Germany through Barrett-Jackson the Scottsdale auction house. Fortunately, I was able to trace someone in the organisation who was most accommodating and helped unravel a little of the transfer saga.

Apparently, the car had been part of a complex trade deal that involved a collection of Ferraris and other exotics, and the chap in Scottsdale was able to provide me with copies of various documents that showed the path from US ownership to the fellow in Hanover. I also made contact with the lady at Lycos Engineering who keeps an informal record of all the 300 SLs around. I was at least able to ascertain that nothing negative was known about my car. It had not been reported stolen, crashed or otherwise interfered with. Things were looking up.

You often need a bit of luck, and mine came in the form of a chance conversation between Tom and one of his pilot colleagues. The fellow listened to the tale of the SL and informed Tom that his cousin was an archivist at the Mercedes factory in Stuttgart. He might be able to help with the potentially worrying numbers we had found. Two faxes later, the very kind gentleman at the factory was able to confirm, on official Mercedes letterhead, that the numbers I supplied all tallied; the car had left the factory in 1962 with all the serial numbers we had found. Good news indeed.

I was particularly anxious to establish that the paperwork really did confirm that European taxes had been paid and that the car would attract no additional UK charges. I'm sorry to say that my initial communications with HM Customs and Exercise were less than illuminating. I was given a lot of conflicting information, at one point being categorically assured that under no circumstances would I be allowed to import the car into the

UK. On another, I was ridiculed for potentially paying far too much for such an old car and more or less told that I had no right to import a foreign banger. Finally, I found an officer who knew what he was doing and provided accurate and useful information. As the vehicle would be coming into Britain from a European location, the issue, he assured me, would not be Customs and Excise related but one for the Vehicle Licensing authority.

At the start I was given the run-around by a number of people I spoke with at various DVLA offices, but eventually I found a very helpful lady at Maidstone who agreed to look over the paperwork I had and tell me, on the basis of the information provided, if she would be prepared to register and tax the vehicle. I faxed the copy paperwork in my possession and somewhat reluctantly she gave me a verbal "yes".

That seemed to clear the main areas of doubt. It had needed about 60 calls, faxes and e-mails. That's dedication for you. Next hurdle was getting the money to the chap in Hanover. I was still as nervous as a kitten and for a while contemplated taking out a briefcase of tenners, but decided that I had to trust someone some time if the transaction was to be done. I wire transferred the cash and received originals of the paperwork by return. The car arrived on the back of a transporter from Munich four days later. I unloaded her and drove straight to the MOT station. The only required change was fitment of a pair of UK spec Halogen headlamps. She passed with flying colours.

That afternoon, armed with fifteen bits of paper, most of them in German, Kathleen and I set off for the licensing centre at Maidstone. We stood in line for about 20 minutes and by the time we got to the front of the queue I was convinced that our cause was lost. I bet Kathleen a pound that it would take the counter clerk less than five minutes to find our wad of documents wanting and turn us away. I handed the chap the papers and watched his face cloud as he quickly flicked through them. "Hold on," he said, and disappeared into the back office.

He was gone less than two minutes. I tried to read his look as he returned. He consulted a list on his desk. "Will JSL 118 be OK?" he asked, and started writing out a tax disc. Kathleen was a pound to the good. Was it sheer good luck or had my diligence paid off? A bit of both I suspect. That afternoon, complete with new UK plates, I was able to go for a long and rewarding test drive.

I'm sorry for this long and potentially boring tale but it does demonstrate the effort sometimes required to get the right car.

All the literature on the subject tells you that you must also acquire a hardtop when you buy an SL roadster. What it fails to add is that most cars don't have them, and they are like hen's teeth to find if you didn't acquire one with your purchase. When I first got the car, I was given the name of an SL specialist who, it turned out, was only a dozen or so miles from my home. When I finally went to visit, he had a hardtop in stock that he was selling on behalf of a customer. So I have managed to acquire one of these rare items at a reasonable price. Apart from one long-distance rally I haven't yet done a great deal with the SL, so to some extent the jury is still out although initial impressions are favourable.

A long time ago there were two things I promised myself I'd never own. The first was a gold Rolex and the second a Cobra. I've kept my promise about the Rolex but I have reneged on the other. There are a couple of things I dislike about these cars. The first is the "steroids" look that was introduced with the Mark III version and the second is that the currency has been so debased by the large number of "fake snakes" around.

I suppose in a way the replicas are a compliment to AC cars and John Tojerio who started the whole thing off in the early '50s with the delightful AC Ace. As is often the case, the car began as a one-off. The inspiration for the subsequent long line of Ace/Cobras was a "special", built on a Tojerio chassis with a Davison aluminium body, that bore more than a passing resemblance to Ferrari's 166 Barchetta. The car had a two-litre Bristol engine and was campaigned very successfully. It was demonstrated to the Hurlocks, then the owners of AC, and luckily they had the foresight to see the potential. The body design was modified to be different enough from the Ferrari to avoid legal fisticuffs and the AC Ace was launched at the 1953 Motor Show. It wasn't a cheap car, and came in for massive competition from companies like Jaguar, Austin-Healey and Triumph. Its road holding and handling qualities however, assured the car a niche market.

The Ace not unnaturally started life with AC's own 2 litre engine, but the success of tuner/racer Ken Rudd with a Bristol-engined version saw the introduction of the Ace Bristol, which remained in production for many years. The car always had sporting pretensions and was one of the most successful sports racers of the '50s. Its most remarkable achievement was probably at Le Mans in 1959, where it decimated the 2 litre opposition and easily won its class. Driven by Rudd, it came an amazing seventh overall. The fact that the race was won by none other than Carrol Shelby (with Roy Salvadori, in an Aston) may have contributed to later developments.

When the Bristol Company announced the end of engine production, it could well have spelled the end for the Ace, but it was Rudd who came to the rescue by suggesting the use of a Ruddspeed tuned version of the 2.6 litre, Ford Zephyr/Zodiac power plant. The only major styling change was the adoption of the longer, tapered bonnet and smaller grill. Sadly, although the new car was quicker and handled better than the Bristol-engined variant, it did not prove popular with the public, who were unwilling to pay roughly twice the price of an Austin Healey for a car with a Ford engine.

This time it really did look like the end of the line, but fate intervened in the shape of Carrol Shelby, who wanted to build a Ferrari-beater and decided that the Ace could form the basis of his dream. So began the legendary partnership between little AC Cars Limited, based at Thames Ditton, England, and Carrol Shelby of America. It was Shelby who introduced the mighty Ford Motor Company into the deal. It wasn't the first or last Anglo-American sports car collaboration but it was a particularly successful one.

The Thin Wall V8

America was wedded to big engines, and the V8 configuration provided a lot of cubic inches in a relatively compact package. The problem was that big capacity also meant heavy weight. General Motors had led the way with the development of a small block, aluminium V8 that would later be sold to Rover and enter service as the mainstay of British Leyland's big engine offerings. Although considerably lighter than the equivalent iron engines of the day, aluminium resulted in other problems such as lack of rigidity, uneven thermal expansion, excessive noise and, of course, extra cost. Ford wanted to avoid the problems, and set about the development of thin wall, cast iron technology. Using their newly developed techniques, they were able to produce extremely strong, wear-resistant and rigid engines that came in at more or less the same weight as their alloy equivalents. The engine used in the Cobra was an immensely strong, over square unit that proved durable and highly tuneable. In standard 4.2 Cobra form, it produced 260 bhp. Weighing in at about 500lbs with all ancillaries, it was only slightly heavier than the two-litre Bristol unit that had produced around 120 bhp. Race-tuned versions were quoted at more than 350 bhp.

The first Ford engines dropped into the Ace were the 260 cubic inch (4.2-litre) Fairlaine small blocks, suitably modified to produce an outstanding 260 bhp. The first leaf-sprung Cobras using the Ford V8 were a revelation. Weighing about the same as the Ace and clothed in more or less the same body, except for slightly flared arches, they developed more than twice the power of the Bristol-engined cars. They even had 100 more horsepower than the stage 5 Ruddspeed Aces equipped with 2.6-litre engines and three DCOE Webers. Performance was brisk without sacrificing road holding or handling, although with their rather primitive transverse leaf-sprung suspension, inherited from the Ace, they could be a handful. People were quoting under five-second 0 to 60 times, which even today is up in the super-car class but which, in 1963, was staggering. The 4.2 engine was quickly replaced by the legendary 289 cubic inch (4.7-litre) that gave more torque and a bit more power. Rack and pinion replaced a steering box, and slightly wider wheels necessitated a fractional extension of the wheel arches.

I'll stop the history lesson. In my humble opinion the basic leaf-sprung 4.7, rack and pinion car, usually known as the MkII, is a true classic. The slightly wider track and elegant flares covering wider wire wheels only enhance the already beautiful lines of the 2.6 Ace.

As is so often the case, perfection was ruined by excess. The MkII became the MkIII with improved suspension, courtesy of coil springs, but wheels got wider and required bigger arches. Beauty was sacrificed to muscle and the cars took on a coarser look. The final incarnation saw the 7-litre, 427 cubic inch, big block V8, shoehorned in place of the 289. Wheels got even wider, as did the flared arches, and with a generally longer and fatter body the ultimate muscle car was born. Hideously noisy side exhausts were also added to the configuration. To me, it was as if a once beautiful young woman had become a bloated old tart, but that is a very personal view.

Production of all forms of the car ceased in about 1969 but, almost 40 years after the first Cobra came off the line at Thames Ditton, the cars are again in production, having restarted in the

My MkII 289 Cobra. A very quick motorcar when required but also quite happy to drift along in genteel fashion.

early '80s on both sides of the Atlantic. The AC Car Company has gone through a range of fortunes, having at various times been bought and disposed of by Ford. Both Ford and AC have jealously protected the Cobra and AC names respectively, stopping the many purveyors of kit Cobra variants from actually badging their products as originals. The problem, however, is that there are now many more replicas than the real thing, and a significant business has grown up selling reproduction parts to build and adorn the fakes. Acquiring stick-on badges and bits to match the originals, costs only a few pounds.

Notwithstanding my earlier intentions, I was eventually tempted by a MKII with an interesting history. From what I have pieced together, the car, chassis number CSX 2360, started life in 1964 when it was shipped from AC to Carrol Shelby's Californian operation. 2360 spent time as a Ford demonstrator before being acquired by its first US owner. Sadly, in the early '70s the car was severely damaged.

The remains were purchased by Brian Angliss who ran Autokraft, a Cobra restoration and parts business. He later took over AC cars. The car was rebuilt at the factory using new and reconditioned parts and was returned to original MKII specification. Although it had been left-hand drive, it was rebuilt in right-hand configuration. In 1976 the car passed to a new owner who, for some reason, never quite got around to using it. Having stood unused at the back of his garage for some 20-odd

The well instrumented but Spartan interior

years, it was finally resold in 1998. The new owner is reputed to have been a racer intending to modify the car for track use, but he never carried out the work. Two years later it was back on the market with just 1000 miles on the clock.

I was initially seduced by what I had thought was a very rare, original right-hand drive car. By the time I had traced the history I had experienced the brilliance of the package and was hooked. I still am. Apart from a clutch that feels like a kick-start on a jumbo jet, it goes and handles beautifully.

I love my understated MKII with its subtle lines and scintillating performance. It's such a simple and basic car, with no frills or creature comforts; weighing in at about 18 cwt and delivering almost 300 horsepower, it goes rather well. I suppose, on balance, it is a good thing that my British racing green rocket attracts scant attention. People are far more inclined to drool over the fat-wheeled, metallic purple one with the white interior and Range Rover engine that sits outside the pub on fine weekends. (That doesn't make me sound very nice, does it?)

I promised myself that there would be no more cars until I got rid of some I already had. Of course, if there were no limits, there are hundreds of cars I'd like to own, but few that I really crave given the constraints. I'm not interested in owning cars that I don't use and, in any event, there is a limit to the number one can drive in a reasonable timeframe. Nevertheless, I'd like to have at least one American classic, and my first choice would be a 1935/36 Auburn Speedster. Its a flamboyant choice but that, I suppose, is my style; it certainly fits right in with the others. I've put out the feelers but as yet nothing has come up. There were a few right-handed cars produced and, if I am able to lay my hands on one, it will be one of those.

I hope that my love of old cars comes through this narrative. I have to say that some of my happiest moments are in the motor house just being with my old, as well as my newer, acquisitions. I'll swear that they have personalities, but I'd better shut up before I show myself up as an eccentric old fool.

Investing in Old Cars

Will prices rise again? Should old cars be thought of as investments? Is it wise to include a classic car element within a mixed investment portfolio?

I think the answer to all three questions is probably, no. Actually, I have no idea if prices will one day again go mad and hit the crazy heights of the late '80s, but I wouldn't bet on it. I suppose that if you want to invest for growth the stock market is probably your best bet (although recent down-turns make you wonder).

There now, that's the sensible bit out of the way. Let's look at that third question again. If we leave in the word "wise" then I guess the answer is still "no", but there may be an alternative point of view. If you are crazy about old cars, have the bulk of your estate wrapped up in sensible things like houses, building societies and stocks and bonds then maybe, just maybe, there's a place for something that will make your heart pound a little faster.

Remember, you can't polish your unit trust certificates or experience the joy of negotiating tight country lanes in a corporate bond. Provided you don't expect to make a fortune, are prepared to buy carefully and spend on regular, proper maintenance, then there is no reason why you shouldn't be able to enjoy an outstanding old motor car and come out even, or maybe ahead of the game. The big question is; will the market

I'd really like one of these 150 horsepower, supercharged Auburns.

get better over time? No one knows, but the odds are that for the right cars we won't see significant falls. It helps if you are in a position to sit out a mini-crash in the event that things do go a bit pear shaped. If you need to sell in a hurry then it's odds on you'll lose your shirt. Also keep a watch on the development of technologies that are likely to make the petrol engine obsolete, and get out at the first whiff of a breakthrough. But please don't take any of this as prediction or recommendation.

The first rule is to buy with your head but also with a huge chunk of your heart. This is not out-and-out investment territory. You must use and enjoy your car, experience the pleasure of owning and driving a fine, old motor to the full and then maybe in time, if you can bear to, part with it for more than you paid.

What should you buy? There are no absolute rules, but there are some guidelines. Guideline one; buy pretty. Beauty, they say is in the eye of the beholder but do not completely trust your own judgement. There are lots of cars that are universally acclaimed as beautiful, so stick with accepted market judgements but avoid designs that come and go with fashion. Two, always go for excellent performance. Don't ever consider anything that won't hold its own in modern traffic. Big engined, sports orientated cars best fit the bill. Three, with some notable exceptions, open, two-seater cars are generally thought to be the most desirable. Four, go for makes and models that were originally expensive and exclusive. So Aston, Ferrari and Bentley are likely to be better bets than Austin, Morris and Triumph.

Five, seek out scarce cars of which relatively few examples were made. Don't take this too far. Whatever you choose must be numerous enough to have established a market presence and value. Finally, always go for cars in excellent condition. It's worth paying a bit more for superb panel fit and finish as well as exemplary mechanics. For the average owner there is nothing to be gained from acquiring cheap, shoddy examples. Always get an independent expert to examine thoroughly any prospective purchase. The appropriate car club should be able to help.

CHAPTER 14

Competition

In the early '90s I began to wonder what to do with my old cars. A number of people I knew were beginning to use their classics for rallies and other forms of competition and I started to think I'd like to have a go. Kathleen, against her better judgement, was persuaded to give it a try and I called Roger Deeley, the organiser of the well known Claret and Classics rally. It was still January and the event was not until June, but I was turned away: the competitor list had long been filled to capacity. As luck would have it, at the time Roger was considering a new event he had christened the "Bilbao Classic". It was to be run in the Basque regions of France and Spain. The timeframe was late September, and he promised us a place if he managed to get it off the ground.

We decided to take the V12 E-type, and got into a flurry of preparation. I amassed a vast array of spare parts, obtained rebuilt wheels and fitted new tyres. I had the car thoroughly

Kathleen and I at the finish of the 1st Bilbao Classic. We were given a wonderful reception at the Remelluri vineyard in the heart of Rioja country.

serviced at least twice and generally went completely over the top. Even so, when the time came to set off on the long trek to the start at Bordeaux, the blooming car wouldn't start. Our first port of call was the local garage for a new battery. It is hard to believe the trepidation with which we faced our first event.

I don't want to burden the reader with a detailed account of the workings of regularity rallying (for the interested few there is a simple description later in this chapter) but the gist is that competitors are given a set speed (usually quite low – about 30 mph) and a detailed set of route instructions to follow for each section. The objective is to get to an undisclosed location somewhere along the route (you know when you're there because rally marshals will be waiting at the side of the road) at exactly the right second so as to have averaged the set speed for the complete section. A rally is made up of multiple sections.

We armed ourselves with a set of stopwatches but not a set of average speed tables, (for those not familiar with regularity rallying the need for such items will not yet be apparent). As we had not done any previous rallying, I was not aware that I would need these tables nor that they were readily available. So I devised my own somewhat convoluted method of keeping to time.

In the paperwork that arrived before the start, we were given our average speed (50 kph) for the whole rally. The tables I produced were a straightforward matrix. One axis showed the time (which the navigator would read from the stopwatch) and the other the mileage (to be read from the odometer). The intersection point gave the speed in miles per hour that the driver would have to drive over the next two miles in order to bring the journey average to 50 kph. In order not to frighten Kathleen, when this speed was greater than 100mph I inserted dashes. Both my speedo and trip were inaccurate, so I built what I had calculated to be the appropriate compensation factors into the numbers.

If you know about this type of competition, you'll realise that my approach bordered on farce and if you don't, suffice it to say it was ludicrously baroque and woefully inadequate. We nevertheless came 7th from a field of about 40 and were hooked (at least I was), and I vowed to go back the following year and try again.

Later in the year someone gave me a video of the 1989 Classic Marathon and I found the whole thing so compelling that I decided to prepare one of my cars to FIVA specification so that I could enter international events. We started with the series 2 E-type but, as it was a 1969 car, the rule book requirements were so arduous that I abandoned the plan and decided to use my XK150 instead. It being a 1958 model, the level of preparation was less stringent. This is the car that had come back to the UK from America and had lain more or less untouched at the back of the garage for rather a long time. I decided on a complete rebuild and a change of colour.

In order to give us something to aim for, I entered the Henry Lidden rally, which was a one-day, navigational event run by the Bath Motor Club. Work started on 9th January, while the event was scheduled for 17th March. In that time the car was completely stripped, the engine rebuilt and up-rated and the suspension rebuilt and improved. The bodywork was found to require a minimum of repair and was painted inside and out in Carmen red. Brian retrimmed the interior and fitted a new hood. I got the car back a week before the event and, to run it in, drove it down to Devon and back without incident.

We fiddled about with last-minute preparation and got in reasonable fettle to the Bath start-in, where it easily passed scrutineering. After a bit of confusion about who was to be my co-driver, an enthusiastic neighbour stepped into the breach and did a creditable job. The format was a little arcane and the whole thing a bit of a mystery; we never really knew exactly what we were doing or what was happening. We seemed to be going all right most of the time, although I made a hash of the auto-tests. When it was over we both thought it had gone quite well, since we had got round the course and had found all the controls. We later discovered that we made a technical error somewhere along the route and were left with a piece of paper too many. In any case, we were disqualified and it all ended rather disappointingly. As a result, I decided that one-day navigational events probably weren't my bag. I had adored the Bilbao but not the Lidden, although I suppose if we had done well it might have been a different story. The car held up magnificently, a tribute to Brian Stevens and his work force.

The next event began at 6.30 one Sunday morning in April, when we set off for the start of the "Highland Fling". Preparation had started badly when we discovered that the clutch, which had got us through the Lidden, was not man enough to make it through the Fling. So, on the Thursday before we set off, out came the engine and gearbox and in went a replacement clutch assembly. With one thing and another, we finally got home with the car more or less ready on Saturday evening at 10 o'clock. It was not without some apprehension that we set out for Scotland on the Sunday morning.

I had heard of the Highland Fling through a classic car magazine and knew very little about it, apart from the fact that it was a four-day event run in the far north of Scotland. To find out more I called one of the organisers, who persuaded me that even as a novice I'd be able to cope and have a good time into the bargain. A few days after I had paid up and was committed, I mentioned what I planned to an experienced competitor and was a little alarmed to be told that in his view it was too tough for someone with so little experience. When it came to the crunch, the only person who was prepared to have a go at it with me was my daughter, Sarah, on Easter break from university. She had never done anything remotely like it before and the published

Highland Fling competitors
at Inchnadamph

information told us very little except that the competition consisted of 30 or so "tests" of various types. These included hill climbs, auto-tests, regularities and navigational runs. Most of it was on tarmac roads, but as it turned out there was also a bit of off-road competition, some of it quite rough.

The drive to Glasgow was mercifully fast and uneventful, and we got to the hotel where the rally was to start in time for lunch. As the other competitors began to arrive, however, we suffered further blows to our already faltering confidence. Not only were most of them veterans of the Fling and other major events, but their equipment looked terribly professional. The Healeys were particularly impressive, bristling with Haldas, (special distance measuring devices) roll cages and arrays of spotlights. Several of them had headsets and microphone communication between driver and navigator. All in all we felt out-classed and out-gunned, and we spent a troubled night wondering what we had got ourselves into. On the positive side, the event was run by a couple of fabulous characters; Malcolm Nicholson and Roy Campbell. They were both helpful and charming and very, very funny. When we weren't rallying they kept us laughing.

In the course of the first day we drove 300 miles to the far North-west. The route took us past magnificent scenery that included places like Glencoe, Fort William, Invergarry, the Muir of Ord and Ullapool. Between the fast road sections we stopped for a number of auto-tests, a regularity, and an incredible hill climb. The Corkscrew climb was run on what can best be described as a mountain track consisting of seven 180º turns up a steep hillside. Not a scrap of tarmac in sight. We had no idea what we faced before the start, and just before we set off a marshal suggested that the '150 wouldn't be able to make it around the hairpins and that I should take it easy. In the event we got around all but one, and gave it our absolute best shot. We also found the auto-tests hard going and, having never done anything of that type before, I made a pig's ear of things. The most difficult part was remembering the course, which from the driving seat always looked utterly different from the diagram provided by the organisers. Anyway, probably because of my lack of experience with both the car and the event, I found the XK150 a handful around the tight courses. By early evening, however, we made it to Inchnadamph in the north-west Highlands.

We knew that we had not had a "good" day but hoped we had acquitted ourselves not too badly. But it was not so. The morale-sapping news was posted on the results board just before dinner. Car Number 20, Jaguar XK150S, was last. Apart from our placing, we had had a thoroughly enjoyable day, and we kept telling ourselves that this was all that mattered; but we weren't convinced. I have to confess to being a little down at the close of day one.

We set off on a drizzly Tuesday at 7 am, last car to start. Well, at least we couldn't do any worse. The day consisted of several auto-tests, a couple of regularities and some fast road sections. We got back to the hotel around 6 o'clock after a hard day's rallying. Dinner was at 7 and then first car away at 9 pm for a two-hour night section. With lights ablaze we hurtled around a couple of regularities and another auto-test. By this time, regardless of where we were placed, we were having a good time. We got back around a quarter to midnight; luckily the bar was still open. Before turning in for the night Sarah and I learned we had moved up to sixteenth overall. We had enjoyed it more than expected, having spent the best part of 12 hours in competition that day.

Day three was another tough one. It started with a hill climb on a closed road at Dourne. We had hoped to do well, but the road was covered in mud and we managed only to fishtail our way up the straights, having got the back swinging widely through the turns. Unfortunately, our uncontrolled antics didn't do much for our speed. We also had four regularities that day which we managed rather well. Even our auto-test results weren't too bad. We ended the day with the Rumpster hill climb where, on a dry track, we were able to blast our way to the top. Unfortunately, we were too quick and incurred a 16-second penalty for beating the set time. But it was great fun and well worth the measly few points we lost.

At the end of the Fling, my daughter Sarah, showing off her cup for coming third in class.

We got back to the hotel around half-past six and, as there was no night section, we once more settled down in the bar. When the results were posted we discovered we had had our best day, moving up to ninth overall. We were surprised and thrilled. I could claim very little of the credit, the plaudits going to my daughter Sarah for her excellent navigation and regularity time keeping.

Our fellow competitors warned us not to get too ambitious on the last day. "Try and hold your position", they advised, "ninth for a first time on this event is good going." But that night I slept even less soundly, tossing and turning and worrying about holding on to our hard-won place.

The main test on the last day was a long navigational section, based on an ordnance survey map, around Wick, Thurso and John O'Groats. The section contained an element of "plot and bash", whereby we were given a navigational puzzle to solve while we were on the road. A lot of people got lost, and cars came whizzing past us in all directions. Sarah kept her nerve and ignored what the others were doing. A couple of further auto-tests, when we put in adequate if unspectacular times, and we were back in the hotel for dinner, prize-giving and, sadly, the end of the event. We had managed to get through it and the car stood up to the pounding, never missing a beat. Another cheer for Mr Stevens. On the last day we pulled up one more place, finishing third in class and eighth overall. We felt a real sense of achievement. The whole thing was a hugely enjoyable experience and we made a lot of new friends. Sarah was the hero of the week, although I've never since tempted her back into a rally car with me. I wonder why?

I vowed to do the event again the following year, hence the acquisition of the Tiger and the story already told in Chapter 12. Sadly, 1995 was the last Highland Fling; the event never ran again, which is a great shame.

For one reason or another, I had not competed in another hard driving event until we had a go at a couple of quite tough foreign rallies in 2000. I have, however, gone back each year for Roger Deeley's Bilbao, which he later christened the Basque Classic. The fifth and last was run in 1999 when, together with my co-driver Tom Coldicott, we managed a win.

Kathleen and I have done a number of events together including a Claret & Classics and the Norman Conquest in the SS 100. We have also competed in a Tour of Ireland in the XK150 (I've done two other Irish Tours with a different navigator), a Tour of the Dordogne in the DB6 and another the following year in the Mercedes 300SL.

In general, I have settled for fairly gentle, non-car-breaking events where the emphasis is as much on good company and socialising as on competition. In 2000, however, I competed in four events, each with a different car and navigator. The first two were quite tough, although not as challenging as the Fling. The first was an odd event that started near Spa in Belgium, where we loaded the cars on transporters which were then sent down to Spain. John Lockyer and I, with the other drivers and navigators, followed by air to Barcelona. We spent two days in the mountains near Lloret and then rallied back through France into Belgium. Although we almost did well, a mistake near the end forced us down the field. We really put the Ferrari through its paces, though.

A few weeks later, Tom Coldicott and I had a go at the Liège-Rome-Liège in the XK150. The regularity sections were little more than hill climbs or road races, and a lot of cars went over the

John Lockyer beside my XK 150 at the end of the 1997 Classic Tour of Ireland. John has been my co-driver twice on the event. Although victory has eluded us, we have always come away with a few pots. We hope to have another crack at it again soon.

Little and Large. This isn't a trick photograph but it shows something of the variety of cars on historic rallies. The Rolls is a 20 horsepower and the Austin Seven is a special that proved to be a much faster car. I followed it on the motorway at 80 mph.

Loading on to the ferry for the 1999 Tour of the Dordogne. The Aston behaved impeccably apart from trouble with an electric window, which is the Achilles heel of these cars. If you ever leave the car for more than a month without use you can be sure that the windows will play up when you try to use it again.

Kathleen did a sterling job of navigation and we came 5th overall and second in class. She loves the comfort, wet weather protection and load carrying capacity of the DB6.

edge. We came 5th from 106 starters, so acquitted ourselves well enough, I suppose. Later in the year I had go at the Norman Conquest in the SS, this time with my old friend John Williamson as co-driver. We didn't do particularly well but had a good time.

Four days after the finish of the Conquest, Kathleen and I took the 300SL on our second "Tour of the Dordogne". She did a sterling job and we got around without a single navigational error. Minor problems with the speedo kept us out of the big prizes, but we still managed to collect a few pots.

No year would be complete without at least a couple of long-distance, continental classic car rallies.

My start in motor racing at an advanced age was, as usual, driven by events and not the result of careful planning. In December 1995 I attended a Brooks auction with the specific objective of bidding for a low mileage XK120 fixed-head coupé. (This was before I obtained the rebuild project described in Chapter 12.) There I saw and fell in love with Holly. Holly was a pre-war, 4.3-litre Alvis sports/racer special with the registration number HOL 56. She had been built and raced in the '50s by one Harold Barr, who was reputed to be a madcap special builder. Most of her important bits had started life as part of a 1937 Charlesworth bodied saloon. The chassis had been cut and lightened and the engine was a long way from standard. In the '80s she was acquired by an unlikely but brilliant club racer called Albert Sparrowhawk. Albert is not only a charming and unassuming man, but also a gifted and talented engineer. He did an enormous amount of work on the car, including transforming the handling and road holding by repositioning the engine in the chassis. Albert commissioned a stylish new body from Rod Jolly, the world-renowned coachbuilder, before the firm achieved its current elevated status. He also converted the engine to racing specification and campaigned the car in VSCC events with great acclaim. He was one of the most successful racers of the day. In the early '90s Albert sold Holly to another racer, who continued the improvements and was also very successful. The car came with an

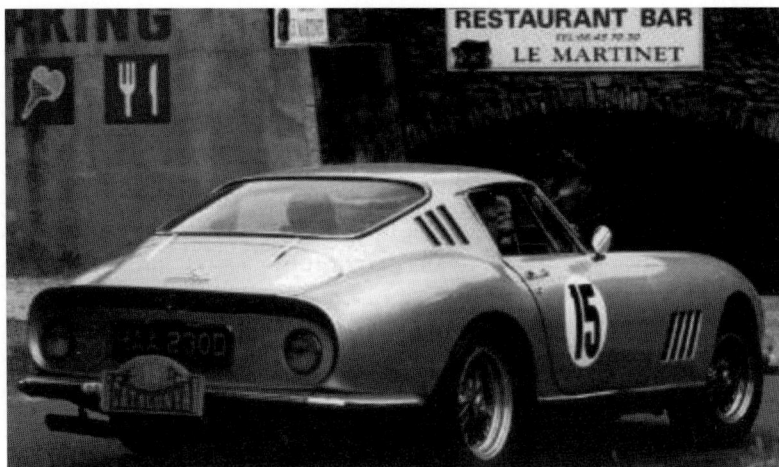

I contested the 2000 Catalunya Marathon with John Lockyer. We drove to Jalhay near Spa in Belgium where the cars were loaded on to transporters and shipped to Lloret in Spain. In this picture the Ferrari is on its way through France back to Belgium. We did very well until the penultimate day, when we took a wrong turn.

John Williamson navigated on the 2000 Conquest Normande. We were not at our best and managed only a lowly 10th. Although there were lots of prizes we came away empty-handed. It was an excellent rally, however, and we had a good time. As always, the SS was a star. A major feature of the week was the French petrol strike, which had us scurrying for fuel at every opportunity.

The Mercedes 300SL on its first event, the 2000 Dordogne. Kathleen didn't put a foot wrong all week and we were never off the rally route. Sadly, the trip meter was faulty and ruined our chances. We nevertheless came first in class. By doing lots of arithmetic and having several stopwatches, which we started at different times, we also managed to win the last day of the rally and got a nice prize for our trouble. We were photographed getting ready to leave a control. The marshal is organiser Carol Corp.

Historic Regularity Rallying

For those unfamiliar with this type of rally, a few words about the basics may be useful. The main objective is to have fun in old cars without endangering life, limb or motorcar and at the same time provide some challenging competition. The longer events usually take you through delightful countryside, with the mornings devoted to competition and the afternoons and evenings free for sightseeing, a few drinks and dining with your friends. Each team consists of a driver and a navigator. The navigator's job is to guide the driver around a route provided by the organiser. This is usually in the form of a set of brief instructions and "tulip" diagrams, which are schematic drawings of road junctions showing the directions of entry and exit. There are no maps involved, so you have to follow each instruction precisely to stay on course.

To make the process more taxing, the team must maintain rigorous timing. The organiser will set a specific average speed for each section, say 30 mph. A day is broken down into several sections with undisclosed controls at the start and finish of each one. Because the competitors have no idea where the controls are located, they are forced to maintain the average speed through the whole section. The organisers will have accurately measured the distances and have worked out, based on the given average speed, the exact time it should take. You lose one point for each second late or early at a control. It sounds impossible but, with the aid of stopwatches, average speed tables and a bit of practice, scores in single figures and even zeros are not uncommon.

enormous history file and an enviable reputation as a race winner.

She stood on the floor of the auction room looking provocative, and I spent a lot of time wandering around her and trying her out for size. At one point a man in a deerstalker hat came along and started chatting to me. It was a while before he introduced himself; he was none other than Albert Sparrowhawk,

The Alvis 4.3 Special at Silverstone, rebuilt by Brian Stevens after the incident at Mallory.

who had come along to see how his old car would fare in the sale. I guess I caught the bug of enthusiasm from him and soon we were talking like mad about how I could make a start in vintage racing with a wonderful machine like the Alvis. Frankly, knowing what I know now I wouldn't advise anyone to start their racing career in a 4.3-litre monster like Holly, particularly as vintage racing is usually conducted without benefit of safety aids like harnesses or rollover bars. But some of us are more foolhardy than others.

I've searched my memory a number of times to try and reconstruct the events leading up to that fateful bidding session. I have to admit that my best recollection is probably not totally accurate. I do recall that the XK120 I had gone to buy was sold at too high a price and I was wandering away from the action, when Holly came up for sale. The catalogue estimate was huge, certainly more than I would have paid for a car I had not intended to buy in the first place. I was also aware that it would be a pointless acquisition for, although I had flirted with the idea, I was certainly not committed to track racing. I think at the time my view was that the car was enormous fun but in no way part of my plans for future motor sport. As I stood there in full view of the auctioneer (it was Robert Brooks himself), the bidding died at a figure considerably below the lower estimate. I suppose it sounded like a bargain and, on crazy impulse, I put up my paddle and went the next £1000. I'm not quite sure why. The bidding restarted and

A much-modified Alvis engine showing off triple SUs and lots of polished alloy. These racing versions develop almost twice as much power as they did in original form.

went up another £3000 in a flash and then stopped. Brooks looked directly at me but I kept my paddle down. No further bid. The difference between a good auctioneer and a great one is the instinctive ability to sense the winning move. He fixed me with questioning eye, "I'll take a £250 increase," he offered. I gave it only a moment's thought before nodding assent; the car was mine. I didn't know whether to be elated or horrified until Albert and a whole gang of Alvis racers came through the crowd to congratulate me. I was a provisional member of their exclusive club, and I felt honoured.

Brian took charge of the car, which in truth was in very poor shape beneath its glossy exterior and required a lot of work. We didn't get it to the track until April 1997, more than a year after purchase.

Some American friends, knowing I was about to start racing, invited me to join them on a competition course at Lime Rock in Connecticut a few days before my first appearance at Silverstone. The schedule was tight. The races were on a Saturday with a practice on the previous Friday afternoon. If I went to Lime Rock, I would arrive back at Heathrow on Friday morning. I decided, nevertheless, that four days of immersion tuition would be worth the trouble. We spent the time in America roaring around the Connecticut circuit in Formula Dodge single-seaters, which were about as far removed from a 1930s Alvis Special as you could get. After four nonetheless useful days, I got into Heathrow in the early morning, had a shower and set off for Silverstone to try out the Alvis in afternoon practice. I think it would be accurate to describe my mood as apprehensive.

I had never driven the Alvis on a track before. The four days at Lime Rock had been very controlled and very sanitised, and even then there had been moments of sheer terror. When the officials ordered us to muster at the entry to the circuit, words cannot describe the utter panic that welled up inside me. The previous session was running late and the big entry gates were closed. Sitting in the car I could see nothing of what was happening on the circuit but I could hear the cars going round. The terrifying sound gradually built, rose to a crescendo and then faded as the cars approached and then flew past. The roar as they went along the pit wall, sometimes three abreast, was deafening. I suddenly realised I could not to go through with it. The thought of joining that maelstrom of roaring machinery filled with experienced racers on one of the world's major circuits convinced me this was no place for a greenhorn like me.

I turned in absolute terror to see if I could reverse my car out of the crush of racers waiting to get on the circuit. It was hopeless: being new and knowing little of the procedure I had been one of the first cars at the gates and I was completely hemmed in. Other, eager competitors were all around, blipping their throttles, anxious to get on with things as they waited for the gates to open and let them on. We sat there for another five minutes as my sinking feeling plumbed new depths and my insides turned to water. Suddenly everything went quiet as the cars that had been flying round a few moments earlier left the circuit, allowing the next practice session to get under way. The gates were flung open and the marshals gesticulated wildly, trying to get us on as quickly as they could. "Go, go, go!," they screamed above the roar of racing engines and I suddenly found myself accelerating hard through the gates and up the pit lane exit onto the circuit. There were cars all around. It was only a practice session but for me it was the race of my life. I overtook car after car in my excitement at being on the track in my own racecar for the first time.

I drove like a lunatic, forgetting everything my instructors had taught me at Lime Rock. Racing lines and track position were tossed to the winds as I was caught up in the exuberance of my first 20-minute practice. I came in exhausted but happy with a smoking engine and worn down tyres.

My first event the next day was what they call a high speed trial, where novices go out for 30 minutes and are given a set number of laps to do in the time. It was good practice in more or less race conditions, and I duly did the appointed number of circuits and got a little cup for my trouble. Earlier that morning I had gone out to qualify for the scratch race, which I had entered but didn't do terribly well, ending up somewhere around the middle of the field. Actually I had an engine problem, not improved by charging around for 20 or so laps in the trial. I ended the race with smoke pouring out of just about everywhere. Frankly, I doubt it made any difference to the result, but I'd got through my baptism of fire and anxiously awaited my next outing.

June Silverstone was run in glorious sunshine, and I was entered in a scratch as well as a handicap race. The handicaps are enormous fun but you need to keep your wits about you. The field consists of cars of all types and capacities. The fast cars are at the back and the slow ones at the front. The grid positions are based on the handicapper's assessment of what each competitor can achieve on a good day. With a 4.3-litre car, one is always going to be towards the back of the grid. The slower cars take off minutes before the faster ones, which tear off in pursuit when it is their turn. It can be frustrating meeting Austin Sevens firmly on the racing line as you come into the bends, but it's all good fun. My excuse that day was that there just weren't enough laps, and I think I ended up about fifth on the track but way down on handicap. The scratch race was more interesting and I qualified seventh, tore off the line and finished the race fourth. When the results were announced however, the second man had been disqualified for some minor infringement and I was given third, but I knew I had really been fourth.

I was growing in confidence and recklessness by the time we went to Mallory Park for the next meeting. I went to a track day the week before to practise and, although I ended up blowing an oil pipe off my engine, I managed some quick times. Came the day of the race: I was determined to do well and shot off in the qualifying session going extremely quickly. I passed a blown MG on the pit straight but was balked by a slower car coming out of Gerrard's bend and the MG went by me. As we came out of the bend towards the "esses", I decided to try and go past him. It was a stupid move

The Family at June Silverstone 1998, where I had a very good day. I came 4th and was given 3rd. Holly performed well.

and completely pointless, as we weren't actually racing and it is odds-on I would have caught him on the pit straight anyway. The next thing I recall, the Alvis was going sideways at high speed. I was probably too inexperienced to catch the slide in any event, but when I got on to the grass I realised it was all over. It seemed to happen in slow motion. I'm told I hit the tyre wall at about 70 mph. The impact demolished both the wall and the Alvis. I was badly shaken but, apart from some very lumpy bruises, I was not seriously injured. The Alvis was a write-off. The officials at the meeting were heroes as always and got the wreckage loaded up on our trailer. Brain Stevens, who was acting as my racing mechanic for the day, left the scene with one very broken racing car and a very chastened driver. We took no further part in events that year.

Brian worked miracles. He took the chassis apart, and not only repaired it but made it a good deal better than it had been before. In May the following year we made it to Donnington Park. We went up the night before, and after dinner Brian and I took a stroll to check the weather. It was a beautiful evening without a cloud in the sky and all looked set for a dry day's racing. Both Holly and I are pretty hopeless in the wet, and I hate damp tracks, so the prospect of clear skies was good news.

The next morning I woke early to the sound of pouring rain. Qualifying was a nightmare: the conditions were the wettest to date, and most of the time I just couldn't see the track through my visor. I spun the car twice at the Old Hairpin and didn't even bother to look at my qualifying times, so convinced was I that it had been a disaster. The first event was a handicap and I did disappointingly poorly. It was partly the wet, but I suppose the crash at Mallory was also taking its toll. I was certainly a lot less gung-ho than I had been. When it became time for the scratch race, if I'm honest, I would have been glad to have found some fault with the car, made my excuses and dropped out. As I drove to the grid from the muster area I gave myself a good talking-to. There was no point in going racing unless I enjoyed it and was prepared to give it my very best shots. I'm not sure I convinced myself.

I was, however, surprised by my position on the grid: I was sixth, with a lot of very seriously quick machinery behind me. Perhaps the timekeepers had made a mistake. The good news was that the rain had stopped and, mercifully, the track was dry. The even better news was that two cars in front of me hadn't made it to the start, so I was effectively fourth. We did a parade lap, but before the starter could bring down his flag, the chap right in front of me held up his hand: his engine had stalled. The starter was having none of it. "Get him off!," he screamed at the marshals and the erstwhile competitor was ignominiously wheeled off the track.

I was third on the grid when the flag came down. I shot off the line like a bullet and, for the first time in my life, I was in the

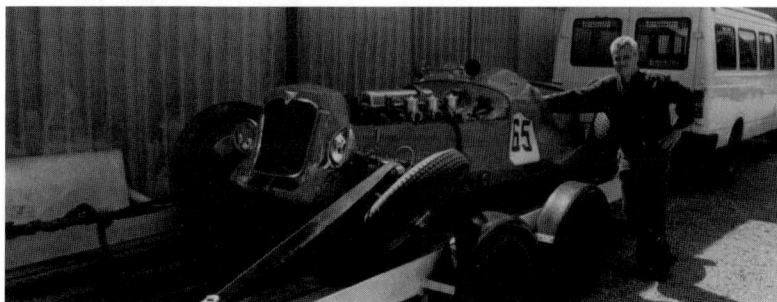

The remains of poor Holly returned to Brian's workshop after the Mallory crash.

lead. On the second lap I was caught by a big Bentley special that went by me up Starkey Straight on sheer grunt. I out-braked him and myself at Goddard's chicane and my chassis just touched his rear wheel. The effect was to slow me down enough to regain control and gently to push him off the track. I was back in the lead. I was caught and passed on Wheatcroft Straight by Julian Bronson's blown Riley Blue Streak Special (Julian wasn't driving at the time or I would never have been in contention). This is a wickedly fast and well sorted car and I knew that if it got away I would never be able to catch it, so I decided to try another outbraking manoeuvre. I went in too fast and too deep at Redgate curve and spun the car. The Riley shot off and the big Bentley hurtled past. Luckily, I ended up facing the right way and went after them before another car came round. I went like the clappers for a while and began to reel in the Bentley, but it got dangerous when we started to catch the back markers, who were for the most part unaware that they were being lapped and weren't being overly co-operative. I settled for third. It was my finest race up to that date, particularly helped by being run in good company.

As I passed the finishing line I came off the gas and applied the brakes and, although the pedal was rock hard, there was no effect whatsoever. The drums, now glowing red, had cracked in a dozen places and were offering no resistance to the shoes. In the heat of battle I hadn't noticed that I was running without brakes. If the race had been a lap longer, I probably would have.

Later that year we went back to Mallory Park. It was a strange feeling to be where I had crashed so heavily the year before. I wasn't sure I wanted to play. As usual, we were called to the muster area before the start of the previous race and, as we watched the battle play out, a beautiful Alvis-engined Frazer Nash ploughed heavily into the tire wall exactly where I had gone in the year before. It took the ambulance crew 50 minutes to lift the driver from the wreckage. Apart from the fact that I felt rotten for the poor chap (who incidentally made a full recovery and is back racing), I have to admit to having a bad moment or two.

I had been moved up to fourth on the grid, because the pole position man had not made it to the start. But having the long wait had given him the chance to repair his car, an amazingly quick Morgan three-wheeler, and after 45 minutes he suddenly appeared and took his rightful place. I made another good start but the Morgan was already a speck in the distance. For me, it developed into a ding-dong battle with a Riley which wasn't as fast as me but more nimble around the circuit. He would pass me on the outside around the long Gerrard's bend, and I would catch and re-pass him on Kirby Straight. The game went on until the last lap, when I was determined to hold him off around Gerrard's and I just made it. We got into back markers, and I managed to put a slower car between us before the 180° Shaw's hairpin. It was all over, and I went past the chequered flag in second place. The third place man in the Riley very sportingly gave me the thumbs-up as we came off the track.

All this sounds as though I'm an ace driver waiting for my moment of glory, but I'm not. In fact I have very little natural talent for racing, but I enjoy the whole business of being involved and the adrenaline rush when I do well. I have recently gone through a series of spins, minor shunts and mechanical breakdowns that have rather diminished the enjoyment, but I hope I have another season or two left in me before creaking

The '120 racer in action at Snetterton. A somewhat easier drive than the Alvis.

bones force me to hang up my helmet.

In late 1998, the Jaguar Enthusiasts' Club announced a race series exclusively for XK sports cars. The idea was born in June of that year during the XK 50-year celebrations at Donnington. As part of the festivities, the organisers put on an informal XK race which attracted cars from all over the world. The enthusiasm that was generated persuaded the organisers to promote a series in 1999.

When the races were officially announced, I was rather caught on the hop. Being an XK lover of long standing, as well as an enthusiastic racer, it seemed the most natural thing in the world for me to be involved, but the more I considered entering one of my cars, the less suitable they all seemed. Frankly, I just wasn't prepared to start cutting holes in the bodywork to fit rollover bars and cages. After a lot of consideration I decided not to compete but, as the first race date drew nearer, I began to waver and, when an aluminium-bodied XK120 racer came up for sale, I relented and acquired my fifth XK. With Brian's help I spent a lot of time trying to get the car right, but my decision to fit a Toyota five-speed gearbox proved a disaster. The gearbox difficulties, coupled with a persistent starter problem, rather put paid to the 1999 season, in which I finished only one of the four races I entered.

My experiences with the XK demonstrate the frustrations and difficulties of club racing. There are occasions when real dedication is needed in the face of continuing setbacks. In the first race at Silverstone, I had problems changing gear but managed to qualify fourth. In the race, however, coming up to the tight turn at Becketts, I couldn't find third and freewheeled my way into a spin. Unfortunately, another competitor ran into me and took us both out. At Brand's Hatch I had no excuse except that, as I have already said, I am not at my best in the wet. The car was playing up and wouldn't re-start with a hot engine. I qualified way down in ninth place and raced my way up to about fifth before spinning off at Druids in torrential rain. I might have got going and possibly maintained station but the car wouldn't restart, so I was out. At Castle Combe I had a better race,

Typical XK Challenge Grid

qualifying fourth and getting within a second of the pole man. I finished third but still had terrible gear selection problems and lost seconds on every lap. The last race at Snetterton was another disaster in the wet, with me failing to get second gear just after the start and dropping down to last before the first bend. I battled back up the field and then spun at Riches. A lot of the front men crashed out ahead of me and, if I had been able to restart, I might have made some useful progress, but it was not to be.

I'm not complaining, just highlighting a not untypical racing season for an average club racer. I do it because it can be enormous fun. When things go well it's wonderful, and when they don't I lay my plans for the next time out. I'm looking forward to next season, which is as it should be. I'm hoping spring will see me back on the track and taking part in a host of classic rallies. I suppose it's a case of "Gather ye rose buds while ye may".

I imagine I'll stop racing in the not too distant future, partly because it's an enormous drain on resources and partly because my family has always been unhappy with the idea. Historic rallying, on the other hand, will go on for a number of years. In some ways, hands-on restoration and competition are the two extremes that seem to exemplify why I love old cars and the activities that surround them.

Conclusions

One of the nice things about living in Britain is the number of old cars one still sees on the roads. Every year, when the good weather arrives, people bring out all manner of machinery that has spent the winter tucked up in cosy garages. A particularly heartening aspect of this enthusiasm is that so many of the cars are ordinary family saloons that owners, over the years, have carefully cherished and maintained. I often wonder, however, what the future holds for what has been called the classic car movement. (Classic in this context seems simply to mean old.) On the positive side, judging by the large number of shows and activities, old cars seem more popular now than they ever have been. But is the trend set to continue? I'm not sure. I think there are threats from a number of quarters.

It is hard to gauge the extent to which trends in 'political correctness' will affect things in the future. There is no doubt that there are a number of people who have been persuaded that private car ownership is anti-social and that older machines are particularly polluting. I suspect that those put off in this way were never destined to be enthusiasts in the first place, but to what extent the anti-car lobby will affect the hobby is hard to judge.

More significant is the fact that people tend to relate to cars of their own era and not to those from other periods. This to a large extent explains why less exotic 1930s cars are becoming increasingly harder to sell, as the population that remembers

them first hand starts significantly to decrease. I have heard it
argued that the early '70s saw a major change in the way people
began to think of motorcars and motoring. The important
question is: will people in the future consider old cars to be
classics or just scrap metal?

Perhaps the greatest threat comes from advancing technology.
I am firmly of the school that believes if you can't use them, then
they are not worth having. Already there are many old, particularly
pre-war, vehicles that I would use only with reluctance on roads
like the M25. High cruising speeds, modern tyres and driving aids
like ABS and traction control make the use of older cars less safe
in some circumstances. The fact that so many modern drivers are
unaware of the limitation of older vehicles and drive without the
necessary consideration, is also alarming.

At some point, whenever that may be, there must at least be the
possibility that technology will make the car, as we know it, obsolete.
It is quite amazing that the basic elements have changed so little
from their beginnings in the late 19th century. Apart from
overcrowding and the cut-and-thrust of modern traffic, today's
infrastructure of roads and the availability of fuels and services
better support the running of a car, of whatever description, than
was ever the case. But will this be true in the future? If, at some time,
a technology emerges that obviates the need for readily available
petrol supplies, then the internal combustion engine, at the heart of
old cars, will cease to be a viable proposition. In Britain, the demise
of leaded petrol has already caused a scare. There is much talk of fuel
cell technology which, I believe, uses hydrogen. Given the bad
publicity associated with the airships of the past it is hard to believe
that this very volatile fluid will be available at every street corner. I
have heard of the notion, however, that methanol could be the fuel
of the future, used to generate the required hydrogen. It may be that
older engines can be modified to run on methanol, I don't know.
Perhaps we have a few more years yet.

Crystal ball gazing has never been my forte, so I'll stop. There
is no doubt that at the present time the old car fraternity (and

sorority) seem to be enjoying their old cars with enormous vigour; long may it continue.

A number of my friends have asked me about my preferences in the list of cars I have owned. Although I would find it very difficult to pick out a single all-time favourite, there are a number of old friends that I remember with special affection. My particular favourites have already been mentioned in the preceding chapters, although they are surprisingly few. My first Jaguar XK sports car, the green '120 fixed-head coupé, will always have a special place in my affections. She was the first really fast car I owned and I was particularly pleased and gratified to discover that I was able to handle her with moderate competence. She initiated a long association with Jaguars in general and XKs in particular, and her successors still fill my garage.

My one and only MGA is remembered as another favourite. Apart from the fact that they are very handsome and nicely proportioned, MGAs have excellent road manners and are a joy to drive, particularly around country lanes in the summer. With a little more urge, the "A" would be a great car.

Both my Michelotti-designed Triumphs were excellent cars that provided reliable and stimulating motoring. I suppose I would choose the TR5 in preference to the 4A, mainly because of its excellent performance. Would I have another? Probably not, but on a recent event one of the other competitors had a most beautiful, "jasmine yellow" TR5 and I have to admit to feeling very envious indeed. These Triumphs have a rugged and stalwart character that no other manufacturer could quite achieve.

My first Alfa Romeo, the 1750 GTV, comes near being an all-time favourite. I recently saw a 2-litre version in superb condition and, if my circumstance were different, I would consider having it as everyday transport. The Alfa twin-cam is really a fine engine, with a well deserved reputation for hard work and long life. For many years I have harboured the notion of building myself a special which would be made up from a 1600 MGA body and chassis and an uprated, 2-litre Alfa twin-cam engine and gearbox.

I have no idea whether it is a practical proposition. I suspect there might be problems getting the very wide Alfa sump between the narrow front, MG chassis rails but no problem is insurmountable. I might give it a try one day.

Another car for which I have a particular soft spot is the little Flying Standard 8 that I bought in the '60s for £15. At the time I treated it cruelly and drove it into the ground, but it was a delightful and characterful car. An added bonus was a reasonably watertight top and wind-up windows. I met someone the other day who told me that the drop-head coupés were extremely rare. I think he said that only a handful were produced, but I may have got that wrong.

On reflection, if I had to select one car from the list I think it would be the little Standard. Last summer I attended a car show with my youngest daughter, Elizabeth, who at the time was not quite five. Being a sentimental and romantic old fool, the idea of having a little car to pootle around in, with her at my side, attending the occasional show, seemed like it might be fun. I can imagine us having picnics besides Elizabeth's beautifully presented Flying 8.

If I were forced to choose one car from the current set, it would be easy. For me the SS 100 is my favourite. I hankered after one for a very long time, and not without reason. On a beautiful summer's day there is nothing so glorious as being behind the wheel of that lovely car. It's one of Elizabeth's favourites as well.

Elizabeth aged one and a bit, about to start automotive appreciation classes with the SS.

An added attraction is that, when asked to, the old SS can respond to the throttle and motor quite well. I remember being on a rally with Kathleen where we got hopelessly and comprehensively lost. It took us an age to get back onto what we hoped was the rally route. As we flew along, hoping to find a control before it closed, we came upon a pair of Porsche 356s, also lost and knocking on quite quickly. We, however, were in a real hurry and when I was able to, I trod on the throttle and went past them both. One was being driven by the editor of a well known classic car magazine.

"It isn't often," he said coming up to me at the end of the day, "that you see an SS 100 going flat out past a pair of Porsches."

Have you ever looked at classic car prices and wished you'd kept that old motor you once foolishly sold for £100? There are scores of times when I've looked at a modern car and wondered if it was destined to be one of tomorrow's classics. Frankly, I've never really seen anything that I believed in enough to buy, put aside and then over the years see blossom into a valuable asset. That is, until a few years ago, when I was on the driving course at Lime Rock mentioned in Chapter 14. There, for the first time, I saw the newly released (1996) Dodge Viper GTS. I hadn't been impressed by its predecessor, the open Viper RT/10, which to my mind was little more than a concept car hastily converted into a "just about saleable" proposition. It had all the right ingredients but lacked detail and the styling, to my eye, missed the mark.

The GTS coupé is altogether a different kettle of fish. Subtle it isn't, with huge wheel arches covering wide 10-inch front and 13-inch rear wheels with ludicrously low tyres (35 profile at the back). The glass fibre and plastic body is almost a pastiche of how the ultimate muscle car might look, but it is completely practical and usable, with electric windows (believe it or not, the RT/10 has side screens), air and a CD player. When I saw my first GTS, the only colour option was metallic mid blue with two broad, white stripes running the length of the car. (They were subsequently offered in red, yellow, silver and black.) The roofline features an eye-catching double bubble contour that makes it look a very

My GTS, vamping on the
dealer's forecourt

mean machine. In their wisdom, the Chrysler designers have gone for Chinese eye lamps flowed into the bodywork rather than pop-ups, and they look absolutely right. The styling, like it or hate it, is aggressively macho and anything but bland.

Performance is definitely in the super-car league, with 0 to 60 coming up in just over 4 seconds, 0 to 100 in under 10 and the standing ¼ mile in 12.5 seconds. In true American fashion, it's all achieved without benefit of sophisticated or highly stressed mechanics. Chrysler's Team Viper group started work with their all alloy, pushrod V10 that was sleeved to 488 cu ins and given a set of 9.6:1 Lambo worked heads (Lamborghini was a Chrysler company at the time.) Fuel delivery is by electronic multipoint injection, but the package delivers only a very modest 56 bhp per litre. Of course, given the near 8-litre capacity, this comes out at a thumping overall 450 bhp with 490 ft/lbs of torque. The quoted top speed is reputed to be around 190 mph, achieved by using a six-speed box with a 0.5 ratio top. They say she will cruise at 100 and give 25 mpg?

When the GTS first hit the American streets, the sticker price was the equivalent of a bargain £37,000. When the car was finally imported into the UK (LHD only), this was translated into an irritating £60,000. A few years on, second-hand cars are now available at relatively low prices, certainly fractions of what you would expect to pay for equivalent Porsches and Ferraris. I've wanted one since the time at Lime Rock, and when an

immaculate but slightly used example came up I decided to stick it at the back of the motor house (at the front actually, so I can use it sometimes) and see if in the next twenty years it will, as I expect, become a classic. I know it goes against the guidelines I rattled out in an earlier chapter, but it may be the exception that proves the rule.

A number of unkind people have suggested it's just a substitute for flagging virility, but if I decided I wanted to turn back the clock in that area, I'd have needed one ten years ago.

Well, that's it. I hope that some of the preceding pages amused and interested you. I hope also that my love of old cars comes through in this book. If you are ever at, or taking part in, an old car event and spot me in the crowd, please remember to say Hello, and stop for a chat.

Receipts

I've kept a large number of the receipts associated with the cars I've owned, far too many to include, but I thought the reader might want to skim through a few, so here are some of the early ones. Those from dealers, as one would expect, were normally produced on specially printed forms, but others were usually on scraps of paper. In some cases, for obvious reasons, I have obliterated the vendor's address and/or phone number.

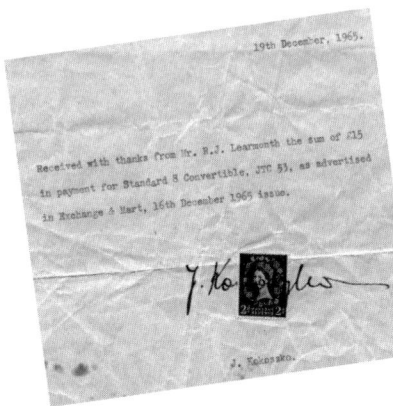

This rumpled piece of paper was part of the documentation that came with my 1947 Standard 8. Note the use of a postage stamp that was required in those days to make the thing legal. Looking at the receipt again after many years, I notice that the owner has me as R.J. and not R.A. Learmonth. I'd never noticed that before. It is odds-on that JTC 53 no longer exists, which is a shame because she was a delightful little car.

The Standard 10 I bought after disposing of my Triumph TR2/Standard Vanguard hybrid cost only £25. It was one of a number of nondescript cars that I owned in the days after my first marriage. I remember it as a perfectly adequate vehicle that could have provided years of service; a typical small British car of the period.

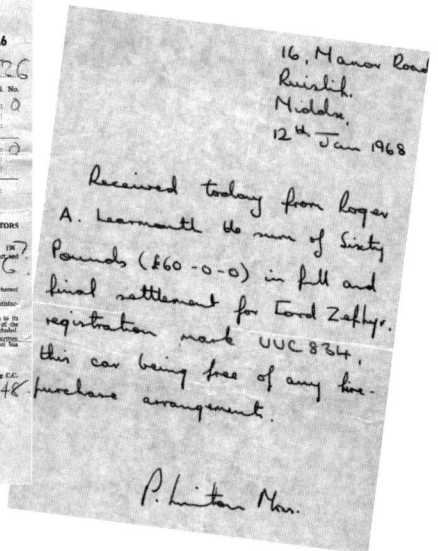

This was for the Zephyr Automatic that I bought from my work colleague and pal, Linton Moss. Another of my nondescript cars. If only it had been able to go uphill backwards, I might have had it still; but probably not.

The MGA is a car I remember with particular affection. The A40 it replaced was a dog by comparison. I did a sort of low budget, running restoration on the "A" and it turned out an excellent car. Another of the few I think of as my " favourites".

This messy piece of paper is a memento of the worst car I ever owned, the nastiest XK150 imaginable. It's one car I hope hasn't survived. If it has I'd be prepared to destroy it with my bare hands. The entire front was constructed from filler paste and cardboard and not very well at that. I bought it in the pouring rain and never made the same mistake again. The thought of that awful monster still sends shivers down my spine.

I finally got rid of the '150 by exchanging it for a problematic XK140 fixed-head, but anything was better than the dread '150. I can't remember why, but the documentation seems to indicate that we sold our respective cars to each other. When I started going through these old receipts for inclusion in this section, I noticed for the first time that the owner of the '140 has put down the wrong registration number (678 EBB was the number of the XK150). Was it just a slip or was there some other motive?

The first seriously smart car I owned was this Riviera Silver Blue MGC GT. Unfortunately, it was more than I could afford and drained my meagre resources beyond their limit. When it became time to give it up, however, I was a sorry fellow.

Received from Mr R Learmonth the sum of £410 for MGB 274 STT in full payment.

W. Stevenson.

16th Sept 70

Given over to Mr R Learmonth 's type Jaguar registration Mark EPL 889B in part exchange for MGC sports car PRX 792F

15/2/72
Mr Learmonth.
40, Fifinot Cons-
S.G.19.

Rec'd £500 cash on full payment for MUSTANG FLH 3.C. for above.
DS FULL PAYMENT.

O. Riley
11 Ladbroke News
W.11.

The MGC had to make way for cheaper transport, but selling proved difficult. I was finally forced to take a 1964 Jaguar S-type in part exchange. I was terrified lest the big, complex automatic should let me down, but it never did. (The only other auto I had owned had been the dreaded Zephyr.) The Jaguar was an altogether lovely machine that wafted me around in great comfort. My heart, however, was always into sports cars, and the S-type quickly made way for an MGB.

My first MGB was taken in part exchange for the S-type. For a reason I can't remember, the owner of the MG and I exchanged receipts for the full respective sale prices. The MG had been repainted Ford Aubergine and after I had fitted a white hood it didn't exactly look like the classiest piece of machinery in town. It nevertheless went extremely well for the period. Since then I've had a soft spot for Bs.

The Mustang convertible was my first American car. By coincidence my wife Kathleen bought a new Mustang convertible when we went to live in America some ten years later. They had very little in common other than the name. The 1965 model was a surprisingly good car that ran and stopped without incident or drama. I have since that time cast many a covetous glance at some of the fine US restorations I have seen, particularly the Shelby 350 and 500 GT Fastbacks.

Only £480 for the very nice E-type I bought from a talented auto mechanic. For some reason the receipt shows the car as a coupé, but it was definitely a roadster. It was another of the cars I treated to a white top. It was without doubt the quickest motor I had owned to date and I managed to frighten myself and quite a few others before it was sold.

25 Blandford Ave
Beckenham
Kent
17th Feb 1973

Received the sum of £480-00. being the full purchase price of Jaguar E type Coupe 674 CUW as seen and approved.

Michael White

By comparison with the earlier Cooper, I remember this Mini (it was the Clubman variant) as a particularly nasty little car with a rusty body and a worn engine. It was, however, extremely useful for moving house. Once the passenger seat had been removed it provided serious bulk carrying capability.

My second MGB was a Glacier White roadster in very good condition, being under five years old. I part-exchanged the Clubman and got more than I paid, so I suppose it was a reasonable deal. The B was an ideal touring car and was happy to cruise at 90 miles an hour for long periods. By the mid '70s, performance was no longer the B's strength, but reliability and build quality were exemplary.

The GT6 was another nice car, apart, that is, from a noisy back axle that got steadily worse as time went by. I have heard people refer to this model as the poor man's E-type and I can see what they mean.

Performance was a little better than the MGB GT, but the car didn't have the carrying capacity of a B. Mine was Signal Red and very much looked the part.

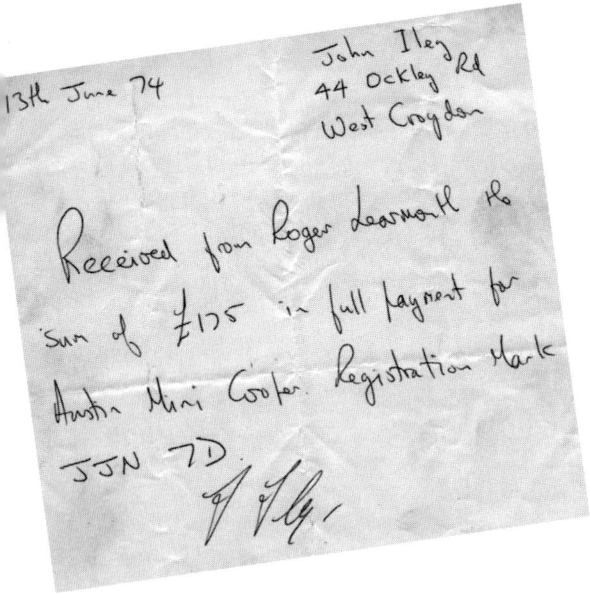

13th June 74

John Iley
44 Ockley Rd
West Croydon

Received from Roger Learmonth the sum of £175 in full payment for Austin Mini Cooper Registration Mark JJN 7D.

19th August 1975.

Received from Roger Learmonth the sum of £650-00 being payment for Triumph 1500 JYT 597K. The car is not subject to any Hire Purchase agreement to my knowledge.

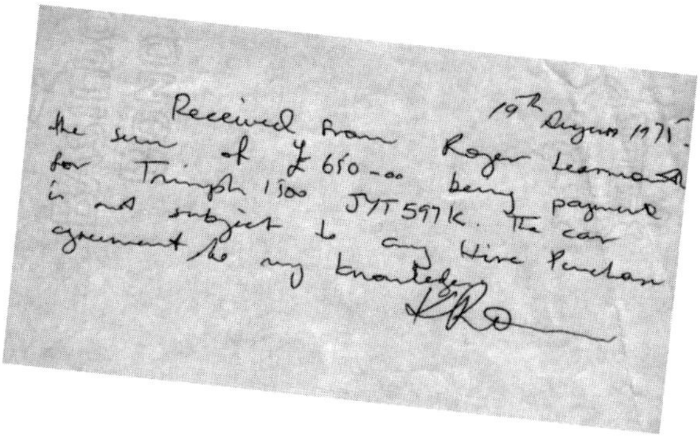

Receipt for the wretched front-wheel drive Triumph 1500 with which I had so much trouble, most of it, I have to admit, my own fault.

My one and only Mini Cooper was red with a black roof. It was another example of the British genius for designing motor cars. In its day the Mini was a fabulous package that was hard to beat. I would roar around in my little red car, causing all kinds of mayhem. At the time I also owned a TR5 and the pair made a nice combination. I haven't yet seen the new 2001 Mini that is to replace the classic design, but it certainly has a lot to live up to.

35

52 Bell Green,
Sydenham,
S.E. 26.
16th Feb. 76.

Received from R. Learmonth, Esq., 50 Keats House, Porchester Mead, Beckenham, Kent. the sum of £700-00. as full and final payment in respect of one used Alfa Romeo 1750 GTV reg. no. SMW 92 J. Above vehicle complete with registration book, current M.O.T. certificate and road tax to March 1976.

With thanks,

P. Clemence.

P. CLEMENCE.

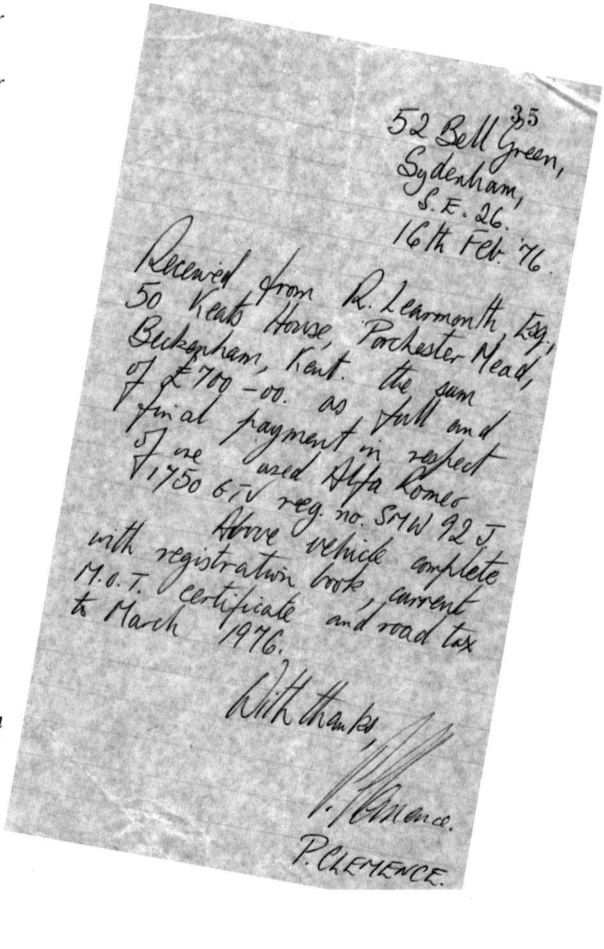

I bought my Alfa 1750 GTV Bertone from a car dealer who was also a neighbour. I needed an occasional four, and parted with my trusty two-seater B to get it. It turned out to be a fabulous motor. I'd love another. As with a lot of Italian cars, tin worm was the main enemy and I worked hard on eradication. The car converted me to Alfas and I had another two in succession. Neither was a match for the Bertone.

I bought this lime green Midget as a stopgap between rather more up-market transport. It temporarily cured me of the desire to drive bangers. Good examples are fun cars, but this wasn't one of them. It did its job, however, and was quickly passed on to a new and, I hope, more appreciative owner.

The receipt for the TR5 project car I bought to restore. I paid way too much and in the end never got around to finishing the job, as my interests moved towards more exotic machinery. But I did a lot of work and learned a great deal. I'm still sorry I didn't see the project through, if for no other reason than that I lost my shirt on the deal.

There are many more receipts I could include but enough is enough. Reading through them after all these years, it seems that I was obsessed with the dangers of acquiring a car that had an outstanding hire purchase debt. I never did so and, if I had, I doubt that the wording on a receipt would have saved me. I also notice that a lot of them are in my own hand, so I was clearly keen to get the wording right.